D1083796

BECOMING RONALD REAGAN

BECOMING
Ronald Reagan
The Rise of a Conservative Icon

ROBERT MANN

Potomac Books
An imprint of the University of Nebraska Press

All rights reserved. Potomac Books is an imprint of the
University of Nebraska Press.
Manufactured in the United States of America.

Library of Congress Cataloging-in-Publication Data
Names: Mann, Robert, 1958– author.
Title: Becoming Ronald Reagan: the rise of a
conservative icon / Robert Mann.
Description: Lincoln: Potomac Books, an imprint of
the University of Nebraska Press, 2019.
Includes bibliographical references and index.
Identifiers: LCCN 2019008146
ISBN 9781612349688 (cloth: alk. paper)
ISBN 9781640122536 (epub)
ISBN 9781640122543 (mobi)
ISBN 9781640122550 (pdf)
Subjects: LCSH: Reagan, Ronald. | Reagan, Ronald—
Childhood and youth. | Motion picture actors and
actresses—United States—Biography. | Governors—
California—Biography. | Dixon (Ill.)—Biography.
Classification: LCC E877 .M35 2019 |
DDC 973.927092 [B]—dc23 LC record available at
https://lccn.loc.gov/2019008146

Set in Questa by Mikala R. Kolander.

For Dave Norris, my teacher, mentor, and friend

Contents

Illustrations

Following page 132

1. Young Ronald Reagan with parents
2. Announcer at WHO in Des Moines
3. As Drake McHugh in *Kings Row*
4. With Jane Wyman and their children
5. Scene from the 1942 film *Desperate Journey*
6. Working for the Army Air Corps
7. Scene from 1943's *This Is the Army*
8. Testifying before the House Un-American Activities Committee in 1947
9. Meeting of the Screen Actors Guild in 1950
10. Reagan and Nancy in 1953 on a movie set
11. Newspaper ad promoting *General Electric Theater* in 1954
12. Publicity photo for *General Electric Theater*
13. GE president Ralph Cordiner
14. With GE plant employees in 1955
15. Newspaper ad for General Electric
16. With GE workers in October 1955
17. With Nancy in their "Home of the Future"
18. Advertisement for the "California School of Anti-Communism"
19. Album cover for Operation Coffeecup
20. On the set of his last movie, *The Killers*
21. Senator Barry Goldwater in March 1964

Acknowledgments

I am grateful for the kindness, sharp eyes, and honesty of those who read this manuscript in whole or in part: Bob Ritter, Alisa Plant, Louis Day, Glo Weaver, Norman Sherman, John O'Brien, and Jay Shelledy. I appreciate the incisive, helpful review by the anonymous reader for Potomac Books, as well as the careful copyediting of Elaine Durham Otto. The staffs at several archival collections were most helpful and hospitable during my research. Those include the Arizona Historical Foundation at the Arizona State University Library; the David M. Rubenstein Rare Book and Manuscript Library at Duke University; the Department of Special Collections at the University of California Santa Barbara; the Kislak Center for Special Collections at the University of Pennsylvania; the Ronald Reagan Presidential Library; the Briscoe Center for American History at the University of Texas at Austin; and the Vanderbilt TV News Archive at Vanderbilt University.

Thanks to Valerie Yaros, historian/archivist for the Screen Actors Guild–American Federation of Television and Radio Artists, for her assistance. For decades, the LSU Middleton Library has been a second home where I conduct my research. I am grateful to the library's dedicated staff members, led by Dean Stanley Wilder, for their assistance. I especially appreciate the help of the library's interlibrary loan section and mass communication librarian, Rebecca Kelley.

Thanks also to the following individuals: Alisa Plant, who is not only a remarkable and wise editor but also a good friend; Sheridan Wall, my industrious and resourceful student researcher; the

Manship family, who established the endowed chair that provided so much of the funding for my research; Dean Martin Johnson, former dean Jerry Ceppos, and other wonderful and gifted colleagues on the faculty and staff of the Manship School of Mass Communication at Louisiana State University; my students, who inspire me; Dean Jonathan Earle and others at the LSU Roger Hadfield Ogden Honors College for their support of my teaching and research; and Bill Geerhart, whose long fascination with Ronald Reagan's famous October 27, 1964, speech inspired me to tell this story. (Bill has an outstanding website dedicated to the speech at http://conelrad.blog-spot.com/2014/10/a-time-for-credit-men-who-put-reagan-on.html.)

I dedicate this book to Dave Norris, my economics professor at the University of Louisiana–Monroe more than forty years ago and a treasured friend and mentor in the years since. As mayor of West Monroe, Louisiana, for four decades, Dave was one of the most respected and gifted public officials in my state. He now enjoys a well-earned retirement from elected office. I attribute much of who I am and how I view the world to the friendship and guidance of wise and caring mentors like Dave.

More than thirty years ago, as I began writing books, I worked for U.S. senator John Breaux of Louisiana. When Breaux learned I wanted to write a biography about his Senate predecessor, Russell B. Long, he instantly became my cheerleader and remained so through my first three books, giving me the time and space to research and write while keeping me on his staff part-time. I can imagine few political leaders who would have been so supportive of a staffer who wanted to write books on the side. Breaux's encouragement and friendship made all the difference in my budding writing career, and that paved the way for my rewarding years in academia. Regarding academia, I owe an enormous debt of gratitude to my former dean and current faculty colleague at LSU, John Maxwell Hamilton, who supported hiring me in 2006. I will never be able to thank Jack enough for what he has done for me and for the students, faculty, and staff of the Manship School.

Finally, I am thankful for my wise and loving wife, Cindy, who supports and encourages me in everything I do, and for our daughter and son, Avery and Robert. I love the three of you more than life itself.

Introduction

In the spring of 1954, Ronald Reagan was a washed-up Hollywood actor with few prospects for reviving a film career that had never delivered the stardom he desired. Early that year, Reagan was nearly broke. In desperation, he had agreed to a humiliating two-week stint as the master of ceremonies for a music-and-comedy revue at a Las Vegas hotel and casino. It seemed his once-promising career in entertainment was almost over. By late summer, however, Reagan's fortunes had changed. General Electric hired him to host a weekly television drama series it sponsored on CBS and gave him the side job of goodwill ambassador for the manufacturing giant. The show was a hit. Overnight he was a star again.

When Reagan began his work for General Electric, he was a liberal Democrat and the former head of the Screen Actors Guild, the AFL-affiliated union that represented Hollywood actors. In 1948 he had campaigned for President Harry Truman and Hubert Humphrey, the liberal Democratic mayor of Minneapolis seeking a U.S. Senate seat. Although he had supported and voted for Republican Dwight D. Eisenhower in the 1952 presidential election, Reagan did so only after urging the retired general to run as a Democrat. In the late 1950s, Reagan underwent a radical transformation, becoming a respected, popular spokesman for conservative causes. By 1960 Republican presidential nominee Richard Nixon admired Reagan's influence among conservatives so much that he invited the actor to campaign for him in his race against John F. Kennedy. Two years later, during Nixon's ill-fated run for California governor, he enlisted Reagan again (Nixon lost). Only four years later, Reagan would become the Republican candidate for California governor and would defeat the incumbent, Edmund "Pat" Brown, by a million votes.

President Ronald Reagan is familiar to most Americans over the age of forty. Reagan, the actor and political activist, is not so well known. His presidency has been an interesting field of study for twentieth-century historians and others for decades. Just as interesting is Reagan's fascinating life during the 1950s and early 1960s, the period of evolution from struggling film actor to respected political figure. In our current era, when a former reality television star with no prior political experience is president, such a feat may seem unremarkable. In the 1960s, transitioning from acting to politics was rare. Reagan was not the first to do it (his onetime film costar George Murphy won a U.S. Senate seat from California in 1964). But Reagan was the first actor to jump from the screen to the stump to immediate credibility as a presidential contender. Reagan's transformation from struggling liberal actor to influential conservative spokesman in five years—and then to California governor six years later—is a remarkable and compelling story.

This book explores Reagan's early career: his budding desire in high school and college for acclaim, his political awakening as a young Hollywood actor, his ideological evolution in the 1950s as he traveled the country for GE, the refining of his political skills, his growing aversion to big government, and his disdain for the totalitarian leaders in the Soviet Union and elsewhere. All this and more shaped Reagan's politics and influenced his career as an elected official.

This book also explains how the skills he learned and lessons he absorbed during his political apprenticeship from 1954 to 1964—when he would visit each of GE's 130-plus factories to speak to plant employees and local citizens—made him the inspiring leader so many Americans remember from the 1970s and 1980s. To do so, I devote special attention to Reagan's GE years, a period of his political and intellectual life that has often been opaque. What makes Reagan's GE years clearer in this book is the extensive use of contemporaneous newspaper accounts about his speeches in cities and small towns across the United States. While available to researchers in libraries in hundreds of communities, these accounts were almost impossible to search and acquire before the advent of three major genealogy websites that have archived thousands of newspapers across the country. Searching for details of Reagan's speeches and his travels became exponentially easier because of these technological advances. No other biography of Reagan yet has made use of this extensive and valuable source material.

I began this book out of a long admiration for and fascination with Reagan's nationally televised speech in October 1964 for Republican presidential nominee Barry Goldwater. That speech—one of the best of Reagan's career—interested me by how it propelled the former actor into the California governor's race. I suspected the story was not that simple (it was not). What I did not fully appreciate was how important Reagan's speeches and after-dinner talks had been to his early political career. I did not understand the extent to which his ideology and positions on a host of issues emerged from the work he did on the road, speaking for his employer, from late 1954 to early 1962. I knew Reagan had delivered some speeches. I did not realize how much those speeches were the product of his own thinking, reading, and research. What began as a book primarily about this October 1964 speech evolved into something much broader: an examination of the decades-long personal, political, and ideological journey toward that key moment. Reagan's "A Time for Choosing" speech is not the focus of this story but the culmination of it, the climactic moment in Reagan's post-acting career that launched his quest for elective office.

I had always viewed Reagan as an incurious, befuddled man who relied on a team of speechwriters to tell him what to believe and say. Studying Reagan from the 1950s and early 1960s disabused me of this. Not that I now see Reagan as an intellectual giant or a rigorous student of public policy. He was not. He was untrained in public policy yet fascinated by politics. (This might describe half or more of the current membership of the U.S.

Congress.) Reagan was often careless with his research. He rarely thought deeply or looked for ways to challenge or reassess his strongly held assumptions. Over the years, he repeated many false statistics and shared fanciful anecdotes to support conservative policies. Many of the qualities Americans associate with Reagan as president—inattention to detail, a less-than-complete command of policy, and inaccurate factual assertions—were evident from his first days of public speaking on political issues. Of course, Reagan was not unique in this regard. Many politicians exaggerate, obfuscate, and twist facts. (Compared with President Donald Trump, for example, Reagan's rhetorical excesses were tiny. Unlike Reagan, Trump is a purposeful, congenital liar. Reagan was sloppy and careless; Trump is often malevolent in his mendacity.) Nonetheless, examining a future U.S. president's adherence to fact and truth in his early years is a worthwhile endeavor if one desires a complete understanding of his presidency.

In the beginning of my research, I admired Reagan's oratorical skills but not much more. Perhaps I am like many of those in the Republican Party who view him so fondly because of Trump's well-publicized deficiencies. That may be why Reagan has risen in my estimation: as flawed as he was, he was not in Donald Trump's league as a fabulist.

My research into Reagan of the 1930s through the 1960s bolstered my opinion of him for another reason: I discovered a man who was working out his ideology, his views on the issues, and his attitudes about Communism and the role of government in an earnest if sometimes careless fashion. I do not agree with much of what Reagan believed about government (although in my twenties I voted for him twice). History has proved him wrong on many fronts, including the importance of a strong, well-funded Social Security system and establishing Medicare. Like his good friend Barry Goldwater, he was too eager to confront the Soviet Union militarily in the 1960s, which might have sparked a nuclear holocaust for both countries and others. While personally without outward racial animus, he was no champion of civil rights.

This does not mean there is little about Reagan to admire. One can disagree with his policies—particularly his shocking neglect of the AIDS crisis in the 1980s or his ill treatment of the poor—and still applaud his immense love for the United States. I respect his faith that he could persuade, not coerce, people to see issues his way because of a belief in the innate goodness of people. Reagan believed in the power of words to inspire and persuade. He believed leadership involved wooing, not bullying. And he did not make his politics personal. In almost every way, I found that Ronald Reagan was a decent, charismatic, and likable man with whom I disagreed on almost everything politically. In other words, he was just like many of my friends and neighbors.

1

My Heart Is a Ham Loaf

I n September 1966 as the former liberal actor campaigned for California governor, a *Time* magazine reporter asked Ronald Reagan about his emergence as a prominent conservative activist. "You have to start with the small-town beginnings," Reagan replied. "You're a part of everything that goes on. In high school, I was on the football team and I was in class plays and I was president of the student body, and the same thing happened in college. In a small town, you can't stand on the sidelines and let somebody else do what needs doing; you can't coast along on someone else's opinions. That, really, is how I became an activist. I felt I had to take a stand on all the controversial issues of the day; there was a sense of urgency about getting involved."[1]

As a New Deal liberal and then an archconservative, Reagan saw himself as a product of rural Illinois, not Hollywood. Even as he lived and worked among the movie stars who became his good friends in the late 1930s and 1940s, Reagan celebrated the midwestern values of the small towns he believed had shaped him and which would, by the mid-1950s and early 1960s, become the training ground for his nascent political career. The title of Reagan's 1990 memoir, *An American Life*, paid homage to his improbable journey that began in America's heartland. "Times were tough," Reagan said of the Great Depression in February 1984 when he visited his boyhood hometown of Dixon, in northwestern

Illinois. "But what I remember most clearly is that Dixon held together. Our faith was our strength. Our teachers pointed to the future. People held on to their hopes and dreams. Neighbors helped neighbors."[2] In another setting, Reagan observed about growing up in a small town during the Great Depression: "As in any kind of calamity people were closer together."[3]

Ronald Wilson Reagan was undeniably the product of a small town. He was born February 6, 1911, in the northwestern Illinois town of Tampico (population 849), the younger son of John Edward "Jack" and Nelle Wilson Reagan. His parents, who remained married until Jack's death in 1941, were an unlikely couple. Jack was a handsome, hard-drinking Irish Catholic shoe salesman whose work barely supported his family. Nelle was a stalwart, teetotaling member of the Disciples of Christ who regarded her husband's alcoholism as more addiction than sin. That did not mean she quietly tolerated his drinking. Ronald Reagan once confided to his son Ron that he heard "a lot of cursing from my parents' bedroom when my mother went after [Jack] for his drinking."[4] In one of his memoirs, Reagan recalled that his father would vanish "suddenly" and be gone for days: "Sometimes when he did return, my brother and I would hear some pretty fiery arguments through the walls of our house."[5] He recalled: "I was eleven years old the first time I came home to find my father flat on his back on the front porch and no one there to lend a hand but me. He was drunk, dead to the world." Reagan dragged him into the house and put him to bed. He pitied his father, explaining that Jack was "filled with contradictions of character."[6]

Nelle understood her husband's weaknesses and practiced forgiveness, which is why she remained with Jack despite his absences and bouts of heavy drinking. "She told Neil and myself over and over," Reagan recalled, "that alcoholism was a sickness— that we should love and help our father and never condemn him for something that was beyond his control."[7] Nelle did not wallow in self-pity over her family's plight. Instead, she devoted herself to helping those less fortunate. Friends from Dixon remembered she often visited the state's mental institution and the local jail to care for inmates. Sometimes young "Dutch" tagged along. (He earned the nickname that followed him into adulthood from his father, who reportedly exclaimed at his birth, "He looks like a fat little Dutchman.")[8] "She was very good at reading the Bible," one friend recalled about Nelle. "The [prisoners] looked forward to her coming. Some of them were released in her custody and slept on a cot in Nelle's sewing room until they found another situation." Another friend from Dixon remarked: "If Nelle had had the education, I think she would have mounted the pulpit."[9] From his devout mother, Reagan said he learned "the value of prayer, how to have dreams and believe I could make them come true." From his less-devout, gregarious father, Reagan said he learned "the value of hard work and ambition, and maybe a little something about telling a story."[10]

Jack's declining job opportunities in the years before and during the Depression forced the family into several moves. "My father was constantly searching for a better life and I was forever the new kid in school," Reagan remembered. "During one period of four years, I attended four different schools. We moved to wherever my father's ambition took him." Reagan was nine in 1920 when his family settled in Dixon (population 8,191), where he would live until he left for college in the fall of 1928. "It was a small universe," Reagan would write later, "where I learned standards and values that would guide me for the rest of my life." Although he would spend his professional life in Hollywood, Sacramento, and Washington, Reagan later said the values he absorbed in Dixon shaped his views of politics and the world. "I grew up observing how the love and common sense of purpose that unites families is one of the most powerful glues on earth and that it can help them overcome the greatest of adversaries," he wrote in *An American Life*. "I learned that hard work is an essential part of life—that by and large, you don't get something for nothing—and that America was a place that offered unlimited opportunity to those who did hard work." He continued:

> I think growing up in a small town is a good foundation for anyone who decides to enter politics. You get to know people as

individuals, not as blocs or members of special interest groups. You discover that, despite their differences, most people have a lot in common: Every individual is unique, but we all want freedom and liberty, peace, love and security, a good home, and a chance to worship God in our own way; we all want the chance to get ahead and make our children's lives better than our own. We all want the chance to work at a job of our own choosing and to be fairly rewarded for it and the opportunity to control our own destiny.[11]

In the small Illinois towns where Reagan spent his formative years, professional entertainment was rare. "People had to rely on themselves for entertainment," he wrote, "and, at this, my mother excelled." Nelle was a passionate amateur actor and leader of a local group that staged dramatic readings of famous poems, plays, speeches, and books at local churches and other settings. "Whether it was a low comedy or high drama," Reagan recalled, "Nelle really threw herself into a part. She loved it. Performing, I think, was her first love."[12]

Hoping to instill in him her passion for performance, Nelle coached nine-year-old Dutch on memorizing and delivering a short passage of poetry, "About Mother," that she hoped he would deliver during a reading at the Tampico Church of Christ in May 1920.[13] "Summoning up my courage," Reagan wrote, "I walked up to the stage that night, cleared my throat, and made my theatrical debut. I don't remember what I said, but I'll never forget the response: *People laughed and applauded*." He was hooked. "This was a new experience for me and I liked it," he admitted. "I liked that approval. For a kid suffering childhood pangs of insecurity, the applause was music. I didn't know it then, but, in a way, when I walked off the stage that night, my life had changed."[14] Reagan later praised his high school English teacher, B. J. Frazer, for challenging him to write and think with originality and for grading him on it. "That prodded me to be imaginative with my essays," he recalled. "Before long he was asking me to read some of my essays to the class, and when I started getting a few laughs, I began writing them with the intention of entertaining the class.

I got more laughs and realized I enjoyed it as much as I had those readings at church. For a teenager still carrying around some old feelings of insecurity, the reaction of my classmates was more music to my ears." That led Reagan to audition for parts in school plays. By his senior year, he said, "I was so addicted to student theatrical productions that you couldn't keep me out of them."[15]

In Dixon, Reagan also reveled in a different type of acclaim—the local notoriety of his summer job as the lifeguard at Lowell Park beach, north of town. It was from the dangerous, swift waters of the Rock River that Reagan rescued seventy-seven struggling swimmers over seven summers.[16] The *Dixon Evening Telegraph* sometimes covered his exploits, conferring on him local-hero status. On July 23, 1932, for example, the paper reported: "There have been several narrow escapes and thrilling rescues, both of adults and children at the beach. On one occasion a Dixon young man slipped from the diving tower and fell, striking against the ladder and, becoming unconscious, fell into the deep water. Reagan, after several dives, rescued him and saved him from drowning."[17]

Reagan loved the limelight, but his swagger masked a lifelong fear of intimacy. "I wish I had a dollar for each of the friends and family members who complained to me that Dutch never let them get anywhere near," his biographer Edmund Morris wrote.[18] Ron Reagan recalled his father "was often wandering somewhere in his own head."[19] Even Reagan recognized this. "Although I always had lots of playmates," he recalled, "during those first years in Dixon I was a little introverted and probably a little slow in making really close friends. In some ways I think this reluctance to get close to people never left me completely. I've never had trouble making friends, but I've been inclined to hold back a little of myself, reserving it for myself."[20]

During his first performance in Tampico, Reagan had moved an audience with someone else's words. Not until he arrived at Eureka College in the fall of 1928—a small Disciples of Christ liberal arts school in a town of the same name in central Illinois—did he find his own voice before a crowd. In his first semester, he was among the students alarmed by the school's plan to fire several faculty members, cancel some courses, and impose budget cuts in response to a recession in the Midwest that preceded the 1929 stock market crash. News came that athletics might be next to get the ax. Two years earlier, Eureka president Bert Wilson could not persuade his board to approve his recommended cuts. With the budget even tighter, he had offered another proposal. "When the students and faculty got wind of the plan," Reagan recalled, "resentment spread over the campus like a prairie fire because the cutbacks meant many juniors and seniors wouldn't be able to take classes they needed to graduate." Reagan and other students were angry not only with Wilson's "underhanded" program but also because they believed Wilson should have consulted them about alternatives.[21]

At a meeting of students and faculty on the night of November 2, organizers wanted a freshman to present their grievances to the student body.[22] "Because I was a freshman and didn't have the same vested interest in avoiding the faculty cutbacks that upperclassmen did," Reagan wrote, "I was chosen to present our committee's proposal for a strike."[23] A classmate of Reagan's had a slightly different recollection of his prominent role in the meeting: "We put Reagan on because he was the biggest mouth of the freshman class; he was a cocky s.o.b., a loud talker. Dutch was the guy you wanted to put up there."[24]

Reagan remembered his speech as a barn-burner. He described how the cuts would harm not only students but also the school's reputation. He excoriated administrators for ignoring students and for hoping to enact their plan when school was out. "Giving that speech—my first—was as exciting as any I ever gave," Reagan wrote. "For the first time in my life, I felt my words reach out and grab an audience, and it was exhilarating." Reagan recalled the "roar after every sentence, sometimes every word" and said, "It was as if the audience and I were one." Finished, Reagan called for a vote. The crowd approved the strike by acclamation. No student appeared for classes for a week, Reagan said, and not long thereafter Wilson resigned "and things returned to normal at Eureka College."[25]

Reagan's maiden speech was not as influential and decisive as he later imagined. "The earliest manifestation of his greatness as a political orator it may have been," biographer Iwan Morgan observed, "but the address did not pave the way for student victory as his memoir suggested." Faced with fury from the school's trustees, who threatened to fire several faculty members they considered "ringleaders" of the strike, students dropped their demand for Wilson's ouster. As Morgan noted, Wilson quit because the faculty turned on him. The school's trustees, meanwhile, "implemented his retrenchment plan in full."[26]

In his first memoir, *Where's the Rest of Me?* published in 1965, Reagan's recollection of his joy and exhilaration in that moment was vivid and emotional, if not entirely accurate. He wrote:

> I discovered that night that an audience has a feel to it and in the parlance of the theater, that audience and I were together. When I came to actually presenting the motion there was no need for parliamentary procedure: they came to their feet with a roar—even the faculty members present voted by acclamation. It was heady wine. Hell, with two more lines I could have had them riding through "every Middlesex village and farm"—without horses yet.[27]

"He was not shy in front of a crowd," Ron Reagan noted about his father. "But this was evidently the first time he had ever felt the electric jolt of a rapturous audience response directed at not a fictional character mouthing someone else's words, but at Dutch Reagan himself, speaking his own words."[28] An adoring audience is intoxicating, but so is the realization one can speak words that educate, excite, and inspire. Reagan was learning, as someone once observed, "They may forget what you said—but they will never forget how you made them feel."

An incident a few days after his Eureka speech deepened Reagan's attraction to performance and oratory. While home in Dixon, he took his girlfriend to a nearby town where a touring company presented *Journey's End*, a popular play by British playwright R. C. Sherriff, set near the Allied trenches of France during the First World War. One actor played a Captain Stanhope, who drank to cope with the horrors of war. The performance mesmerized Reagan. "War-weary, young but bitterly old Captain

Stanhope carried me into a new world," Reagan wrote thirty-five years later, adding:

> For two and a half hours I was in that dugout on the Western front—but in some strange way, I was also on stage. More than anything in life I wanted to speak his lines to the young replacement officer who misunderstands and sees callousness in his effort to hide grief. That deep silence, the slow coming to his feet, then the almost whispered, 'My God, so that's it! You think I don't care! You bloody little swine, you think I don't care—the only one who knew—who really understood.' He was, of course, referring to the death that day of the beloved older officer. If I had only realized it, nature was trying to tell me something—namely, that my heart is a ham loaf.[29]

At Eureka College, Reagan continued "investigating a new, wonderful world, possibly more fascinating than any other, the world of drama." Maybe the impulse that drew him deeper into acting was primal. "The fact was, I suppose, that I just liked showing off," he admitted.[30] Years later, after he left the White House, Reagan acknowledged that an intrinsic need for acclaim had motivated much of his career. "As I've grown older," he wrote in 1990 at age seventy-nine, "perhaps there's always been a little of that small boy inside me who found some reassurance in the applause and approval he first heard at nine or ten."[31]

FEW EVENTS WOULD INFLUENCE Reagan's generation more— its politics and outlook on life—than the Great Depression. "They were cheerless, desperate days," Reagan later wrote. "I don't think anyone who did not live through the Depression can ever understand how difficult it was."[32] A few of his contemporaries in Dixon escaped its worst effects. The most fortunate did not lose their livelihoods. Those less fortunate took help from local charities or accepted government assistance for the unemployed. Like many of his contemporaries, Reagan knew poverty. "When I left home at seventeen to go to college," Reagan later recalled, "we had never lived in a house we owned." But he claimed to have never considered his family impoverished. "Only later in life did the government decide that it had to tell people when they were poor."[33] Jack Reagan, his son wrote, "passed on to me . . . the belief that all men and women, regardless of their color or religion, are created equal and that individuals determine their own destiny; that is, it's largely their own ambition and hard work that determine their fate in life."[34] His father, Reagan remembered, was a "sentimental Democrat who believed fervently in the rights of the workingman—I recalled him cursing vehemently about the battle of Herrin in 1922, where twenty-six persons were killed in a massacre brought about by a coal-mine strike—he never lost his conviction that the individual must stand on his own feet."[35]

And yet his hard-drinking father often found it hard to stand, literally and figuratively. Finances were a constant struggle for the Reagans. "He was in and out of work usually as a shoe salesman on straight commission, no salary," Reagan told a correspondent in 1982. "My mother got a job in a dress shop at fourteen dollars a week. On one of my years in college I shared my summer earnings with them to help pay the grocery bill."[36] Reagan recalled a gloomy Christmas in 1931 during his final year in college. As he and his brother, Neil, prepared to leave for dates Christmas Eve night, a special delivery arrived. "I can still see the tiny apartment living room and Jack reading the single blue page the envelope contained. Without raising his head, he quietly remarked, 'Well, it's a hell of a Christmas present.' The blue page was the traditional blue slip: he was fired. Before that year was out, I would send fifty dollars home from college, to apply on the grocery bill so credit could go on."[37]

The following summer, in 1932, the Democratic Party nominated New York governor Franklin D. Roosevelt to challenge Republican president Herbert Hoover for reelection. Jack Reagan was a fierce FDR supporter who "pinned his hopes on a reward for toiling in the political vineyard." In other words, his father trusted that volunteering for Roosevelt would earn him a government job. After Roosevelt won, his father found work running Dixon's outpost of the federal government's food relief program. "Jack's job was handing out the foodstuffs the government bought and shipped in, as well as the scrip the government issued permitting the unemployed to go to the grocer and buy, the government in turn redeeming the scrip from the grocer for cash."[38]

Judging by the two pages Reagan devoted to it in his 1965 memoir, his father's New Deal work influenced the younger Reagan's views of government and its role in the lives of the poor. Reagan admired his father's near-religious devotion to feeding his Dixon neighbors and helping them find work. "It took him only a few weeks to start rounding up every odd job, every put-off chore from raking yards to thinning the woods at Lowell Park for the Park Board," Reagan recalled.

His father ran afoul of bureaucrats who, Reagan said, descended on Dixon "with loads of furniture and, of course, the card files—enough to require a whole floor of offices in a downtown building." In time, the men his father had been helping spurned the work he found for them. "To his stunned surprise," Reagan wrote, "he was told the last time they took his jobs the new welfare staff had cut them off relief." Predictably Jack arrived home that night drunk, Reagan said. But Jack's hard drinking did not hinder his promotion. He became head of the Works Progress Administration (WPA) office in Dixon, where Reagan recalled his father ensured there were no "boondoggles." Reagan also claimed, "There was no bureaucracy at Jack's level." The position allowed his father to give locals even better jobs, but Reagan said local welfare officials fought him. "Using every pretext, including physical unfitness, those in charge of direct relief resisted releasing their charges to WPA," Reagan wrote. "Jack's life became one of almost permanent anger and frustration." Jack reserved his ire for the local bureaucrats, Reagan remembered. "Being a loyal Democrat, he never criticized the administration or the government."[39]

There is one problem with Reagan's recollection of his father's heroic struggle to secure work for the down-and-out men of Dixon: it did not happen like Reagan described, as biographer Garry Wills discovered when he examined records of the Lee County, Illinois, Civil Works Administration (CWA). Wills found that Jack Reagan "did not hand out the work relief jobs; that was the task of the registration officer (in Dixon, Tim Sullivan). When

Jack became county director of the CWA, he needed a full-time registrar under him to keep the elaborate work rolls required by the administration." To Reagan's claim of "no bureaucracy," Wills observed:

> When Jack Reagan stayed up nights finding new jobs for people, he was filling out forms for the Chicago field office, applying for certification of projects. If this certification was denied . . . there would be no work for Jack's beneficiaries. What Reagan points to as his father's great achievement—the combining of two projects to make the second one possible in the case of Dixon's airport hangar—was a *bureaucratic* maneuver that showed Jack had learned to play well the game of satisfying the field office's requirements. He improvised by knowing the rules well enough to use them to his advantage.[40]

Like most young people, Reagan's parents influenced his political thinking and no one more than Jack, whose livelihood and revived fortunes depended on the new Democratic president's administration. "I had become a Democrat, by birth, I suppose, and a few months after my twenty-first birthday, I cast my first vote for Roosevelt and the full Democratic ticket," he remembered in 1990. Like his father, Reagan "idolized" Roosevelt. "He'd entered the White House facing a national emergency as grim as any the country has ever faced," Reagan wrote, "and, acting quickly, he had implemented a plan of action to deal with the crisis."[41] Reagan never forgot the sunny September day in 1936 he saw Roosevelt in a parade in Des Moines. He recalled watching "from a distance of about 30 feet as he passed by" in an open car.[42]

Reagan not only favored Roosevelt's politics; he admired Roosevelt's easy way of communicating with the public. Years later, long after Reagan had abandoned liberalism, he still extolled Roosevelt's singular way of speaking to the American people. "During his Fireside Chats, his strong, gentle, confident voice resonated across the nation with an eloquence that brought comfort and resilience to a nation caught up in a storm and reassured us that we could lick any problem," he wrote. "I will never forget him for that." Reagan believed FDR's New Deal policies "set in motion the forces that later sought to create big government and bring a form of veiled socialism to America." But he defended his hero, noting "many people forget Roosevelt ran for president on a platform dedicated to reducing waste and fat in government." Perhaps a bit too charitably, he suggested, "If he had not been distracted by war, I think he would have resisted the relentless expansion of the federal government that followed him."[43]

Happy for his father's change of fortune and delighted with the new president, Reagan graduated from Eureka College in 1932 to bleak job prospects. "When I graduated college," he later recalled, "it was a time when . . . the government was putting ads on the radio urging people not to leave home looking for work because there was none. Even though I had graduated with a degree in economics, I didn't know what I really wanted to do." But in a way, he did know. "I knew that I wanted something in the entertainment world," he admitted. "My two biggest joys through high school and college had been football . . . and dramatics."[44]

He had discovered he enjoyed the limelight. "I love three things: drama, politics, and sports, and I'm not sure they always come in that order," Reagan would write in 1965. He credited his love of performing to his heritage. "As a first-line Irishman, I relished it," he wrote. "There seems to be something blarney-green in the blood of most Sons of the Old Sod . . . that gives zest to the shillelagh psyche." Finally Reagan admitted to himself, "I wanted some form of show business. Actually I wanted show business, period, but the problem was how to go about it. Broadway and Hollywood were as inaccessible as outer space." But there was the show business of radio in nearby Chicago. During a job-hunting trip to the city, Reagan realized he had overshot his ambitions. No station would hire an amateur college actor with no announcing experience. "This is the big time," a sympathetic employee at a large radio station told him after several days of rejection. "No one in the city wants to take a chance on inexperience." The woman counseled Reagan to find a job at a radio station in a smaller market and learn the business. "I think you will make it," she told him. "Come back and see me after you have some experience."[45]

Reagan took her advice and in the fall of 1932 he scored a weekend job at woc radio in Davenport, Iowa, announcing college football games. The station paid him ten dollars a game and bus fare. It was not enough on which to live, but it was a start. He moved back in with his parents in Dixon and commuted to games. The first contest Reagan called was a rain-soaked meeting between Iowa State and Minnesota, a regional broadcast originating from woc. But the station relayed Reagan's voice to who in Des Moines, which meant listeners all over the Midwest heard him. His first venture into his new medium brought him instant acclaim. His "crisp account of the muddy struggle," a *Chicago Tribune* critic wrote, "sounded like a carefully written story of the gridiron goings-on and his quick tongue seemed to be as fast as the plays." The temporary job soon became permanent. Reagan moved to Davenport, where he announced games and, more often than he liked, worked as an announcer who introduced musical selections.[46]

By the spring of 1933, woc merged with the larger who in Des Moines, an nbc affiliate. The station promoted Reagan to chief sports announcer and doubled his pay. Over the next few years, radio audiences throughout the Midwest became familiar with the resonant voice of Dutch Reagan. "Those were wonderful days," he recalled. "I was one of a profession just becoming popular and common—the visualizer for the armchair quarterback."[47]

By 1934 Reagan was who's voice of the Chicago Cubs and Chicago White Sox. Reagan honed his broadcasting skills by calling the teams' home games, not in person but by extemporizing and elaborating on the details of games sent by teletype from reporters at the ballparks in Chicago. "To millions of sports fans in at least seven or eight midwestern states," the *Dixon Evening Telegraph* informed readers in August 1934, "the voice of 'Dutch' Reagan is a daily source of baseball dope. Every afternoon at 2 o'clock 'Dutch' goes on the air with his rapid-fire play-by-play visualization of the home games of Chicago's major league baseball teams the Cubs and the Sox. . . . Sitting in his studio in Des Moines, 'Dutch' builds a word picture of every detail of play so vivid that hundreds of thousands of fans feel that they are almost 'seeing' the teams in action."[48] Reagan earned decent money, sent checks to support his parents, and alleviated his father's "economic problems for the first time in his life." That help was vital to Jack and Nelle's survival after Jack's debilitating heart attack, at age fifty-three, in 1936. "Now he was not only unemployed, but was physically unable to work," Reagan wrote, "but, as Nelle confirmed later, it never entered his mind that he could apply for public assistance."[49]

After several years of calling Cubs games from Des Moines, Reagan asked his bosses to send him with the team to its 1935 spring training camp on Catalina Island, off the Southern California coast near Los Angeles. He also picked up a sports reporting assignment from the *Des Moines Dispatch*. As he roamed around sun-drenched Hollywood on his days off, Reagan's long-dormant dream of an acting career bloomed. "In this world of scores and sweatshirts," Reagan wrote, "it had been a long time since the acting bug had stirred within me, but when it did it came out like a butterfly from a cocoon."[50]

Back in Des Moines the following year, Reagan also indulged a growing attraction to politics. During the 1936 presidential election, he sometimes touted Franklin Roosevelt's reelection on the air. According to biographer Anne Edwards, he performed "loving imitations of Roosevelt's fireside chats to the amusement of WHO staffers, although not all were in the president's corner."[51] His real passion, however, was acting. The local and regional acclaim he had achieved in Des Moines, combined with his trip to Los Angeles, only stoked his budding need for fame and success in Hollywood. "I spoke at quite a few banquets at that time," Reagan told the Dixon newspaper in 1941. "Some of my material was a bit corny, but it did get laughs. I received such a kick out of hearing and seeing audiences react to my talks that I made up my mind to try to become an actor."[52]

After two spring training trips to Catalina Island, the twenty-six-year-old Reagan conspired to make his 1937 trip count for more than enhanced coverage of the Cubs. With the help of Joy Hodges, a young movie actress from Des Moines, Reagan secured a screen test at Warner Bros. studios. The test went well, but Reagan left for Iowa before studio chief Jack Warner could view it. "It was only on the train that suddenly the horrified feeling came over me that maybe I had blown the whole thing," Reagan wrote years later. He was wrong. Leaving town, he later understood, had been "the smartest thing it was possible to do. Hollywood just loves people who don't need Hollywood." He had scarcely dropped his bags in his Des Moines apartment when a telegram arrived from his agent in California: "WARNER'S OFFER CONTRACT SEVEN YEARS, ONE YEAR'S OPTION, STARTING AT $200 A WEEK. WHAT SHALL I DO?" Reagan's immediate reply: "HAVE JUST DONE A CHILDISH TRICK. SIGN BEFORE THEY CHANGE THEIR MINDS."[53]

2

Mr. Norm Is My Alias

During Reagan's early days in Hollywood, an industry veteran advised him that studios sometimes took six months to cast a new actor in a role. He prepared to wait. Within days of arriving, however, the lucky newcomer was making his first film, *The Inside Story* (later changed to *Love Is on the Air*). It was a B movie, meaning it would get second billing to the bigger productions that featured the studio's top stars. The Bs were the industry's minor leagues, where Reagan would work if and until Warner Bros. saw the star quality that justified a promotion. Over time, and to his great disappointment, the Bs would become his habitat. He would later joke he became the "Errol Flynn of the B pictures." On another occasion he quipped, "I was as brave as Errol, but in a low-budget fashion."[1]

His first movie was forgettable, although Reagan was not. The *Hollywood Reporter* noticed him, declaring Reagan "a natural, giving one of the best first picture performances Hollywood has offered in many a day."[2] In the sixty-minute movie, which took only three weeks to film, Reagan played a crime-fighting small-town radio announcer. It would not be the last time the studio gave him a role requiring little dramatic muscle as he portrayed a version of his wholesome off-screen persona. Although this was not the movie's leading role, it was a thrilling debut in the business that had captured his imagination years earlier. Writing an account of his early months in Hollywood in the *Des Moines Register*, one of more than a dozen he would pen for the paper that year, Reagan described acting in his first scene: "I was surprised to hear [the director] shout 'Cut!' and almost dropped dead when he okayed the scene on the very first try. A warm glow swept over me, and I glanced rather proudly at the sidelines. I'd made my first movie scene. I was an ACTOR."[3]

Persuaded that Reagan had potential as a star, Warner Bros. gave him a raise and picked up his option for another six months. Feeling confident he could earn a living in Hollywood, he sent for his parents and found his father a job at Warner Bros., where he managed his son's fan mail. Now, he said, "I faced the same kind of problem I faced during my first year at Eureka College when [Coach Ralph] Mac McKenzie relegated me to the fifth string of the football squad: I had made the team; now I had to make the first string." In his first eighteen months, Reagan had roles in thirteen movies. Most took three or four weeks to film. "I was proud of some of the B pictures we made," Reagan later asserted, "but a lot of them were pretty poor. They were movies the studio didn't want good, they wanted 'em Thursday."[4] His wait for a role in an A movie frustrated him. "It seemed like my term of apprenticeship would never end," he said in 1941.[5]

Reagan would get some decent roles, and he would win praise for his acting in a few films. He admitted, however, to "a lot of disappointments" in his movie career. "You'd make an A picture and think you did okay and then find yourself back in the B's, a little frustrated and saying unkind things about the studio's judgment."[6] He was not as bad at acting as some critics later claimed, but he would be recognized rarely—in acting talent, at least—among top ranks of Hollywood performers. Colleagues knew him as a "dependable guy, never late, hung-over, or difficult to work with."[7] One fan magazine described Reagan as "the clear-eyed, clean-thinking young American in uniform. You can see a montage of American Background when you look at him—debating teams, football, ski parties, summer jobs in a gas station, junior proms, fraternity pin on his best girl's sweater, home for Christmas, home for Easter. Your mother would approve of him. Your dad would talk politics with him while you dressed." He knew he was no rakish, bad-boy charmer like Flynn or Charles Boyer. "Mr. Norm is my alias," he once said.[8] As *Current Biography* wrote, "Critics generally considered him a competent performer and his scrubbed wholesome, 'typically American' appearance made him a favorite of motion picture audiences."[9] As another critic would write in 1947, "He was just a pleasant fellow, a bit on the colorless side, lacking fire or whatever you call that 'something' which really big stars have."[10]

Ron Reagan noted one quality his father lacked that prevented him from achieving major stardom: "While he was an astonishingly good-looking, extremely photogenic man—I'll bet even the shot on his driver's license was a keeper—he, nevertheless, generally failed to project on-screen the urgent sexuality, the heat, that made some of his contemporaries like Flynn, Clark Gable, even Humphrey Bogart genuine movie stars."[11]

Writing in 1985, biographer Garry Wills observed Reagan was not as obsessed with acting as with being a star. "He learned his lines; was winning, conscientious, dependable; but did not agonize over character. He never aspired to *become* the character he played. Even in what he considers his greatest feat of acting intensity [his 1942 A movie, *Kings Row*], he emphasizes that he screamed well [in the role of] Drake McHugh only because he thought of the scene as showing 'Ronald Reagan with his legs cut off.'" Reagan longed to star in action-adventure films, but Warner Bros. cast him mostly in light comedy roles. For his book on Reagan, Wills uncovered research by the Gallup polling organization that the studio commissioned on the young actor and his on-screen persona. "It showed," Wills wrote, "that Reagan was more popular with women than men (an interesting contrast to his presidential polls) and most popular with women in the twelve-to-seventeen age bracket (an important audience at the box office). He was the bobbysoxers' hero, the Tab Hunter of his day." As one observer later concluded, "Obviously, Fate had not designed him to be a movie star." Rather, as Wills wrote, "Reagan failed in Hollywood because he was not satisfied with his proper rung, with the range he commanded, but attempted heavier roles he could not sustain."[12] Reagan wanted complex roles, but he was best at playing himself. This would inhibit his Hollywood career but would prove invaluable when he entered politics in the 1960s.

There was another reason Reagan never achieved the super-stardom about which he had dreamed: his attention to movies competed with a growing fascination with public affairs. Some fellow actors did not believe he was serious about acting. Bette Davis, the fabled screen star with whom Reagan appeared in the 1939 film *Dark Victory*, saw him as nothing more than a "silly boy." Others, before they came to know him well, regarded Reagan as shallow or unserious. "To his co-workers, he appeared to lack the ambition and dedication needed to be a great actor or even a top star," biographer Anne Edwards wrote. "Those who did not know him judged him by the naive or brassy characters he generally portrayed on screen and by his mediocre talent, and pretty much dismissed him."[13]

Cast and crew members, who wanted only to shoot that day's scenes and eat or relax in silence, often viewed Reagan as too serious about politics. When not on camera, he read a book or chatted up crew members or actors about current affairs. "Making movies is a very boring thing to do, particularly for actors," Reagan's occasional co-star Larry Williams wrote in 1980. "Ronnie was never bored. You noticed it at once. There was something about all that idle time on the movie set that seemed to stimulate him in some private way. Far from finding the long dreary hours a drag like the slothful rest of us, Ronnie seemed to embrace them as a happy challenge. To him this time appeared to represent a splendid opportunity for serious social discourse, a chance to express his animated views on an infinite variety of subjects to us, his fellow actor-captives."[14] From a young age Reagan had a photographic memory. "I could pick up something to read and memorize it fairly quickly," he wrote years later.[15] Williams witnessed the power of Reagan's memory, as he recalled:

> Ronnie was so charming and earnest as he went about this task, it couldn't help but invigorate us—at least during the

first part of each working day. His general attitude toward our common boring situation just seemed so much nicer than ours, causing the bellyachers among us to feel guilty, and made us frown with enormous interest as we listened to Ronnie's astonishing fund of statistics.

For statistical information of all sorts was a commodity Ronnie always had in extraordinary supply, carried either in his pockets or in his head. Not only was this information abundant, it was stunning in its catholicity. There seemed to be absolutely no subject, however recondite, without its immediately accessible file. Ron had the dope on just about everything: this quarter's up-or-down figures on GNP growth, V. I. Lenin's grandfather's occupation, all history's baseball pitchers' ERAS, the optimistic outlook for California sugar-beet production in the year 2000, the recent diminution of the rainfall level causing everything to go to hell in summer [in] Kansas and so on. One could not help but be impressed.

Williams described, tongue-in-cheek, a typical encounter with Reagan: "Larry, before I run down for you this Far Eastern concept I'm sort of kicking around in my mind, answer me a background question: What would you say is the current population of Formosa?"

"Ronnie, I don't know things like that."

"Right. Most Americans don't. No need to apologize."

"I'm glad."

"I've got the figure right here, but before I give it to you maybe I should just jog your memory a bit about Chinese history in the last three thousand years."

"Swell, Ron, but I think I see somebody over there waving for us to come to the set."[16]

Unlike many actors who wiled away downtime with idle pursuits, Reagan became a bookworm. Words, a former colleague would recall, "are what he stockpiled. The bulk of his perceptions—and this is strange for a man who is in a visual arena, pictures and so on—came through words."[17] Irving Wallace, a screenwriter who served with Reagan in the Army in the 1940s, remembered avoiding political arguments with him. "The statistics-quoting was unnerving," he told journalist Jessica Mitford in 1965, "it went on endlessly, a fountain." Wallace recalled Reagan's response to the weekly arrival of the post's *Reader's Digest*. "He'd grab it like a starving man grabbing for food. Then he'd read it from cover to cover, absorb it. Then he'd tell us everything he'd read in it, launch into long and serious discussions about the articles." Wallace, however, was unimpressed with Reagan's mind. As he told Mitford, "He's a man who parrots things—shallow and affable."[18] Actor Robert Cummings recalled: "He did expound on the set a lot, even in 1941. He was a passionate Democrat."[19]

Reagan's reading diet included the *Wall Street Journal*, *Washington Post, Christian Science Monitor, Reader's Digest*, and sometimes pages of the *Congressional Record* that friends shared with him. A colleague from his early film days, however, recalled, "No one was quite sure he was accurate, but he sure as hell sounded accurate."[20] As Reagan would prove in the coming decades, he was not a sophisticated, discriminating consumer of information. "Reagan was sort of an equal opportunity reader, who tended to believe anything he saw in print was true," biographer Lou Cannon observed, "particularly if it reinforced his point of view. He had a powerful but indiscriminate memory that rarely distinguished between the actual and the apocryphal."[21] As Larry Williams wrote in 1980, "It recently struck me as rather odd that none of us ever seemed to question Ron about the reliability of the sources of his often quite alarming information. On reflection I suppose the answer is that we were afraid he might tell us."[22]

Reagan not only enjoyed sharing what he read; he sparred with his more conservative friends. "They had made many films together, but arguing politics drew them together," actress June Allyson said of Reagan and her husband, actor Dick Powell. "It was a riot to listen to Ronnie, a staunch Democrat, trying to convert Richard while Richard argued just as hard to turn Ronnie Republican."[23] Hoping to coax his friend over to the Republican side, Powell once told Reagan that he should switch parties. Powell said he had well-connected friends who could finance a campaign if Reagan wanted to run for Congress. Reagan laughed off the suggestion.[24]

One person who grew weary of Reagan's fascination with politics was his wife, Jane Wyman, a gifted young actress he met when they starred in the 1938 film *Brother Rat*. In the first years of their marriage, Reagan had dazzled Wyman and she tolerated her husband's interest in politics. Wyman was as single-minded in her devotion to the acting craft as Reagan's loyalties were split between acting and politics. Early on, however, June Allyson noticed Wyman's occasional annoyance with Reagan's long-windedness when Allyson asked Reagan a question about politics as a ploy to enter the conversation between him and her husband. "He answered me carefully, methodically," Allyson recalled. "When Ronnie got through explaining something to me, Jane Wyman leaned over and said, 'Don't ask Ronnie what time it is because he will tell you how a watch is made.'"[25]

Those not bored by his diatribes or distrusting of his facts often found Reagan a fascinating character. "As far back as I remember, he was always interested in issues," said Lee Annenberg, whose husband, Walter (he would later publish TV *Guide*), first met Reagan in 1937. "I always thought he was a very thoughtful and discerning man. He wasn't just a Hollywood star, he was a thinking man. A lot of people didn't realize that." Jane Bryan, who co-starred with Reagan in the 1938 film *Girls on Probation* and was the wife of his good friend Justin Dart, remembered Reagan in those days as someone who "followed the political news as enthusiastically as he followed events in the motion-picture industry."[26] A Republican business executive, Dart recalled the Reagan he met in the early 1940s as "a rabid Democrat. The night we first met we fought like cats and dogs. My wife warned me not to talk politics with him."[27]

If well informed—or at least well read—Reagan was also a political innocent. He was a liberal Democrat with an inherited ideology. Of his political views in the 1940s, Reagan recalled: "I was a near-hopeless hemophilic liberal. I bled for 'causes'; I had voted Democratic, following my father, in every election. I had followed FDR blindly, though with some misgivings. I was to continue voting Democratic through the 1948 election—Harry S. Truman can credit me with at least one assist—but never thereafter. The story of my disillusionment with big government is linked fundamentally with the ideals that suddenly sprouted and put forth in the war years."[28]

Lou Cannon, an astute journalist who covered Reagan in California and in Washington, regarded his liberalism of the 1940s as something far less than the "hemophilic" condition Reagan described. "Even in his relatively liberal phase," Cannon wrote, "Reagan was no indiscriminate joiner, and most of his political activity in the postwar years was limited to the Screen Actors Guild. He took a brief fling with the utopian-minded World Federalists, but at a time when liberal-sounding Communist-front organizations were a dime a dozen in Hollywood, Reagan joined only two." Cannon believed Reagan "left both groups as soon as he realized that Communists were running the show."[29] Journalist Joseph Lewis, who studied Reagan's early years, decided that, like many in "the movie colony," he "had not arrived at liberalism by working out his own position; he simply struck a pose."[30]

BY 1941, REAGAN HAD attained the status of sometime-A-movie actor. Only thirty years old, he was among the highest-paid stars in Hollywood, having appeared in several successful films. In 1940 he had scored the iconic role of University of Notre Dame halfback George Gipp in *Knute Rockne, All American*, co-starring his friend and mentor Pat O'Brien. (Whence came Reagan's nickname later in life, "The Gipper.") That year he also played George Armstrong Custer in *Santa Fe Trail* with Errol Flynn and Olivia de Havilland (it was one of the year's top-grossing films). And as the United States entered the world war in December 1941, Reagan wrapped up work on the best role of his film career. In 1942's *Kings Row*—based on the 1940 best-selling novel of the same name—he played a rich playboy, Drake McHugh, who lost his legs after an operation by an unscrupulous surgeon. In the film's signature scene, Reagan's character awakened to discover his limbs missing and cried, "Where's the rest of me?!" The memorable line would become the title of his 1965 memoir.

The movie earned three Academy Award nominations, including Best Picture and Best Director. Reagan lamented that he did not receive a nomination, but the film was not without its rewards for him. Warner Bros. gave him a seven-year, $1 million contract extension, and he soon filmed his next movie, a wartime story with Errol Flynn.[31] "I couldn't be happier," Reagan told his home-town paper, the *Dixon Evening Telegraph*, in September 1941.[32]

As Reagan's star rose, war brewed in Europe. And the growing conflict presented the opportunity for his foray into political advocacy—as a movie character. "Fully one-third of Reagan's first thirty movies, several of them made in cooperation with military authorities, encouraged military preparedness or warned of threats to security," historian Stephen Vaughn wrote.[33] In particular, Reagan made a series of movies in 1939 and 1940 in which he played Secret Service agent Bass Bancroft, including *Secret Service of the Air*, *Code of the Secret Service*, and *Murder in the Air*. The films were overtly patriotic and featured implicit warnings about the crisis in Europe. One of Reagan's 1941 films, *International Squadron*, based on the daring Royal Air Force in which he played brash American pilot Jimmy Grant, promoted preparedness. In the movie, Reagan's character is at first skeptical of the Nazi threat but eventually is persuaded of the moral urgency to help Britain against Hitler. "It is wrong to think of ourselves," Grant says finally. "There is so much to be done." At the movie's end, Grant flies a suicide mission behind German lines. (The movie was a remake of a 1936 film, *Ceiling Zero*, starring James Cagney. "Reagan gives the role his all," one reviewer wrote, "and that's good enough, but he never quite makes his screwball pilot the first-class heel that Cagney made him.")[34] The next year, Reagan co-starred with Errol Flynn in another patriotic pro-war film, 1942's *Desperate Journey*, an absurd story about an RAF bomber crew shot down over Nazi Germany that Reagan believed trivialized Nazi atrocities.[35]

Americanism—which studio head Jack Warner described as "antifascist as well as anticommunist"—was a frequent theme of Warner Bros. movies before America's entry into the war. In May 1940 Jack and his brother Harry had urged President Roosevelt to organize the film industry to fight Nazism. "We would rather die in an effort to be helpful," the Warners said, "than live to see barbarism triumph."[36] In another setting Warner had said, "I tell you, Catholic, Protestant, Jew, or whatever faith you may observe, we must all be Americans first, last, and always."[37]

Warner would later cite the studio's pro-war films in testimony before the House Un-American Activities Committee (HUAC) as evidence of his studio's and his actors' patriotism. As a leading star in the Warner Bros. stable, Reagan's heroic characters had helped alert the public to the dangers that Nazi Germany posed. It was not surprising, then, that these and other roles burnished Reagan's public image. As Stephen Vaughn noted, his popular appeal before, during, and after the war "was strongest among moviegoers under age eighteen. Whether they or others who attended movies distinguished between Reagan, the private citizen . . . and the image they saw on screen is uncertain, but by late 1941, few Americans were more visibly associated with military valor."[38]

Just as Reagan's acting career accelerated, the Army summoned. In April 1942, done filming *Desperate Journey*, Reagan responded to his draft notice and reported for a physical exam. He had served as an Army Reserve cavalryman since his days in Des Moines (where he had bluffed his way through the requisite eye exam). When the Army administered a vision test in Los Angeles, however, doctors ruled him ineligible for combat. But the military branches did not exempt those with poor eyesight from service, and they assigned soldiers like Reagan to noncombat duties. The Army sent Reagan to Fort Mason at the San Francisco Port of Embarkation, where for several months he served as a liaison officer supervising a company of ROTC cadets loading supply ships bound for Australia. He returned to Los Angeles in June to work in the First Motion Picture Unit of the Army Air Corps in Culver City. The unit leased the fourteen-acre Hal Roach Studios. Lieutenant (and later Captain) Reagan spent much of the conflict there (except for eleven months in 1944 in New York, where he helped campaign for the Sixth War Loan Drive) as an adjutant and personnel officer who also made training and propaganda films. Some in Hollywood would ridicule the unit's mission as fighting the "Battle of Beverly Hills" and joked that its motto was "We kill 'em with fil'm." The *Hollywood Reporter* called Reagan a "Cutting Room Commando."[39] But there was no shame in his stateside wartime duties. Some able-bodied film stars—including John Wayne and Roy Rogers—avoided military service altogether. At "Fort Roach," Reagan served with other Hollywood actors assigned to the unit, including his good friend William Holden (who would serve as best man at Reagan's second wedding), Alan Ladd, DeForest Kelley, and Van Heflin.[40]

Reagan starred in only one full-length movie during the war: Irving Berlin's 1943 musical *This Is the Army*. The Army lent him to Warner Bros. to make the patriotic movie that benefited the Army Emergency Relief Fund. In the film he played Johnny Jones, son to the character played by song and dance man George Murphy. The two would become lifelong friends, a relationship born of their movie careers and cemented by politics. (The Republican Murphy would win a U.S. Senate seat from California in 1964.) The Army Air Corps also featured Reagan in several short films as a narrator and sometimes as an actor. A 1942 propaganda film that Reagan narrated, *Beyond the Line of Duty* (about the exploits of an American bomber pilot, Capt. Hewitt T. "Shorty" Wheless, in the Philippines), won the Academy Award for "Best Short Subject" in 1943. Other films Reagan helped make included *Mister Gardenia Jones* (1942), *Cadet Classification* (1943), *The Rear Gunner* (1943), *For God and Country* (1943), *Target Tokyo* (1945), *The Fight for the Sky* (1945), *The Stilwell Road* (1945), and *Wings for This Man* (1945). Theaters featured some of the movies between the first and second films of double features or sometimes in place of the first film.[41]

Beyond movies, several popular magazines displayed a uniformed Reagan with Wyman and portrayed them as the perfect war couple. Reagan's fan mail swelled so much he persuaded Warner Bros. to hire his mother to answer it (Reagan gave her the job that had been his father's before he died of a heart attack in 1941 and paid her seventy-five dollars a week, to be deducted from his contract after the war). As Vaughn observed of the "wide publicity" given Reagan's wartime service, "If people missed his training pictures, millions saw him in *This Is the Army* or in magazines. No twentieth-century president, except for Dwight D. Eisenhower, had been seen in uniform by more people."[42]

Reagan rarely talked about having avoided combat, but there are indications it embarrassed him. His friend actor Eddie Albert, having fought heroically in the brutal battle of Tarawa in the Pacific, returned to Hollywood in 1945 and recalled, "Ronnie was the first person I went to see. I had something for him." Albert presented Reagan with a *netsuke*, a button-like ornament he had removed from the uniform of a dead Japanese soldier. "I handed it over and explained what it was, and he was appreciative—but I've never forgotten the way he looked," Albert told Reagan biographer Edmund Morris. "Like I'd humiliated him." When Morris asked Reagan about the episode, he gushed with admiration for Albert's heroism and added, "I was legally blind. Lucky to have been allowed to do what I did."[43]

REAGAN LATER WROTE THAT his experience with the Army's bureaucracy prompted his first doubts about liberalism and faith in government. As the post's adjutant and personnel officer, he worked closely with the civilian bureaucrats at Fort Roach. He recalled:

And it didn't take long for me to decide I didn't think much of the inefficiency, empire building, and business-as-usual attitude that existed in wartime under the civil service system. If I suggested that an employee might be expendable, his supervisor would look at me as if I were crazy. He didn't want to reduce the size of his department; his salary was based to a large extent on the number of people he supervised. He wanted to increase it, not decrease it. I discovered it was almost impossible to remove an incompetent or lazy worker and that one of the most popular methods supervisors used in dealing with an incompetent was to transfer him or her out of his department to a higher-paying job in another department.[44]

While Reagan's wartime Army films had burnished his fame, his stature as a serious actor waned. When he reentered civilian life in September 1945, newer and better actors—who were not finishing a four-year hiatus from dramatic, nonwar movies—had supplanted him. As biographer Bob Spitz observed, Reagan's "relatively bland, one-dimensional persona—the idealistic, likable best friend—felt dated in this new atmosphere."[45] Between his lone 1943 film, *This Is the Army*, and his first 1947 film, *Stallion Road*, Reagan did not appear in one Warner Bros. production. "Coming out of the cage of the Army back into the free-for-all civilian life, I was well fixed," Reagan wrote later. "My $3,500-a-week contract was running; Warner's were casting about for a movie script that would pay them off." The studio, however, did not find much for Reagan in those postwar years and nothing of the quality offered him before the war. To occupy his time, Reagan said he built model ships and decamped for a time to nearby Lake Arrowhead, where Wyman was making a movie on location. There he raced a rented speedboat around the lake. The boat's owner worried about him. "It's all right," Reagan said he told the man. "I just want to know that the boat is there at the dock any time I want to take a drive on the water. I can't walk on it anymore."[46]

With so much time on his hands, Reagan reflected on the societal and governmental changes the war had wrought and said it influenced his political views. "Like most of the soldiers who came back, I expected a world suddenly reformed," he wrote in his 1965 memoir. "I hoped and believed that the blood and death and confusion of World War II would result in a regeneration of mankind."[47] In his 1990 book, Reagan credited his political awakening to a growing disenchantment with the New Deal. "At the end of World War II, I was a New Dealer to the core," he wrote. "I thought government could solve all our postwar problems just as it had ended the Depression and won the war. I didn't trust big business. I thought government, not private companies, should own our big public utilities; if there wasn't enough housing to shelter the American people, I thought government should build it; if we needed better medical care, the answer was socialized medicine." But Reagan did not see the New Deal addressing the many problems afflicting veterans. "I learned that a thousand bucks under the table was the formula for buying a new car. I learned that the real-estate squeeze was on for the serviceman. I discovered that the rich had got just a little richer and a lot of the poor had done a pretty good job of grabbing a quick buck. I discovered that the world was almost the same and perhaps a little worse."[48]

Although he was correct in noting the postwar housing shortage for veterans, Reagan offered a distorted portrayal of the treatment of veterans. In his version of the postwar years, he omitted any mention of the 1946 federal legislation appropriating funds to buy automobiles for returning servicemen who had lost a leg. By 1950 the legislation helped more than 25,000 returning veterans buy cars. He also did not mention the Serviceman's Readjustment Act of 1944—better known as the GI Bill—that enabled 2.2 million veterans to attend college and helped another 3.5 million to study at a trade or vocational school. "Legislation affecting veterans did not stop with the GI Bill," historian Mark D. Van Ells wrote in his 2001 history of returning World War II veterans. "Indeed, the volume of federal veterans' legislation produced during the war was staggering. Between passage of the Selective Service Act in September 1940 and the end of the war in 1945, the federal government enacted 187 laws affecting veterans. By July 1948 that total had risen to 462."[49]

Nevertheless, it was the perceived disrespect for returning soldiers that prompted Reagan's first political speech on December 8, 1945, at the Santa Ana Municipal Bowl for "United America Day." Organizers planned the event to discourage discrimination against Americans of Japanese ancestry who served in the armed forces. Reagan joined Gen. Joseph Stilwell in honoring a local Nisei veteran, Staff Sgt. Kazuo Masuda, who died in battle. (*Nisei* was a term used to describe the American-born children of Japanese immigrants.) Wearing his Army uniform for the last time, Reagan thanked Masuda's parents for their son's sacrifice and added: "The blood that has soaked into the sands of the beaches is all one color. America stands unique in the world—a country not founded on race, but on a way and an ideal. Not in spite of, but because of, our polyglot background, we have had all the strength in the world. That is the American way."[50]

Some saw Communism as the greatest threat in postwar America, but Reagan worried about "the rise of fascism in our country, the very thing we had fought to obliterate." What he meant was that "scores of new veterans' groups had sprouted up around the country and were trying to peddle some of the same venom of fascist bigotry that we had just defeated in the war."[51] Reagan said he watched more than forty veterans' organizations form, "most of which seemed to be highly intolerant of color, creed, and common sense." He joined the left-leaning American Veterans Committee (AVC) "because of their feeling that the members should be citizens first and veterans afterward—and, as it worked out, I became a big wheel in their operations."[52] He chaired the AVC's Hollywood membership board and recruited hundreds of veterans. Recalled the AVC's founder, Gilbert A. Harrison, who recruited Reagan to join the organization: "I've never known a man ask such careful, probing questions before agreeing, after long thought, to give us his support. It was as if *he* were recruiting *me*."[53]

Reagan also enlisted in the California Democratic Party, helping James Roosevelt—state party chairman and eldest son of FDR—keep the party afloat in 1946. In the fall elections, in which Democrats lost badly across the state, Reagan supported the party with a $1,000 loan. Perhaps Reagan warmed to the Democrats' cause for the chance to support and work with the chairman, whose father had been his political hero.[54] Regardless, his role in the campaign suggested that, while he might have been disappointed by Washington's treatment of war veterans, he was far from disillusioned with the Democratic Party or its candidates.

Reagan was passionate enough about what he saw as the dangers of "native fascism" to write a column in the American Veterans Committee's publication, the AVC *Bulletin*. In its February 15, 1946, edition, he wrote that fascism "is a great menace, and is closely aligned with part of the present attack on labor and price controls. It is the obvious hope of homegrown fascists that runaway inflation with its resultant depression and army of unemployed would give the hatemongers the fertile field necessary to realize their dream of a strongman government in America."[55]

Reagan also joined several other liberal groups, including the Hollywood Democratic Committee, Americans for Democratic Action, the United World Federalists, and the Hollywood Democratic Committee.[56] He said during these early postwar years, "I was blindly and busily joining every organization I could find that would guarantee to save the world." As his activism caught the attention of various groups, Reagan received speaking invitations. "I became an easy mark for speechmaking on the rubber-chicken and glass-tinkling circuits," he said, admitting the attention "fed my ego, since I had been so long away from the screen." Although his subject was what he saw as creeping fascism, Reagan acknowledged, "I was not sharp about communism."

That changed in the spring of 1946 when he finished a speech to a men's club at the Hollywood Beverly Christian Church, to which he belonged. His pastor approached him with compliments about his remarks. But he added, "I think your speech would be even better if you also mentioned that if Communism ever looked like a threat, you'd be just as opposed to it as you are to fascism." Reagan replied that he had not given Communism much thought, but he would consider the suggestion.

The next time he spoke to a Los Angeles civic organization, as a substitute speaker for James Roosevelt, Reagan delivered his usual warnings about fascism to "riotous applause" but added a new line: "I've talked about the continuing threat of fascism in the postwar world, but there's another 'ism,' Communism, and if I ever find evidence that Communism represents a threat to all that we believe in and stand for, I'll speak out just as harshly against Communism as I have fascism." In Reagan's recollection of the moment, he walked off the stage to "a dead silence" and "into the clasp of a friend whose face reflected my own amazement."

"Did you hear that?" the friend whispered.

"I didn't hear anything," Reagan replied.

"That's what I heard," the friend said.

Two days later, Reagan said, a letter arrived from a woman who had been in the audience. She congratulated him on his stance against Communism and explained why his listeners had greeted his denunciation with silence: "I think the group is becoming a front for Communists." The experience caused him enough dismay that he stopped giving speeches. "I had been shooting off my mouth without knowing my real target," he admitted. "I determined to do my own research, find out my own facts."[57]

Among those who nudged Reagan toward the anti-Communist cause was Sam Wood, the director of Reagan's 1942 film *Kings Row*. Wood was an ardent political conservative who had opposed U.S. entry into World War II because he feared that forcing Nazi Germany into a two-front conflict would embolden the Soviet Union. Although Reagan did not see the war through Wood's eyes, his friend's hostility toward the Soviet Union impressed him and influenced a gradual awakening about Communism in Russia and the United States. Wood had also tried to persuade Reagan to join the Motion Picture Alliance for the Preservation of American Ideals, a conservative group formed secretly in 1943 and unveiled in February 1944 by some of Hollywood's top stars and movie executives.[58] Reagan said he declined because of the group's covert creation.[59]

Reagan's anti-Communist feelings deepened in the summer of 1946 when an organization he had joined before the war rejected a resolution denouncing Communism. First called the Hollywood Democratic Committee, the Hollywood Independent Citizens Committee of the Arts, Sciences, and Professions (HICCASP) was a liberal organization that had backed Franklin Roosevelt's policies. James Roosevelt chaired the organization. Hoping to demonstrate the committee's independence from Communist and other radical movements, Reagan proposed a statement declaring HICCASP "has no affiliation with any political party or organization, Republican, Democratic, Communist, Socialist, or other." Some members, including Olivia de Havilland, believed the statement "didn't go far enough" in denouncing Communism. During the debate, Reagan recalled, one "well-known musician sprang to his feet" and volunteered to "recite the USSR consti-tution from memory, yelling that it was a lot more democratic than [the Constitution] of the United States." Then, Reagan said, a prominent writer declared he would side with Russia in a war with the United States. "Well, sir," Reagan remembered, "I found myself waist-high in epithets such as 'Fascist" and 'capitalist scum' and 'enemy of the proletariat' and 'witch hunter' and 'Red-baiter' before I could say boo."[60]

Reagan said the meeting and its outcome shook him. "You can imagine what this did to my naiveté," he wrote.[61] HICCASP's rejection of the resolution opened his eyes. "It was all the proof we needed: HICCASP had become a Communist front organization hiding behind a few well-intentioned Hollywood celebrities to give it credibility." Reagan said he and several other actors serving on the board, including de Havilland, resigned in protest. Shortly after he denounced Communism in a speech to SAG members, Reagan said he arrived to speak to a veterans' organization in Los Angeles. "As soon as I sat down, every member on the board who had been sitting on that side of the aisle got up and moved to the other side, leaving me to sit alone." Reagan said he later learned "the group had become another front for the Communist Party in Hollywood." [62]

Reagan's version of his resignation from HICCASP may not have been accurate. If scandalized by discovering HICCASP's Communist leanings, he was not concerned enough to resign immediately. He waited several months to quit the group and remained associated as "an observer" through October 1946.[63] One informant told the FBI in Los Angeles that Reagan's "professions of anti-Communism" did not ring with candor. "These Johnnies-come-lately raise in me a question as to their basic sincerity."[64] Reagan's brother, Neil, a Hollywood public relations executive, also recalled that he badgered him for months about leaving HICCASP. "Get out of that thing," he said he urged his brother. "There are people in [HICCASP] who can cause you real trouble." Neil claimed he was, at the time, helping the FBI spy on the organization's meetings, believing its members were "not exactly American."[65]

Regardless of its timing and intensity, Reagan's opposition to Communism was genuine, if not deep or well informed. "The zealousness with which Reagan turned to anticommunism," journalist Will Bunch asserted, "was part of a lifelong habit of basing his broad policy ideas on life experiences, part of his preference for the anecdotal over the ideological, for the personal over the polemical."[66] There was another important reason for Reagan's growing passion: as an actor eager for better roles from Warner Bros., he knew well Jack Warner's hostility to both ideologies and the mogul's strong support for so-called Americanism. As Warner told his employees in 1940, "We don't want anybody employed by our company who belongs to [any] . . . communist, fascistic, or any other un-American organization."[67]

Whatever the reason, Reagan's was an enduring philosophy that would influence the rest of his professional life—in the movies, throughout his television years in the 1950s and early 1960s, and during his political career. That it started as a throwaway line did not embarrass or trouble him. He had found his passion and what would become the consistent, animating issue of his public life. "For a long while," he wrote, "I believed the best way to beat the Communists was through the forces of liberal democracy, which had just defeated Hitler's brand of totalitarianism: liberal Democrats believed it is up to the people to decide what is best for them, not—as the Communists, Nazis, and other fascists believed—the few determining what is good for the rest of us." Reagan said he worried "that a lot of 'liberals' couldn't accept the notion that Moscow had bad intentions or wanted to take over Hollywood."[68]

3

Have You Ever Heard Him Talk?

N o matter who he was with—wife, brother, cast and crew members, or friends—Reagan would hold forth about politics. "He's a boring liberal," actress Marsha Hunt told one Hollywood gossip columnist about Reagan. "He would buttonhole you at a party and talk liberalism at you. You'd look for an escape."[1] Recalled director Vincent Sherman: "He was well informed about many subjects and it was kind of a joke around the lot that he could expound on almost anything and frequently did. Some considered him a walking encyclopedia."[2] One good friend, actress Doris Day, recalled her conversations with Reagan about politics in the 1940s. "It wasn't really conversation," she wrote in her 1975 memoir, "it was rather talking at you, sort of long discourses on subjects that interested him. I remember telling him that he should be touring the country making speeches. He was very good at it."[3] June Allyson saw that Reagan's passion for politics tried his wife's patience. "He'll outgrow it," Allyson said she counseled Wyman. "To [Jane] it wasn't funny. But even more annoying to her was the fact that it took Ronnie so long to make up his mind about anything she asked him."[4] Actress Ruth Warrick recalled of Reagan in the 1940s: "He didn't talk; he pontificated, even then. He was a terrific salesman, and he believed the homilies he spouted."[5]

Reagan often talked politics during parties at the homes of

Hollywood friends like Jack Benny and George Burns. Joined by his older brother, Neil, a conservative Republican, Reagan would lecture and debate as long as anyone would listen.[6] "We spent hours arguing—sometimes with pretty strong language—over the future of the country," Reagan wrote about his political squabbles with Neil. His brother's complaints included the growth of the federal government and what he thought was its encroachment into "the American economy from the railroads to the corner store." Neil also believed the United States could no longer trust Russia. "I claimed," Reagan wrote, "[Neil] was just spouting Republican propaganda."[7]

One subject that interested Reagan in the mid-1940s was the threat of nuclear war. Before he resigned from HICCASP, Reagan headlined the group's December 1945 antinuclear rally at the Hollywood Stadium. Reagan read a poem, "Set Your Clock at U-235," composed by radio scriptwriter Norman Corwin. "The secrets of the earth have been peeled, one by one, until the core is bare," Reagan said, reading Corwin's composition. "The latest recipe is private, in a guarded book, but the stink of death is public on the wind from Nagasaki." Jack Warner objected when he learned about Reagan's participation in the rally. Reading the work of another person, Warner told Reagan in a letter, "would be in violation of the exclusive rights to your services as granted to us under your employment contract." Reagan did not fight his studio, but this and other appearances whetted his appetite for the limelight beyond the movies.[8] One example of his growing reputation in Hollywood politics was that Jack Benny, more than twenty years before Reagan would run for office, began calling his friend "Governor."[9]

That Reagan enjoyed debating politics with friends and colleagues was clear. What he lacked was a platform from which he could speak with greater authority—and an official responsibility to imbue his activism and rhetoric with credibility and force. In time, the Screen Actors Guild (SAG) became the perfect outlet for his budding political ambitions. During Reagan's early months in Hollywood, however, he had resented the union. He knew Hollywood actors "had just won a tough five-year battle with studios for the union shop and recognition of the Screen Actors Guild as the exclusive bargaining agent for actors." But he did not like that membership was compulsory. "Making me join the union," he complained, "whether I wanted to or not, I thought, was an infringement on my rights." He was even "uncertain as to why actors needed to have a union."[10] Those doubts evaporated within a few years. In August 1941 he attended his first SAG board meeting as a temporary replacement for British American actress Heather Angel. That good fortune was courtesy of Jane Wyman, also serving as a temporary board member. Wyman had told Jack Dales, the SAG executive secretary, "I don't think you've actually met my husband, Ronald Reagan, but I think he'll make a better alternate than me." Dales recalled "a bright look came" in Wyman's eyes as she added, "He might even become president of SAG one day—or maybe America." In the months that followed, Reagan impressed Dales and board members. "He was articulate," Dales recalled. "He spoke with reason, not with experience."[11]

In February 1946, Reagan returned to the board as an alternate, first for actor Rex Ingram and, the following month, for Boris Karloff. By September that year, members would elect him third vice president.[12] The timing was auspicious. For more than a year, Guild leaders had tried to sidestep a nasty labor dispute between two competing movie industry unions: the 10,000-member Conference of Studio Unions (CSU) and the 16,000-member International Alliance of Theatrical Stage Employees (IATSE). "What had always been, at least compared to other industrial workplaces, a relatively placid shop floor (the mob had seen to that) was roiled by dissension," historian Thomas Doherty wrote. "After a decade of scarcity followed by wartime sacrifice, below-the-line workers demanded a bigger slice of the pie from an industry flush with profits."[13] Herb Sorrell, a combative former boxer from Missouri, led the smaller but more radical union and hoped to establish it as the primary labor representative for the industry's rank-and-file workers. Sorrell and his members called a series of strikes and browbeat SAG for its support. Reagan and other Guild leaders, however, resisted choosing sides, even as some of their members discreetly crossed picket lines.

Reagan's public position on the strike—which amounted to tacit support of the studios and IATSE—angered CSU members, especially after he ignored the picket line while filming *Night unto Night*. (The strike would eventually shut down the film's production, and it would not be completed until January 1947. Warner Bros. released the movie in June 1949.)[14] Reagan believed the CSU was "a vehicle for Communist aims" and that it hoped "to grab something from another union that was rightfully theirs." Even so, he and other SAG board members kept their union on the sidelines. At a tumultuous rump meeting of 350 Guild members at the Hollywood Legion Stadium in December 1946, Reagan defended the board's neutral stance. "I confronted one of the most hostile audiences I ever hope to address," Reagan later said, adding that he told the group the dispute was jurisdictional and he hoped the board would embrace that position. "I launched into a dress rehearsal of the same report I was to give to the mass SAG meeting two nights later. It was giving the opposition ammunition, but it was also a chance to spike their guns."[15] Reagan's virtuoso performance impressed many of those in attendance. "He handled the affair with a courage and intelligence that commended the respect of his most bitter opponents," columnist Hedda Hopper would write in May 1947 after actor Robert Montgomery told her about the meeting. "Without resorting to notes, he reeled off facts and figures with an ease that flabbergasted members of the audience—particularly those who were trying to push their ideas through roughshod." Actor Sterling Hayden called Reagan "a one-man battalion."[16]

In a mail-in referendum, SAG members sided with Reagan and the board, voting overwhelmingly to remain officially neutral while they continued to cross picket lines. For his outspokenness, Reagan claimed he weathered death threats and that his local police department allowed him to carry a gun. In February 1947 the strike failed after SAG and other Hollywood unions repeatedly disregarded picket lines.[17] For Reagan, the experience was searing. He emerged persuaded that "the strike was part of a Soviet effort to gain control over Hollywood and the content of its films."[18]

While CSU had allied with some Communist-leaning organizations during the war, the Communist Party USA had first opposed the Hollywood strike, only later offering support. Its tactics were radical and its leadership was left-leaning, so it was easy for the CSU's opponents to brand it, unfairly, a Communist-controlled organization.[19] "My own conclusion is that [CSU leader Herb] Sorrell was not a Communist: in fact, he squabbled with the Communists frequently," wrote historian Gerald Horne, who studied the 1945–46 strike for his book *Class Struggle in Hollywood, 1930–1950.* "However, charging him with being a Red was useful in destabilizing CSU and bolstering IATSE. Repeatedly Sorrell was dragged before investigative bodies and pummeled with questions about his alleged party membership." Horne noted that because of his racism, "many Communists viewed Herb Sorrell with some contempt."[20]

What Reagan omitted from his telling of the strike story was that the FBI, as late as March 1946, thought Reagan himself might have Communist sympathies. The Los Angeles office had noted his membership in the Los Angeles Committee for a Democratic Far Eastern Policy, which agents suspected of Communist leanings. The FBI had also seen a clipping from the Communist *People's World* in February 1946 that listed Reagan among those supporting freedom for Indochina and an end to U.S. support for Chinese nationalist leader Chiang Kai-shek. In his biography of Reagan, Edmund Morris quoted several sources who intimated Reagan had tried to join the Communist Party shortly after arriving in Hollywood but was dissuaded by friends. Reagan adamantly denied this when Morris questioned him about it decades later. Morris did not believe him and concluded: "So what if Dutch, young and ardent in 1938, thrilled to the message of Marx for a few experimental months? Minds colder and clearer than his fortunately saw that he was not socialist material."[21]

Reagan later claimed his dedication to anti-Communism had hardened during the CSU strike when two FBI agents arrived at his house one evening in the spring of 1947. They told him about a recent meeting of the American Communist Party in Los Angeles, at which one member had said, "What the hell are we going to do about that son-of-bitching bastard Reagan?" Now instead of suspecting him of Communist leanings, the FBI wanted Reagan's cooperation. "Anybody that the Communists hate as much as they do you," he claimed the agents told him, "must know something that can help us." Reagan said he agreed to assist the agents, beginning a long relationship with the agency as one of eighteen informants from the film industry. (His brother and wife did the same.)[22]

The early labor disputes of Reagan's SAG presidency would persuade him the Communists hoped to seize the film industry by infiltrating other civic and professional organizations in Los Angeles. In his postpresidential memoir, Reagan noted American movies then "occupied seventy percent of all the playing time on the world's movie screens." And he concluded that "Joseph Stalin had set out to make Hollywood an instrument of propaganda for his program of Soviet expansion aimed at communizing the world."[23]

Reagan's desire for another dimension to his public career had coincided with his discovery of Communism as a threat to his industry and the United States. He may have shaded the truth, conflated events, and glossed over the sequence of other events in his conversion to rabid anti-Communism, but by late 1947 no informed person suspected him of having Communist sympathies. "Reagan emerged from these experiences as a lifelong anti-Communist but with few personal scars," biographer Lou Cannon wrote. "Unlike radicals or liberals who had looked to the Soviet Union as the hope of mankind and felt disillusioned or betrayed by the purge trials, the Stalin-Hitler pact, or the postwar Soviet takeover of Eastern Europe, Reagan never paid much attention to what was happening in Russia."

Cannon believed Reagan's portrayal of his fight against Communism in Hollywood was exaggerated and "one-dimensional." It was not so much opposition by patriots like Reagan that defeated Communism, Cannon believed, as it was the Communists' "dogmatic behavior." The most strident and inept among them repelled most of their former allies by the time of the U.S. House Un-American Activities Committee (HUAC) hearings in 1947.[24] When he later claimed credit for the exhausted collapse of the

Soviet Union, Reagan imagined his struggles against Communism in Hollywood were more consequential than reality suggests. Not that his opposition to Soviet ideology was insincere or of no consequence. He sometimes saw Communism where it did not exist.

In 1984, elected to a second term as U.S. president, Reagan would suggest to *Time* that the Russians were unhappy about his reelection. "You see, they remember back, I guess, [to] those [SAG] union days when we had a domestic Communist problem. I was very definitely on the wrong side for them."[25] To which biographer Garry Wills observed, "This has almost the ring of General [Douglas] MacArthur's claim that the Kremlin had been out to get him since he prevented the Bonus Army from overthrowing America's government. Reagan proves that such a belief can be held not only sincerely but without megalomania."[26] In her extensive analysis of Reagan's sudden embrace of anti-Communism for the journal *Political Psychology* in 1989, political scientist Betty Glad concluded:

> Reagan's turn to the right . . . was an adaption to a personal and professional crisis. Anti-Communism served certain ego defensive and social adjustment needs for him at a time when his personal and private life had bottomed out. His anti-communist crusade in the late forties not only enabled him to find new ways of making it on the Hollywood scene, it did not require any basic changes in either his personality or his basic worldviews. The communists in Hollywood and the federal government provided safe targets against which he could displace his anger and explain what had happened to him. His views brought him the approval of powerful figures in his environment, and were then reinforced by broader political trends and the opinions of close friends and family members.[27]

Whatever the reason for his newfound vocal opposition to Communism in Hollywood, Reagan's higher profile almost certainly resulted in his election as SAG president in March 1947. "I'll never forget the day he was named president of the union," actor Robert Stack recalled. "It was hairy. People were marching atop the roof of the American Legion Stadium. It was a time when hoods were trying to take over the union, and there were threats on Ronnie's life." Reagan's calm but determined manner impressed Stack. "I saw him act well under pressure."[28]

Hedda Hopper admitted she initially doubted Reagan could handle the SAG job. "He's as green as grass," the gossip columnist told Robert Montgomery, whom Reagan succeeded as union president. Montgomery replied, "Have you ever heard him talk?" Hopper had not, an omission she soon corrected by attending a SAG meeting. Afterward she admitted his superb skills. She had never known a "clearer speechmaker" as he interrupted "the rantings of windy orators by saying, 'Pardon me, but you're mistaken about that. Here are the facts.' And then he reeled them off with shattering logic." Hopper decided Reagan was "the best-informed star in town."[29]

In October 1947 Reagan joined Montgomery and George Murphy—each representing SAG—to testify in Washington before HUAC about alleged Communist influence in the movie industry. The committee's unethical and indiscriminate hunt for Communists in Hollywood would destroy the careers of ten producers, directors, and screenwriters, including prominent writers Dalton Trumbo and Ring Lardner. Jack Warner fingered most of them in his testimony before HUAC the day before Reagan's appearance. Reagan and his SAG colleagues were friendly witnesses, so committee members did not demand that they name movie industry figures suspected of Communist sympathies.

Republican congressman Richard Nixon of California—a first-term HUAC member building a reputation as an ardent Communist hunter—was not on the subcommittee investigating Hollywood. But Nixon had noticed Reagan's role in fighting Communists in the film industry. That spring he met with Reagan and urged him to testify. "I believe that he can be extremely helpful in the committee's investigation," Nixon told one of his prominent supporters. "I am going to make every effort to see that he is called as a witness." It was not that Reagan knew something about Communists in Hollywood that the committee did not; rather, it was that Nixon believed Reagan, as a noted New Deal liberal, could confer respectability and bipartisanship on the subcommittee's investigation. "Reagan would make a particularly good witness," Nixon noted, "in view of the fact that he is classified as a liberal and as such could not be accused of simply being a red-baiting reactionary."[30]

Reagan was not an eager witness, at least when the committee first asked him to testify. The committee's Los Angeles investigator, H. A. Smith, told his bosses in a September memo that Reagan "has no fear of any one, is a nice talker, well informed on the subject, and will make a splendid witness." He added:

> He states that he is a New Deal liberal, and does not agree with a number of individuals of the Motion Picture Alliance [for the Preservation of American Ideals]. I believe we straightened out a number of his differences, in that he felt [conservative actor Adolphe] Menjou and some of the others referred to him, Reagan, as a man who had been a Leftist and then reformed. Reagan resents this very much, as he states he never was a Leftist, that actually he got tangled up in a few committees he thought were all right, but it took him some time to learn they were not. As soon as he discovered that fact, he got out of them.[31]

Appearing before the committee, Reagan struck a professorial pose, wearing a beige gabardine suit and the thick eyeglasses that movie audiences never saw but on which the nearsighted actor depended when not on a movie set. The committee's chief investigator, Robert E. Stripling, did most of the questioning, having briefed Reagan in his hotel room the night before and given him questions he would ask. When Stripling asked him if Communists had infiltrated SAG, Reagan pushed back. He said there was a "small group" that opposed the board's policies. "That small clique referred to," Reagan said, "has been suspected of more or less following the tactics that we associate with the Communist Party." Reagan insisted, however, that Communists did not dominate Hollywood or SAG. They were only "a disruptive force." Asked what steps Congress might take to "rid the motion-picture industry of any Communist influence," Reagan told the committee much of the work was done. He asserted, "Ninety-nine percent of us are pretty well aware of what is going on, and I think within the bounds of our democratic rights, and never once stepping over the rights given us by democracy, we have done a pretty good job in our business of keeping those people's activities curtailed." He added:

> After all, we must recognize them as a political party. On that basis we have exposed their lies when we came across them, we have opposed their propaganda, and I can certainly testify that in the case of the Screen Actors Guild we have been eminently successful in preventing them from, with their usual tactics, trying to run a majority of an organization with a well-organized minority.
>
> So that fundamentally I would say in opposing those people that the best thing to do is to make democracy work. In the Screen Actors Guild we make it work by insuring everyone a vote and by keeping everyone informed. I believe that, as Thomas Jefferson put it, if all the American people know all of the facts they will never make a mistake.[32]

Reagan's testimony won him praise in the press. "If any single member of the Hollywood delegation stole the show with the weight of his testimony," Carl Levin of the conservative *New York Herald-Tribune* wrote, "it was Mr. Reagan." Writing for the left-leaning paper PM, Quentin Reynolds agreed: "Intelligent Ronald Reagan stole the show from his better known colleagues."[33]

Despite the tenor of his testimony, Reagan insisted he was still a political liberal. As he told Hedda Hopper in May 1947, not long before his HUAC testimony, "Our highest aim should be the cultivation of freedom of the individual, for therein lies the highest dignity of man. Tyranny is tyranny, and whether it comes from right, left, or center, it's evil." (Reagan maintained this view the rest of his public life.) He added:

> I believe the only logical way to save our country from all extremists is to remove conditions that supply fuel for the totalitarian fire. I'm not, however, in favor of outlawing any political party. If we ban the Communists from the polls we set

a dangerous precedent. Tomorrow it may be the Democratic or the Republican party that gets the ax. Rather than ban a party, we should force all issues into the public.

Right now the liberal movement in this country is taking the brunt of the Communist attack. The Reds know that if we can make America a decent living place for all of our people, their cause is lost here. So they seek to infiltrate liberal organizations just to smear and discredit them. If you don't believe this, name me one conservative organization that is Communist-infiltrated. Then look at the others. I've already pulled out of one organization that I joined in completely good faith. One day I woke up, looked about, and found it was commie-dominated. And did I pull out of it—but quick.

You can't blame a man for aligning himself with an institution he thinks is humanitarian; but you can blame him if he deliberately remains with it after he knows it's fallen into the hands of the Reds.[34]

While Reagan considered himself a liberal, some of his friends and associates had doubts. "He was a so-called liberal," SAG's longtime executive secretary, Jack Dales, said of Reagan.[35] Later, Reagan wrote that his postwar SAG period was a time of ideological transformation. He would not abandon the Democratic Party officially for another fifteen years, and he would support President Harry Truman in the 1948 election. But his views were changing, spurred by his alarm about Communism and, perhaps much more important, by his closer association with studio heads and other industry titans. "I guess I was beginning to form one of my own principles about government: There probably isn't any undertaking on earth short of assuring the national security that can't be handled more efficiently by the forces of private enterprise than by the federal government," he later wrote.[36] At least one observer was skeptical about the stated reasons for a gradual conservative turn. "When I worked with him," said Stephen Longstreet, the screenwriter for one of Reagan's 1947 films, *Stallion Road*, "it was clear he was a man escaping from the memories of boyhood poverty to run with the present palace guard."[37]

Reagan, however, claimed it was also rapid government expansion in the postwar years that tugged him to the right. "Our government wasn't nationalizing the railroads or the banks," he said, "but it was confiscating a disproportionate share of the nation's wealth through excessive taxes and indirectly seizing control of the day-to-day management of our businesses with rules and regulations that often gave Washington bureaucrats the power of life and death over them. Well, pretty soon my speeches in defense of Hollywood were beginning to take on a new tone."[38]

4

An Ambassador of Goodwill

Reagan believed his SAG responsibilities hurt his film career, and he complained about it publicly. "They don't cast me as an actor anymore," he told one Hollywood columnist in early 1950. "They cast me as president of the Screen Actors Guild. They take sex out and put me in."[1] To another writer, the thirty-nine-year-old actor grumbled, "I have come to the conclusion that I could do as good a job of picking [my roles] as the studio has done. At least I could do no worse." He added, "With the kind of parts I've had, I could telephone my lines in and it wouldn't make any difference. I've had no real acting jobs."[2] The SAG position might have hindered Reagan's film career, but it burnished his public profile as a substantial man of knowledge, power, and influence in Hollywood. "His image had changed considerably," biographer Anne Edwards wrote. "Before he became president [of SAG], he had dressed informally, showing a preference for sports coats, slacks and sweaters. He now wore suits, neckties and, in the evenings, formal clothes more often. He still read every book he believed important as well as most of the political columns.... The charm was retained, but the boyishness and the down-home quality were fast disappearing." One friend who noticed this evolution in Reagan was actor Robert Cummings. His co-star in *Kings Row* said he joked to Reagan, "One day you should run for president," to which Reagan deadpanned, "Yes."[3] In another setting—the winter of 1949, while on location in London to film *The Hasty Heart* with Patricia Neal—an acquaintance asked Reagan what job he would most like. Neal recalled, "Ronnie laughed and said, 'The president of the United States.'"[4]

Reagan's SAG duties and his political activism were more than distractions from his movies. They were also crippling his marriage. From the first days of his SAG presidency, Guild politics consumed him. And this new dimension of her husband's professional life did not please Wyman, who may have regretted suggesting him for the temporary board position years earlier. It was not just that Reagan's and Wyman's careers were going in different directions; his obsession with SAG and national politics bored her. Beyond their young children, Maureen and Michael, they now had little in common. "I think I became too identified with the serious side of Hollywood's off-screen life," Reagan later said.[5] Journalist Jane Wilkie recalled: "I was interviewing Jane when Ronnie hove to and, as he polished his riding boots, held forth without a pause on a political diatribe. It struck me that Jane was faintly bored by the lecturer."[6] Herman Hover, owner of the popular Ciro's nightclub on West Hollywood's Sunset Strip, remembered watching California lieutenant governor Goodwin Knight enter his club one evening while Reagan and Wyman were having dinner. "Knight made a beeline for Ronnie," Hover recalled. "They talked and talked politics, and you could see that Jane was bored. She kept sighing and yawning and making no effort to hide the fact that she thought politics was all very, very dull."[7] When Cummings gushed once to Wyman about Reagan's command of politics, she shot back, "Ooh, politics. He gives me a pain in the ass. That's all he talks about! If you had to sit at home and listen to him like I do—that's all he talks about, how he's going to save the world."[8]

Reagan's political diatribes did not merely bore Wyman. She knew his and her personalities and interests were profoundly different. And their attitudes toward acting—the glue that first bonded them—were worlds apart. "He does not exhibit the born actor's relish at playing a heel; he exhibits the born politician's discomfort at being mistaken for one," film critic Richard Schickel would write later about Reagan. "He has no technique to help him get under this character's skin. Or to distract us from his own discomfort."[9] Wyman, however, inhabited her roles to the point of remaining in character long after the cameras stopped. "In fact," daughter Maureen recalled, "she lived through every role to such an extent that it was hard to recognize her when she came home."[10]

As acting grew less satisfying to Reagan, the pursuit of challenging, complex roles became Wyman's passion. While Reagan was making mediocre movies—like his cringeworthy 1947 film, *That Hagan Girl*, with nineteen-year-old Shirley Temple as a love interest—Wyman was winning critical acclaim for her performances. Her role in the 1946 film *The Yearling* earned her an Academy Award nomination. In 1948 she would win the Academy Award for Best Actress for her part in *Johnny Belinda*. For that role—a deaf and mute young woman—Wyman became so obsessed with staying in character that she wore earplugs off set, learned to read lips, and interviewed psychologists to learn more about her character's state of mind. "The hours were also tough for both of them," Maureen wrote. "It seems one of them was almost always working on the weekend, or too tired out from the busy week preceding it."[11] Their personalities were different. "Jane and Ronnie really made a strange combination," a friend said. "She was so experienced, hard-boiled, intense, and passionate, and he was so pragmatic, down-to-earth, not overly imaginative."[12]

By 1948 the relationship was over. Wyman filed for divorce, claiming "grievous mental suffering."[13] In a court filing she charged, "In recent months, my husband and I engaged in continual arguments on his political views. . . . Despite my lack of interest in his political activities, he insisted I attend meetings with him and be present during discussions with our friends. But my own ideas were never considered important."[14] Wyman complained it was "exasperating to awake in the middle of the night, prepare for work, and have someone at the breakfast table, newspaper in hand, expounding on the far right, the conservative right, the conservative middle, the middle of the road."[15] (Wyman's protests in 1948 lend some credence to Reagan's assertion that his political views were evolving at this early date.)

Had Reagan's acting career commanded more of his attention, politics might never have come between them. Reagan's close friend Dick Powell later said, "They would not have gotten a divorce had their careers not been going in opposite directions— hers up, his down." Neil Reagan recalled that his brother "wept and wept. . . . He didn't want a divorce. He was heartbroken."[16] Even so, Reagan accepted his fate and declined to contest Wyman's suit. By June 1949 their divorce was final.

Single again, Reagan poured himself into his political interests, his SAG responsibilities, and his acting—in that order. Although he might have espoused conservative ideas at the breakfast table, he remained publicly a stalwart liberal Democrat. He supported Harry Truman's reelection in 1948, joining the president and actors Humphrey Bogart and Lauren Bacall and comedian George Jessel at an open-air campaign rally at Los Angeles's Gilmore Stadium in late September.[17] Reagan and Jessel rode with Truman to the stadium, where Reagan served as master of ceremonies and introduced the president to the 15,000-person crowd, almost half of them African American.[18] As SAG president, Reagan chaired a group of twenty-one American Federation of Labor (AFL) unions—the Labor League of Hollywood Voters—that advocated for Truman's election. And he vowed "to take an active part in the present political campaign and to fight against Communism."[19]

Most prominently, Reagan endorsed Truman in a four-minute national radio broadcast in October, which also served as an introduction for a speech by Minneapolis mayor Hubert Humphrey, the Democratic nominee for U.S. Senate in Minnesota. "This is Ronald Reagan speaking to you from Hollywood," he began. "You know me as a motion picture actor, but tonight I'm just a citizen pretty concerned about the national election next month and more than a little impatient with those promises the Republicans made before they got control of Congress a couple of years ago." Reagan attacked the GOP's economic policies, which he said favored big business. "High prices have not been caused by higher wages but by bigger and bigger profits," he said, blaming the Republican-controlled Congress for presiding over a litany of hardships visited on average Americans. "We must have new faces in the U.S. Congress—Democratic faces," Reagan said, declaring the liberal Humphrey "one of the ablest men in public life."[20]

It would be the last time Reagan endorsed a Democrat for president, although he continued supporting Democrats for public office through 1950. For instance, he backed California Democratic congresswoman Helen Gahagan Douglas in her unsuccessful 1950 U.S. Senate race against Richard Nixon. Reagan later told biographer Lou Cannon he formed doubts about Douglas (whom Nixon slandered as the "Pink Lady") and regarded her as "awfully naïve about the subject of Communists." But, unlike Nixon, he hesitated to say so publicly.[21]

Robert Cummings claimed Reagan changed his mind about Nixon before the election. He said that Reagan announced in a late-night call, "We're giving a party for [Nixon] tomorrow night. Can you come?" Cummings replied, "But isn't he a Republican?" Reagan told his friend, "I've switched. I sat down and made a list of the people I know, and the most admired people I know are Republicans."[22] It is unlikely Reagan had any sudden and rational change of heart about Nixon. In her 1982 memoir, Douglas remembered Reagan "worked hard for me."[23] In fact, he taped several three-minute radio spots for her that aired around California.[24] In his 1990 memoir, Reagan claimed he had not supported Nixon and added, "I campaigned against him."[25]

That Reagan still presented himself as a Democrat is clear. Whether he considered himself the same FDR liberal who arrived in Hollywood in 1937 was another matter. "Reagan, in talking about his switch in parties, would refer to a time when he suddenly realized that most of the people he admired were Republicans," biographer Anne Edwards wrote. "In fact, most of his closest friends had always been Republicans. With his father's and FDR's deaths, his own connections to the Democratic Party had become increasingly tenuous."[26]

THE FRUSTRATIONS OF LIFE as a single man and the failure of his movie career pushed Reagan into even greater political activism as he continued speaking about the dangers of Communism. In the January 22, 1951, edition of the magazine *Fortnight*, Reagan urged readers to think about replacing the words "Communist" and "Communism" with "pro-Russian." To Reagan it was not a question of ideology as much as "a hoax perpetrated by the Russian government, to aid in securing fifth columnists in other countries and to mask Russian aggression aimed at world conquest."[27] In July 1951 he was guest writer for labor reporter Victor Riesel's syndicated column. "Never again can the Communists hope to get anywhere in the movie capital," he bragged, writing about SAG's role in beating back the Communists in the 1940s. "And it looks to me as if the die-hard Reds in this country are now concentrating their plotting in other industries such as defense plants."[28]

That year Reagan embarked on a speaking tour as part of Lucius D. Clay's Crusade for Freedom to talk about the Communist threat and Hollywood's success in fighting it. "The Russians sent their first team, their ace string, here to take us over," he told a luncheon meeting at the Biltmore Hotel in Los Angeles in July. "We were up against hard-core organizers." Reagan warned the group, "The Communism fight is never won. It always leaves behind a little Trojan horse."[29] In St. Louis a few days later, Reagan urged vigilance against Communist influence in the United States. He warned, in what may have been a veiled reference to Wisconsin Republican senator Joseph McCarthy's Communist witch hunt, "We play right into their hands when we go around calling everybody a Communist."[30] The following February, speaking to the Hollywood Advertising Club, Reagan defended the film industry as almost Communist-free. He urged members to tell the industry's story to the country. "Actually," he said, "Communism is infinitesimal in the motion-picture industry."[31]

Reagan was speaking out more on political issues, impressing audiences with his earnest passion and common sense. "If the motion picture industry wants an ambassador of good will, and it seems to need many," a columnist for the *Hartford Times* wrote in June 1952, "it would do well to enlist his service."[32] Reviewing Reagan's early anti-Communist activism, Lou Cannon marveled that "he emerged from it in such good mental health. Others on both sides with more complex turns of mind and less balance than Reagan were psychologically trapped by what had happened to them in the great Hollywood Red hunt. Some were forever encumbered by the experience, which became the central reference point of their lives. Reagan was not trapped." Cannon observed that while Reagan's views were changing, "he was only occasionally obsessive about his new opinions."[33] That is not to say Reagan did not sometimes sound alarmist when discussing the perceived Communist and Soviet threats. "This much we can do," he told a Hollywood wire service reporter in May 1952. "Maintain our vigilance to prevent Communists from using our guild [SAG] for their own purposes."[34]

Reagan's views on broader politics were also evolving. By 1952, he joined several other Democrats who sent a telegram to Dwight D. Eisenhower, urging him to run for president as a Democrat. "When Ike decided to run on the Republican ticket," Reagan recalled, "I decided: If I considered him the best man for the job as a Democrat, he still ought to be my choice. So I campaigned and voted for Ike—my first for a Republican."[35] His enthusiasm for Eisenhower, however, did not survive the campaign. He told a friend in Illinois the general "did not grow in stature, and frankly I thought [Democratic nominee Adlai] Stevenson did."[36]

Although he stuck with the general, he was far less enthusiastic about Richard Nixon, Eisenhower's running mate. "Pray as I am praying for the health and long life of Eisenhower," he wrote to a friend in December 1952 about the new Republican president after his landslide victory over Stevenson, "because the thought of Nixon in the White House is almost as bad as that of Uncle Joe [Stalin]." Reagan sized up Nixon as nothing more than "a hand picked errand boy with a pleasing facade and naught but emptiness behind. He has been subsidized by a small clique of oil and real estate pirates, he is less than honest, and he is an ambitious opportunist completely undeserving of the high honor paid him."[37]

IN JUNE 1952, REAGAN went to Fulton, Missouri, ninety miles west of St. Louis, to deliver a commencement address to graduates of William Woods College, then a small Disciples of Christ school for women. His remarkable speech there offers insights into Reagan's changing political views in the early 1950s. He was poetic and inspiring. What he said at Fulton demonstrated—as much as anything he had yet produced—Reagan's innate skill in delivering a message, telling a story, and inspiring an audience. This was Reagan long before writers and aides honed his statements and speeches. His message to students was more than a display of his brilliance as a writer and speaker. The speech highlighted the flag-waving American exceptionalism that would characterize much of Reagan's political career.

Reagan went to Fulton as a favor for one of his Eureka College classmates, Rev. Raymond McCallister, pastor of the Webster Groves Christian Church in St. Louis and a member of the college's board. (McCallister had served on Eureka's debate team with Reagan.)[38] After several humorous stories, Reagan delivered an eloquent, unapologetic defense of American patriotism. "All of us as we grow older have a tendency to grow a little more cynical, to find fault [with America], to see the things that should be done and as we're younger we're a little impatient with sentiment and emotion," Reagan said. "We are a little reluctant to show it, we're impatient for change, and we want correction of those things that are wrong and should be done and so, perhaps, none of us pay enough attention to the very thought behind this land of ours." After he recited the first stanza of "My Country, 'Tis of Thee"—which the graduates had sung in unison before his address—Reagan said:

> It has been said that America is less of a place than an idea, and if it is an idea, and I believe that to be true, it is an idea that has been deep in the souls of man ever since man started his long trail from the swamps. It is nothing but the inherent love of freedom in each one of us, and the great ideological struggle that we find ourselves engaged in today is not a new struggle. It's the same old battle. We met it under the name of Hitlerism; we met it under the name of Kaiserism; and we have met it back through the ages in the name of every conqueror

that has ever set up on a course of establishing his rule over mankind. It is simply the idea—the basis of this country and of our religion—the idea of the dignity of man, the idea that deep within the heart of each one of us is something so God-like and precious that no individual or group has a right to impose his or its will upon the people, that no group can decide for the people what is good for the people so well as they can decide for themselves.

I, in my own mind, have thought of America as a place in the divine scheme of things that was set aside as a promised land. It was set here and the price of admission was very simple. The means of selection was very simple as to how this land should be populated: Any place in the world and any person from those places—any person with the courage, with the desire to tear up the roots, to strive for freedom, to attempt and dare to live in a strange and foreign place, to travel half across the world— was welcome here. And they have brought with them to the bloodstream that has become America that precious courage. The courage that they—and they alone in their community, in their nation, in their family—had in the first place to his land, the unknown, to strive for something better for themselves and for their children and their children's children. I believe that God in shedding his grace on this country has always, in this divine scheme of things, kept an eye on our land and guided it as a promised land for these people.[39]

The speech was a masterpiece. It was free of the torrent of facts and statistics that would become staples of Reagan's speeches. More significant, Reagan displayed what would be the most effective and persuasive tool in his rhetorical arsenal: his ability to use stories to make a point, transport his audience to another place and time, and appeal to their emotions.

For instance, he told a story about the debate over the Declaration of Independence in Philadelphia in 1776, when, as he described it, a mysterious man rose and addressed the delegates. "Sign that document, sign it if tomorrow your heads roll from the headsman's axe. Sign that document because tomorrow and the days to come your children and all the children of all the days to come will judge you for what you do this day." Reagan told the graduates that the man's oratory "was so great, his words so sincere and so moving" that delegates rushed forward to sign the Declaration. When "they turned to find the man that had swayed the issue, they could not find him. The doors were guarded . . . and no one had seen him leave; and no one knows to this day, although his words are recorded, who the man was nor could they find anyone who had spoken the words and caused the Declaration to be signed."[40]

Reagan's story was inspiring; it was also problematic. Members of the Continental Congress voted on July 4, 1776, to declare the American colonies independent of England. However, they did not sign the document until August 2. Voting for independence and signing the Declaration were separate acts that Reagan's story conflated.[41] Despite his claim, the ghostly man's words are not in any official account of the deliberations of Congress. The legendary speaker was the product of the fertile imagination of George Lippard, author of a fanciful 1847 "history" book, *Legends of the American Revolution*. In his book, Lippard described a much longer speech by a mystery orator, whose words were reminiscent of what Reagan told the graduates.[42]

In 1957 Reagan would recount a similar version of the tale when delivering the commencement address at Eureka College, this time informing graduates, mistakenly, that Thomas Jefferson wrote about the strange man and his speech.[43] Sixteen years later, Reagan would repeat the story with far less certainty but with no less drama and enthusiasm. Speaking in January 1974 to the first meeting of the Conservative Political Action Conference (CPAC) in Washington DC, Reagan would tell his audience:

> Some years ago a writer, who happened to be an avid student of history, told me a story about that day in the little hall in Philadelphia where honorable men, hard-pressed by a king who was flouting the very law they were willing to obey, debated whether they should take the fateful step of declaring their independence from that king. I was told by this man that the

story could be found in the writings of Jefferson. I confess, I never researched or made an effort to verify it. Perhaps it is only legend. But story, or legend, he described the atmosphere, the strain, the debate, and that as men for the first time faced the consequences of such an irretrievable act, the walls resounded with the dread word of treason and its price—the gallows and the headsman's axe.[44]

The story's questionable veracity did not trouble Reagan in 1952 or thereafter. It buttressed his point and was a grand tale. To a product of Hollywood's dream factory, this might have been all that mattered to him when urging freshly minted college graduates and other audiences to greater love and admiration for their country.

That Reagan had no interest in the veracity of a story someone told him or that he found somewhere may matter little. It was a commencement speech at a small college, delivered by a fading film star. If Reagan had remained only an actor with a passing interest in politics, his carelessness with history might have gone unnoticed and assumed no great significance. The speech, however, was an early political statement by a future governor of California and president of the United States. It seems fair, then, to hold Reagan—even during his acting days—to a higher standard.

Reagan's subject matter, his assertions, his manner, and delivery also are worth examination. Reagan might not have been Hollywood's greatest actor, but he was among its most politically active and one of its most polished orators. And because he was an actor, skilled at delivering manufactured lines with passion and sincerity, his speeches communicated truth. His sincerity and the intense, clipped certainty of his words led credulous listeners to embrace what he told them. Adding to his credibility, Reagan rarely read his speeches in the conventional way of many other speakers but spoke memorized lines, prompted by the shorthand notes he wrote on cards. He sold his words with an earnestness and conviction that was persuasive to audiences—well beyond the accuracy of his stories and the weight of his facts and statistics.

The *Washington Post*'s David Broder, a respected political writer, first covered Reagan in the mid-1950s, in Bloomington, Illinois, where he wrote for the local paper, the *Pantagraph.* "Eureka was part of my beat, so I heard my first Reagan speeches in 1954 and 1955," Broder recalled in 2004. After he covered Reagan's commencement address at Eureka College in 1957, Broder remembered admiring Reagan's oratorical skills. "These were no more than the standard clichés of a thousand commencement talks, given by successful alumni to current classes," Broder said. "But coming from Reagan, they did not sound like boilerplate. Talking to students afterward, I could tell they had been moved—their sights lifted." Broder believed Reagan was convincing because "he had first persuaded himself of the truth of his utterances. Much later, when someone hung the title 'The Great Communicator' on Reagan, I thought to myself, 'It should be 'The Great Persuader.'"[45]

Reagan's carelessness and lack of attention to facts and sources—displayed in his William Woods speech—would become a lifelong pattern. In the same 1952 speech, Reagan told another fanciful tale, one he could have tried to verify before sharing it. It was a World War II story about the crew of a B-17 "Flying Fortress" bomber returning to base, across France, from Germany. The story, as told by Reagan:

> Disabled by ground fire, losing altitude, they had taken a direct burst in the ball turret underneath the B-17. The ball turret gunner was wounded, and the turret was jammed so they could not get him out. Finally the pilot had to order a "bail out," and as the men started to leave the plane, the trapped wounded kid in the ball turret knew he was being left behind and he cried out in terror. Even the dry words of the citation in military language for heroism cannot hide the drama and the nobility of what took place then. The last man to leave the plane saw the co-pilot sit down and take the boy's hand and he said, 'Never mind, son, we'll ride it down together.' Congressional Medal of Honor posthumously awarded.

The story is fantasy. No record of any such Medal of Honor

exists. Reagan may have found the story in a popular 20th Century Fox war movie from 1944, *Wing and a Prayer* (starring Don Ameche and Dana Andrews), which featured a similar scene. He would repeat this tale over the years, as late as December 1983, when he addressed the Congressional Medal of Honor Society.[46]

REAGAN DID NOT FORGET the stories or facts he loved and embraced. Reagan's longtime aide Michael Deaver, recognizing his boss's remarkable memory, grew careful about what he told him. "My admonition to people always was, 'For God's sake, be sure of your facts before you give them to him, because they'll get in that computer [his brain], and God knows when they'll come out.'"[47]

In 1983 journalist Charles McDowell of the *Richmond Times-Dispatch* sat next to Reagan at the annual Washington Gridiron dinner. McDowell told Reagan about the excitement generated in his hometown of Lexington, Virginia, by the filming of one of Reagan's early films, *Brother Rat*, in 1938. Lexington was home to the Virginia Military Institute (VMI), and the movie was about VMI cadets. McDowell regaled Reagan with stories about the local buzz over the movie. And he told him he had walked many days to campus to watch filming. One day, he said, he spotted Reagan eating lunch at a local drugstore with co-star Eddie Albert. "That just to me captures this marvelous moment in a small boy's life," McDowell finished, adding that Reagan listened to the story with delight. Reagan then said, "I have something serious to tell you." Some scenes were filmed at Lexington, he said, but he had never been to the town. (Most of the movie's outdoor scenes had been shot at the San Diego Military Academy.) "I remember the others coming back from Lexington and telling me what it was like. But I simply wasn't there."

Stunned, McDowell implored Reagan: "Mr. President, how can that be? I've known it all my life. I've told it so many times." Reagan asked McDowell how many times he had seen *Brother Rat*. Five or six, McDowell told him. Reagan replied, "That implanted in your head that I was there. You believed it because you wanted to believe it. There's nothing wrong with that. I do it all the time."[48]

REGARDLESS OF THE ACCURACY of his inspiring speech at William Woods, students and others in the Fulton audience swooned. His message of unabashed patriotism resonated with his conservative (culturally and politically) Midwest audience. Students, faculty, and parents gave him a standing ovation. Some students rushed forward and asked Reagan to sign their yearbooks.[49]

To the graduates in Missouri, Reagan was still a star. But in truth he worked in films sporadically. In 1950 Warner Bros. had released him from his contract. In 1951, he would make three undistinguished movies—including the much-ridiculed *Bedtime for Bonzo*, in which he played second banana to a chimpanzee—and only seven more films from 1952 through 1955.[50] Between films, he focused on SAG business and sulked over the fate of his once-promising career. Reagan had blamed the distraction of his SAG presidency for his acting slump. Ironically, an important change in Guild policy in 1952 would lay the groundwork for his career's dazzling revival in the decade's second half.

In the early 1950s, many in Hollywood began to see television as an existential threat to the movie industry. In 1950, 9 percent of American households had a television set. By 1955, 55 percent would own one. Television was quickly becoming the nation's dominant entertainment industry, and some struggling actors began migrating to New York—the nexus of the new entertainment industry—hoping to find steady work. Motion-picture theater attendance declined precipitously in the early 1950s.[51] Among the consequences of this disruption: SAG's membership shrank by 7,300 members—19 percent—from 1947 to 1951, and film actors' pay slumped. Hoping to arrest their clients' declining fortunes, executives of the Music Corporation of America (MCA)—the talent agency that represented Reagan—had an idea.[52] MCA's elegant, understated president, Lew Wasserman, offered a plan that would allow the agency to create television shows. A subsidiary of MCA, Revue Productions, had been making TV programs since 1949. But Wasserman worried MCA might soon run afoul of a 1939 provision of SAG's bylaws that prohibited agents from engaging in theatrical film production (a conflict of interest, if agencies negotiated with themselves on behalf of clients).[53] SAG had not yet updated the provision to prohibit talent agencies from producing television shows, but Wasserman knew that would happen eventually. In the summer of 1952, to head off that approaching impediment to his company's growth, Wasserman proposed an exclusive "blanket waiver" for MCA that would eliminate any potential conflict for the large-scale television production operation he had in mind.[54]

In years past, SAG had granted limited waivers to agencies that wanted to produce a movie or other theatrical production. But with a long-term waiver, MCA would have no restriction on the number of television programs it could produce for the actors it represented.[55] (By one estimate, more than a third of Hollywood's top stars in the early 1950s were MCA clients.) Recalled Jack Dales, then SAG's executive secretary: "Lew Wasserman and [MCA founder] Jules Stein came to us and said, 'Do you know what's happening? It's all going to New York. Your membership is going to be a New York membership. Your guys here are not going to get a whiff of it."[56]

SAG's staff negotiated the waiver with MCA, and the board took up the proposal at a marathon meeting in July 1952. As board president and an MCA client, Reagan did not oppose the proposal, although one MCA executive insisted he originally objected to it. "Reagan found it awkward to make the decision on Lew's request without looking as if he was favoring MCA," Berle Adams recalled.[57] And one attendee remembered that Reagan did not participate in the board's discussion. "There are a lot of myths about the debate and the waiver, including myths about Reagan's role in same," recalled Chester "Chet" Migden, then a new SAG employee who attended the decisive board meeting. "My recollection is he chaired the meeting and he didn't say a goddamn word. The debate went on with the board members in the room and Ronnie sat there and he recognized the speakers and didn't participate in the debate." Migden recalled most SAG board members were skeptical about the proposal until actor Walter Pidgeon spoke up. "Wait a minute," Pidgeon reportedly said. "We're dying. What's the alternative? To go to New York and work in live television for a couple of hundred dollars? . . . I mean, the worst thing that can happen is it'll work."[58] The argument turned the tide. Pidgeon—who would assume the SAG presidency in November when Reagan stepped down—moved to grant the waiver. The board approved it unanimously.[59] It did not hurt MCA's case that Wasserman had also negotiated a deal with SAG to pay its members residual fees on their television performances, as opposed to the traditional onetime payments for their roles.[60]

Some observers questioned whether Reagan had secretly arranged the waiver in an unethical deal with Wasserman and MCA. In his 1986 book, *Dark Victory: Ronald Reagan, MCA, and the Mob*, journalist Dan Moldea alleged Reagan "engineered" the waiver. He added: "MCA was the only such firm to have been granted such a favored status, giving it the ground floor in television production. It placed the company in a position where it could offer jobs to the actors it represented."[61] Writing for the *New Yorker* in 2003, journalist Connie Bruck was skeptical that Reagan had recused himself: "During the early months of 1952, Wasserman pursued the SAG waiver in ways so deft and untraceable that even subsequent FBI and grand-jury investigations were unable to fully reconstruct what he had done." In her biography of Wasserman, Bruck quoted Billy Hunt, a lawyer for Wasserman: "Lew always told me the waiver was Ronnie Reagan."[62]

One SAG historian, David F. Prindle, argued that the Guild, regardless of any influence by Reagan, would have reckoned with television's explosive growth. "In 1952 it was entirely realistic to anticipate that in another decade television would have killed the movies, just as the movies had killed vaudeville," Prindle wrote. "Without movies, the guild's members would have had to rely on filmed TV, which in that year comprised only 25 percent of everything shown on the tube, the rest being live." Prindle concluded, "If Ronald Reagan had never been born, the guild would still have granted the waiver to MCA."[63]

No matter how it materialized, the waiver changed the face of Hollywood. "MCA became not only the biggest talent agency, which is already was," Migden recalled, "but the biggest television producer. All of a sudden, we had a television industry [in Hollywood]."[64]

Wrote Wasserman biographer Dennis McDougal: "The simple, far-reaching document would shift forever the balance of power in the entertainment industry, yet the waiver didn't even rate a paragraph in the trade newspapers. What was important at the time was that [MCA] had agreed to pay residuals to actors. The waiver itself was regarded as an insignificant bit of union business that no one outside the guild hierarchy knew or cared about."[65] Coupled with Wasserman's negotiating skills and MCA's resources, the lucrative new arrangement would pave the way for the revival of Reagan's acting career. And his career's rejuvenation would offer him a political apprenticeship that opened a path to the White House.

REAGAN HAD BEEN A union leader–cum–political liberal since his early days in Hollywood. Soon he would become a forceful and eloquent spokesperson for big business and right-leaning causes.[66] But there may have been another reason for Reagan's steady drift away from liberalism in the early 1950s: his relationship with an aspiring film actress, Nancy Davis, whom he met in the fall of 1949 and married in 1952.

Born Anne Frances Robbins in 1921, she was the daughter of Loyal Davis, a prominent Chicago neurosurgeon whom her mother, Edith, married in 1929. Davis adopted Nancy when she was fourteen. Nancy idolized her father and may have embraced many of his conservative political views. "I knew nothing about politics," she protested to biographer Bob Colacello in 2002, "and I wasn't even registered when I met Ronnie."[67] Reagan remembered it differently. Early on, he said, a mutual friend assured him Nancy "was more than disinterested in Leftist causes: she was violently opposed to such shenanigans."[68] Nancy knew enough to have strong opinions about alleged Soviet efforts to infiltrate Hollywood. "Damn right there was," she later told a biographer. "And they were trying to get their message into the movies."[69] It is fair to assume Nancy arrived in Hollywood as an ambivalent political conservative (she was a registered Republican) who was more concerned about winning movie roles than elections.[70] Whatever the case, after they married, Nancy's and her husband's political views became virtually identical. "He was all I had ever wanted in a man, and more," she wrote in her memoir of their courtship. "Even then, Ronnie could see that I was totally supportive of him, and that he could trust me. Ronnie's interest in the Guild and in politics had been a source of irritation in his first marriage . . . [but] I loved to listen to him talk, and I let him know it."[71]

Nancy encouraged her new husband's political bent, especially during dinner parties at their Los Angeles home. "Politics was almost always on the menu at the Reagans' dinners," Colacello wrote. "Nancy actively participated in these dinner-table discussions and even cultivated friendships with politically minded people." Before he met Nancy, some of Reagan's friends had been political liberals. Now, under Nancy's subtle influence, Reagan socialized more often with Republican friends in the entertainment business and with wealthy California business executives. Their social friends included Robert and Goldie Arthur (he was a well-known screenwriter and producer and she had been executive secretary to movie moguls Irving Thalberg and Samuel Goldwyn); Randolph Scott, James Stewart, George Murphy, and Edgar Bergen and their spouses; Alfred and Betsy Bloomingdale (he was a wealthy department story executive whose wife would become one of Nancy's lifelong friends); Earle and Marion Jorgensen (he was a steel magnate and she was a prominent philanthropist); and Los Angeles car dealer Holmes Tuttle and his wife, Virginia.[72]

"Nancy thought the exposure to their brand of politics was something of which her husband needed more," Marc Eliot, author of *Reagan: The Hollywood Years*, observed. "The higher up the social scale went, she carefully noted, the more conservative the politics became. Perhaps she believed that wasn't the worst thing in the world."[73]

It is not clear how much Nancy helped influence Reagan's political views or how much he influenced hers. But his political views were becoming more conservative. Nothing, however, would pull him into the conservative orbit more than his decision in 1954 to walk away from movies—he would make only six films between 1954 and 1964—and into the profitable and life-changing world of television drama.

5

That's the Way, Ron

In May 1953, Reagan's neighbors at Malibu Lake Mountain Club, where he owned a weekend getaway, Yearling Row Ranch, elected him their honorary mayor. The following month, the club's newsletter described the gala dinner-dance at which members installed their new leader: "His Honor, Ronald Reagan, Honorary Mayor of Malibu Lake, was a little late for dinner, because he was working, but we are all so happy to know a movie star who is working these days that we didn't mind."[1]

That month Reagan signed up, not for another film, but to chair the reelection campaign of longtime Republican Los Angeles mayor Fletcher Bowron. A reformer who helped transform the city into a modern metropolis, Bowron was also a dry speaker who could have used some of Reagan's charisma. As one of the mayor's aides put it, "If this guy would give a fireside speech, his would be so boring the fire would go out."[2] Bowron lost to his Republican primary challenger, Congressman Norris Poulson, who charged the mayor was weak on Communism.[3] "Sober studio leaders have repeatedly warned their boys and girls against taking sides where the voting public is concerned, but they never seem to take heed," a Hollywood wire service reporter wrote in June after the four-term mayor's defeat. "Ronnie got into the wrong corner again when he rushed to the aid of [Bowron]." The unnamed reporter ended his story asking, "What's [Reagan] doing in movies? Well, as time will permit, he takes an acting job. . . . A dozen years ago Ronnie was one of the two top male stars at Warners—Flynn was the other— but those outside activities gradually leveled off his career."[4]

Reagan kept up appearances. He traveled widely and gave speeches about anti-Communism and other political causes that caught his eye or provoked his ire. "You could add a little to your income by being the speaker" at conventions and dinners sponsored by large organizations, he recalled.[5] In June 1952, after seven terms, he stepped down from his SAG position, which should have given him more time to devote to movies. But Reagan was no longer a contract employee for Warner Bros., which meant he earned money only when working on a movie set. "Ronnie wasn't getting any good picture offers," Nancy Reagan recalled, "and what with the mortgage on the [new] house, child-support payments, and quarterly tax payments on money he hoped to earn later in the year, we quickly found ourselves in debt. It was a year and a half before we could afford to furnish our living room." She admitted her husband "had made a few clunkers in the early years of his career" and had resolved to hold out for better movie offers—which never came.[6]

"I'm living from guest shot to guest shot on television and an occasional personal appearance," Reagan groused to an industry friend who tried to help with an offer to narrate a public service film for a defense contractor, North American Rockwell. "I would like to do that," he told the friend, "but here's my problem. If I do this public service spot, I have to do it for scale—$240. If the word gets out that Ronald Reagan's only work is at scale, my price would go down, and I couldn't make my house payments." He was so desperate for income that he pitched several networks on a radio show, loosely based on his life, about the exploits "of a Hollywood couple, an Actor and Actress who go into ranching."[7]

"We waited for over a year, and we got by only because Ronnie was able to guest star on *Burns and Allen* and other television shows," Nancy wrote. "Neither of us realized it, but Ronald Reagan's Hollywood career had pretty much come to an end."[8] Reagan's appearances on TV dramas were likely his main source of acting income in 1953 and early 1954. During this period, in addition to his August 1953 appearance on CBS's *Burns and Allen*, Reagan appeared once on Milton Berle's *Texaco Star Theatre* (NBC), three times on *The Ford Television Theatre* (CBS), three times on the *Schlitz Playhouse of Stars* (CBS), once on *The Revlon Mirror Theater* on NBC, and once on the *Lux Video Theatre* (CBS). Reagan's friend Holmes Tuttle, a wealthy car dealer and California Republican fund-raiser, knew of his financial troubles. He pushed him to switch careers and run for the U.S. Senate. Reagan rejected that. "I'd like to keep making horse operas," Reagan told him. "I'm a ham—always was, always will be."[9] Asked by a reporter about a possible Senate run in the 1954 election, Reagan said he demurred, "because all I'm interested in is making pictures."[10]

But Reagan also revealed bitterness about the trajectory of his film career. "I'm running for nothing but the actor of the year," Reagan said to columnist Erskine Johnson. "Holding [SAG] office just about wrecked my career. You're seen across the table at a committee meeting and suddenly there are only parts as committee members. Just trying to serve the motion picture industry is the quickest way in the world to get kicked in the pants. I'm not bitter. I'm just going to let the United Nations save the world."[11]

Desperate for steady work, in May 1953 Reagan accepted the hosting duties of a fifteen-minute talk and musical variety television show on ABC, produced by MCA and stocked with entertainment by the firm's clients, including Rosemary Clooney, Rex Harrison, and Eddie Fisher. *The Orchid Award* aired on Sundays at 9:15 p.m., immediately after columnist Walter Winchell's news and gossip program. Winchell often closed his show by giving verbal "orchids" to entertainers. This new show took the bit one step further and awarded real orchids to guests who answered questions from Reagan, in Hollywood, or from the show's other host, Donald Woods, who conducted interviews from New York on alternating weekends. "I must tell you, he was so bad," the show's Los Angeles director, Bob Finkel, recalled of Reagan as host. "He didn't have what was needed for that kind of show." Reagan quit the program in January 1954.[12]

Finances were again so tight that Reagan accepted an offer

arranged by his day-to-day MCA agent, Arthur Park, to headline a Las Vegas variety show for what he said was $15,000 a week (it was likely much lower).[13] The engagement was another humbling comedown for the forty-three-year-old film star. After a few weeks of rehearsal, the show opened in mid-February 1954 for a two-week run at the Hotel Last Frontier. In the ninety-minute show, Reagan presented a comedy monologue, introduced several acts, including a male quartet (the Continentals), a slapstick comedy team (the Honey Brothers), and a musical duo (the Blackburn Twins). The show also featured female dancers and Reagan—wearing a Pabst Blue Ribbon beer apron while feigning a German accent—cracking jokes and enduring slaps on the head with a rolled-up newspaper. Then and later, Reagan and Nancy put the best spin on the situation. He told the *Los Angeles Times*, "I went into it with considerable trepidation so I am doubly happy that it has turned out so well."[14] As Reagan later described it, "The audience's reaction was good, the reviews were good, the pay was terrific, and they invited me to come back. But Nancy and I missed our life in California and neither of us thought much of smoke-filled nightclubs, so when the two weeks ended we were glad to go home."[15]

Despite what he told friends and the press, Reagan surely saw his Las Vegas sojourn for what it was—a humiliating experience. As an entertainment medium, Las Vegas was a notch or two below television. And he was open about his dim view of appearing on television (despite having hosted *The Orchid Show* and appearing in almost a dozen television dramas in 1953–54). He complained to a journalist in February 1954, before the nightclub show, "The studios are driving us [movie actors] into other mediums. Few actors are supported by the studios alone. The others have to spread themselves into radio, TV, legit theater, nightclubs, and wherever their services are in demand." The result, Reagan explained, "is that there's no novelty in seeing most actors on the screen. A person will certainly think twice before paying to see a movie with a star he has seen so often in other mediums."[16] With few prospects for good movies and no desire to work again in Las Vegas, Reagan undoubtedly understood television would be the last and most promising frontier for his acting career.

Years later, he confessed his fears of the new medium. "I was sure a television series could be a professional kiss of death to a movie actor," he wrote. But he did the shows, he said, for the money. "In the end," he acknowledged, "television guest spots not only tided us over financially but led me to one of those unexpected and unplanned turns in the road—the kind that can take you a long way from where you thought you were going."[17]

IN JULY 1953 REAGAN had appeared on a live CBS anthology series, *Chrysler Medallion Theatre*, produced by Revue Productions, the MCA subsidiary that SAG's 1952 blanket waiver had allowed into full-scale television production. The episode, "A Job for Jimmy Valentine," aired on Saturday, July 18, at 10 p.m. Eastern time. For Reagan, it was a forgettable performance.[18] But Wasserman and another MCA executive, Taft Schreiber, had an idea for their client and his foundering career. After Reagan's live performance, Schreiber—now the head of Revue—persuaded the actor to remain in the studio. He wanted Reagan to record a test introduction for a show the company would produce for CBS on Sunday nights. The show was *General Electric Television Theater*, a half-hour drama series sponsored by the manufacturing giant as a vehicle to burnish its corporate image. The CBS television show had debuted in primetime on February 1, 1953, as an occasional substitute for bandleader Fred Waring's musical-variety program (also sponsored by General Electric since 1949), which the network and GE were phasing out. CBS wanted to keep and expand the fledgling show, one Wasserman biographer wrote, "but it needed a gimmick to keep deep-pocketed sponsor General Electric interested."[19] Reagan hoped he would be that gimmick. Reagan's test went well, but the year ended with Reagan waiting to learn whether General Electric wanted him to host its show the following season. While he waited, at Wasserman's urging, Reagan had agreed to his two-week Las Vegas show.

Meanwhile, GE considered actors Eddie Albert, Walter Pidgeon (Reagan's successor as SAG president), and Kirk Douglas for the hosting job. "I was pitched on being the spokesperson," Douglas recalled. "I didn't think, really, that I wanted to do it, but I wanted to hear their case. They made an eloquent address about me being part of the General Electric family. I turned it down."[20] In his book on Reagan's Hollywood years, Marc Eliot claimed Reagan was "ninth on the list of nine possibilities MCA had submitted to GE as potential hosts."[21]

Wasserman and Schreiber were not the only ones helping Reagan score the GE job. Reagan's good friend Walter Annenberg, owner of TV *Guide* and friendly with one of General Electric's top executives, may have helped. "I told him Ron was a great speaker," Annenberg recalled, "that he was a good-looking guy, genial and very able on his feet."[22] Earl Dunckel—the GE executive who directed audience promotion for the new show—admitted the company considered other stars, but said it quickly settled on Reagan. "We looked at several people," he said. "I won't mention who they were. When Ron was suggested, it went through almost immediately."[23]

In April 1954 GE named Reagan as the show's host for the season starting that fall. From New York, columnist Hedda Hopper reported: "Ronald Reagan, here to talk with General Electric's top brass on the fattest TV deal ever signed, tells me he'll have Tyrone Power, Joan Crawford, Jane Wyman, Fred Astaire, Henry Fonda, Joe Cotten, and Paul Douglas as his stars." Reagan expressed delight with the new job, telling Hopper, "Best part of the deal, I can have my cake and eat it, too. My contract allows me to make motion pictures—all of them I want. So I can be a week-end TV actor and carry on my screen work, too."[24]

Reagan, who would make only two movies in the remaining years of the decade, was signing up with General Electric for far more than introducing a weekly television show. MCA listed its New York advertising agency—Batten, Barton, Durstine & Osborn (BBD&O)—as producer of the program. That allowed the firm to take advantage of SAG's blanket waiver and collect the 10 percent commission on residuals for Reagan and the other actors who would appear on the show. GE sponsored the broadcast—that is, bought the TV time—but MCA/Revue owned the program.[25] BBD&O paid Reagan $120,000 a year for his hosting duties— filming brief introductions and closings for each season's thirteen episodes—and for serving as "program supervisor" (more than $1 million in 2019 dollars). He would earn an additional $15,000 for each episode in which he acted and royalties from those episodes after the fifth replay. Revue also guaranteed Nancy roles in at least three episodes every season at $10,000 each. When his five-year contract expired in 1959, MCA would give Reagan 25 percent ownership of the show and make him a partner of MCA-Revue.[26] MCA encouraged the movie stars who would act in the show's thirty-minute dramatic episodes—including comedy giants like Jack Benny and Bob Hope—to choose the roles they wanted to play. To sweeten the pot, after an episode aired four or five times, the stars would get residual royalty payments.[27]

The company also wanted Reagan to travel at least sixteen weeks a year as a goodwill ambassador and visit its 136 manufacturing plants that employed 700,000 people—it was the nation's third largest employer—in twenty-eight states.[28] "My new job called upon me to play a supporting role in an extraordinary experiment by American industry," Reagan later wrote. "Until then, most of America's industrial giants had tended to function under a strong central management with a single geographic region."[29] Under GE's president, Ralph Cordiner, the company had decentralized its operations. The company once had only eight profit-and-loss groups. Now there were more than a hundred, each with remarkable autonomy. The result, one historian noted, was "increased economies of speed by localizing decision making and reducing bureaucratic drag."[30]

That was the upside. The downside was that division and plant leaders and their local employees were fiercely loyal to their respective divisions and understood their missions well. They were not so well versed about or devoted to General Electric as a whole. This is where company officials hoped Reagan would help them, as he recalled: "Sending the host of the GE Theater to the far-flung plants, [Cordiner] thought, would demonstrate that the New York office cared about company employees no matter where they were and would also help forge a closer link between the plants and the communities where they were located."[31] According to Earl Dunckel—the affable former newspaper reporter and conservative GE executive who would be his traveling companion for the first year—the goals of putting Reagan on the road were simple: "to have Ron meet and charm these GE vice presidents all over the country so they would stay off our back long enough for us to get the program moving." Next, he said, the visits were "an audience promotion device" for the show and "an employee communication device."[32]

Reagan made his first visit to a GE manufacturing plant in August 1954, more than a month before the premiere of *General Electric Theater*. He rode a train across country for his tour of the company's massive turbine plant in Schenectady, New York, also the site of GE's Power Division headquarters. As Reagan and his GE escorts roamed the plant's thirty-eight acres, the smoke and fumes forced the actor to remove the contact lenses he always wore on camera or in public. Machines stopped and employees gawked while others gathered around to greet him. It took him a grueling four hours to wind his way through the plant.[33]

Later in the tour, at Erie, Pennsylvania, Reagan and Dunckel arrived at dawn, having taken the red-eye special from New York City. "They met us at the station at six-thirty in the morning," Dunckel said, "grabbed us and put us in a car, put our bags in another car. We never saw the hotel we were going to spend the—euphemistically I say—night, until after midnight. All that time we were walking plant floors, talking to employees." Dunckel recalled female GE employees would rush up to Reagan to ask for his autograph, while most of the men stood to the side and muttered derisive comments about him. "Then he would leave [the women] and walk over to these fellows and start talking to them," Dunckel said. "When he left them ten minutes later, they were all slappin' him on the back saying, 'That's the way, Ron.' He would not leave a department with the men over there scowling and snarling."

Dunckel recalled that at the end of the first exhausting day of their Erie visit, he and Reagan dragged into their hotel. When they asked the front-desk clerk for their room keys, the employee pointed to a young woman who had waited in the lobby for several hours. It was after midnight. "Ron," Dunckel told him, "you can't afford it. You're dead now. We have a tough day tomorrow. Just ask this gentleman to do regrets."

"Dunk," Reagan said, "I'd better find out what it's all about."

Reagan quickly learned the woman planned to strike out for Hollywood hoping to become a movie star. "She was all set, had it in her mind, tickets and everything," Dunckel said, adding, "Ron spent an hour and a half convincing her that, if she was really serious about acting, what she should do is hit the little theater, the local radio and TV stations, the local floor show, whatever."

Dunckel said Reagan dissuaded the woman, telling her, "Always remember, if you can command an audience in Erie, Pennsylvania, you can command an audience anywhere." As they left for their rooms, Dunckel upbraided Reagan for devoting so much time to the woman. "Dunk, I couldn't not afford the time. I'd do almost anything to keep another one of those little girls from going out there and adding to the list of whores in Hollywood."[34]

By September, when he and Dunckel arrived in Bridgeport, Connecticut, for a two-day visit, Reagan was hitting his stride. Based on the rhapsodic review in the *Bridgeport Telegram*, Reagan had shown GE how valuable he would be to the program's success and how well he would serve as a company spokesperson.

Ronald Reagan is the kind of young American you'd expect to find living next door in any small community. He is a family man, first, and television and screen personality second.

This was the advance billing for the gentleman who last week spent two full days meeting and telling General Electric employees and the community about himself.

Now [that] he has left, those whom he met will tell you the publicity men didn't know the half of it.

Beyond telling funny Hollywood anecdotes, Reagan had regaled audiences with stories about his two-year-old daughter, Patti. The newspaper's reporter gushed over his visit:

Throughout his tour of the sprawling G-E plant Reagan's arrival at manufacturing and office areas brought screams, sighs and mad rushes to shake hands and get autographs. Some resourceful employees even brought their own cameras and madly snapped photos of the handsome six-footer as he made his rounds from building to building. Enthusiasm and admiration for Ronald Reagan was not confined to the ladies at the plant who stormed him at each stop. Men, too, waved friendly 'Hi Ronnies' to him from their machines and production lines. All those who met him, liked him, immediately.[35]

6

Progress Is Our Most Important Product

On Sunday, September 26, 1954, a few days before Reagan arrived in Bridgeport, *General Electric Theater* and its new host debuted at 8 p.m., Eastern, on 120 CBS affiliates across the country. Reagan and GE were fortunate that the show's time slot was immediately after the popular variety show *Toast of the Town* (which would become *The Ed Sullivan Show* in 1955). Following Sullivan guaranteed the program a substantial viewership as it worked to build its own audience. The first episode of Reagan's show was a live performance from New York. Entitled "Nora," the episode was based on Henrik Ibsen's 1879 play, *A Doll's House,* and starred Phyllis Thaxter, Patric Knowles, and Luther Adler. (Thaxter replaced what one press report described as a "prominent Hollywood star" who fell ill the week before the show and could not perform live from New York.)[1]

The following week, Reagan introduced Joseph Cotten in his television debut in "High Green Wall," an adaptation of an Evelyn Waugh short story, "The Man Who Loved Dickens."[2] On the show's third week, Reagan and Nancy performed live from New York in "The Long Way Round." Newspaper ads described it as "the tense story of a wife's attempts to help her husband recover from a breakdown."[3] By month's end, Joan Crawford appeared in her television debut, playing Mary Andrews, an American newspaper columnist, in "The Road to Edinburgh."[4]

With its star power and solid scripts, the new *General Electric Theater* was an instant hit. For its first week, it was the third most popular program on network television, behind *I Love Lucy* and *Toast of the Town*.[5] *General Electric Theater* would finish the 1954–55 television season ranked seventh, with an average weekly audience of ten million households and an audience rating of 32.6 (the average percentage of households nationwide with televisions that watched the show). The next season, now an established hit, the show would finish ahead of programs like *The Red Skelton Show* and *The Honeymooners*, with an average audience of 11.4 million and a 32.9 rating. By the end of the 1956–57 season, the show would rank third, behind *I Love Lucy* and *The Ed Sullivan Show*, with an average audience of 14.3 million and an average rating of 36.9.[6]

General Electric Theater's major strength was its ability to attract popular movie stars who had never appeared in television dramas. "Hollywood people would not appear on television," GE's Earl Dunckel recalled. "MCA promised [GE] that they would be able to break that barrier if we would go along with the plan they had."[7] MCA was correct. "The marked increase this season in the traffic of screen personalities between the movies and television is demonstrated by the line-up of important acting talent obtained by the *General Electric Theater* for its 1954–55 production program," the *New York Times* reported in December 1954. "The video outfit has about as much star power for its filmed and live shows as most Hollywood studios have under contract these days."[8] By 1957 some would credit the show with helping transform Hollywood's attitude toward television. "Offbeat casting for the stars also contributes immeasurably to the attraction the shows seem to have for both the performers and the viewers," Walter Ames, TV-radio editor for the *Los Angeles Times*, wrote in October 1957. "The program has always been among the leaders in TV polls, and Reagan gives the casting facet large credit for this situation."[9]

In its first season, *General Electric Theater* featured thirteen filmed dramatic episodes, twenty-two live dramatic performances, and four live musical programs.[10] Most weeks, Reagan would film his introduction and closing segments from a sound stage in the old Republic Studios lot in north Hollywood. (In 1958, MCA would acquire the 423-acre Universal Studios lot and film the show there.)[11] The hosting work for a show like *General Electric Theater* was not heavy lifting. As Otto Kruger, host of a rival NBC television anthology show, *Lux Video Theatre*, remarked: "All I do is come up and tell the people who I am and what we're up to. I don't have a single thing to do with producing, directing, or casting the show. Yet I get letters every week complimenting me on my production, my directing, my casting, even my script adaptations."[12]

Thus began a chapter in Reagan's professional life that would propel him deeper into politics. From 1954 until 1962, when CBS would cancel his show, Reagan would spend many long weeks on the road, trundling across the country by train. He traveled first with Dunckel and then with other GE executives. The visits introduced him to fans and new friends in more than a hundred cities and towns across the country. The show and the plant tours would also revive his acting career. With his trademark sign-off each week—"At GE, progress is our most important product"—Reagan was once again a household name. And as the host of a top-rated television show, he became one the most recognizable faces in the United States.[13]

In 1956, Reagan would allow General Electric to feature his new Pacific Palisades home in GE advertising within the show and in magazine ads. GE would build the home as a showcase of GE's latest electrical innovations. After a show with actor James Stewart in February 1957, the program celebrated the one-year anniversary of GE's "Live Better Electrically" campaign. The program's final commercial featured Reagan and Nancy in the kitchen of their "Total Electric" home. "When you live better electrically," Reagan would tell viewers, "you lead a richer, fuller, more satisfying life. And it's something all of us in this modern age can have."[14] Reagan, Nancy, and their children, Patti and Ron, would also appear in commercials touting the innovative electrical appliances and other products the company installed in Reagan's "Home of the Future."[15]

Reagan and the show did wonders for General Electric's image, as the company flooded the airwaves with positive messages about GE from Reagan and Don Herbert, famous for his role in the popular NBC children's science show, *Watch Mr. Wizard*. As "General Electric Progress Reporter," Herbert introduced viewers to the latest GE inventions and research and, like Reagan, ended his segments with, "At GE, progress is our most important product." A national study by the Psychological Corp. in 1954—before the show's launch—found that only 11 percent of those surveyed knew the GE slogan that would become Reagan's sign-off line. By the following year, recognition rose to 23 percent and to almost 44 percent by May 1957. Sixty-one percent of regular viewers in 1957 could identify the slogan. "General Electric Theatre [sic] has accomplished its public relations goal by reaching large audiences and reaching them in the right way," a BBD&O executive concluded in July 1958. [16]

The telegenic host was considered one of the strongest elements of the show. "Another plus for the show has been Ronald Reagan," *Broadcasting* magazine reported in 1958, "who in addition to being program host on GE *Theatre* [sic], has done an important job as the company's roving ambassador to its employees, community neighbors, and customers, devoting nearly two months a year to these tours." By 1958, Reagan would speak to more than 100,000 people in more than 100 cities and towns.[17] And it was this part of his GE role that would offer Reagan something far more valuable and lasting than fame, riches, and the latest appliances: a new political identity. On long train trips, he would devour newspapers, newsmagazines, and other material supplied by friends and GE executives. These hours of intensive reading—and time spent pondering what he had read—influenced and sharpened Reagan's political views. Over time, as a prominent General Electric employee, he would begin to see the world through the eyes of corporate America. And when his speeches during plant visits transitioned from tales of Hollywood into discourses about political issues, Reagan became much more than a Hollywood actor and TV show host. He evolved into a political force, an actor who not only supported the politicians he admired (during the 1950s, these were mostly conservative Republicans) but also became a leader with his own views on politics—and with a growing political following.

FOR THE FIRST FEW months, during his plant visits, Reagan hewed to the messages he, Dunckel, and GE executives had agreed upon: regale audiences with stories about Hollywood, impress on them that actors, like him, were normal people, and learn as much as possible about the products GE made and the people who made them. More than anything, Reagan would tell GE's story to those employees with only a faint idea about their company's larger values and goals. "It didn't seem at all unusual in GE to make millions of dollars in refrigerators and freezers, and at the same time have the X-ray branch experimenting like crazy to develop a method of preserving food without refrigeration," Reagan later wrote. He added that decentralizing GE created several problems that corporate chiefs hoped Reagan could help solve: "One, how to keep employees in some distant small town from feeling they were forgotten by the company. Two, how to encourage management personnel in those scattered plants from isolating themselves from the community and thinking of themselves as on a temporary assignment with no civic responsibilities at all."[18]

Reagan attacked the plant tours with such vigor that they exhausted him and Dunckel. He called them "murderously difficult" and recalled that he could lose ten pounds in three weeks "and eat anything I wanted." As he wrote in his 1965 memoir: "The first lesson we learned was that no one could do an eight-week tour without ending up a paper-doll clipper. After the second tour that year [1954], which brought the total time to sixteen weeks, we settled for a greater number of tours but shorter—no more than three weeks at one haul." Despite the tours' intensity, Reagan loved being an adored celebrity again. As he wrote: "I enjoyed every whizzing minute of it. It was one of the most rewarding experiences of my life. There was an understandable glow of being welcomed so warmly, but in addition it was wonderful to encounter the honest affection most people had for the familiar faces of Hollywood. No barnstorming politician ever met the people on quite such a common footing. Sometimes I had an awesome, shivering feeling that America was making a personal appearance for me, and it made me the biggest fan in the world."[19]

In his early speeches, Reagan veered occasionally into politics, even though he and Dunckel had agreed his main topic would be "a defense of Hollywood." In October 1954, while visiting GE's Power Division headquarters in Schenectady, New York, he learned that a large dinner event to mark the 100th anniversary of the city's school system had lost its guest speaker to a sudden illness. When the event's organizers asked if Reagan could speak, Dunckel declined, telling them Reagan had no time to prepare a presentation. "Dunk," Reagan said, "let's give it a try."

"Ron, I haven't got time to—"

"Don't worry," Reagan interrupted. "Don't worry."

The next day, Reagan arrived at the gathering, having had little time for preparation because of GE business all morning and into the early afternoon. As Dunckel recalled: "He got up there and gave a speech on education that just dropped them in aisles! He got a good ten-minute standing applause afterward. This is when I finally began to realize the breadth and depth of his knowledgeability. I subsequently came to know that virtually everything that went into that mind stayed there. He could quote it out like a computer any time you wanted. He did read widely, and he remembered what he read. He tended to mesh everything together to get a pattern out of things. It was an amazing tour de force."[20]

"Well," Reagan later wrote about the speech, "that changed everything. From then on, whenever I went to a GE plant, in addition to meeting workers, they'd schedule a speech or two for me to a local organization like the United Fund or Chamber of Commerce; before long, the company began to get requests for me to speak before larger audiences—state conventions of service organizations and groups like the Executives Club in Chicago and the Commonwealth Club in San Francisco."[21]

Paul Gavaghan, the GE publicity director who accompanied Reagan on plant visits after Dunckel's tenure, told biographer

Garry Wills: "There was a formula we always followed. He was taken to meet the top people at the plant, then there was a brief assembly with the workers, in the dining room or some such area. At night we always tried to arrange a banquet with some civic group—the Chamber of Commerce, for instance—where he would be the principal speaker. His speech was always the same; he had it polished to perfection. It was old American values—the ones I believe in, but it was like the Boy Scouts code, you know, not very informative. But always lively, with entertaining quotes."[22] Biographer Lou Cannon described Reagan's early speechmaking:

> The message was authentic, and its construction unique. Unlike anyone else on the national political stage, Reagan composed his central speech on lonely train trips where he had no resort to researchers, speechwriters, fact-checkers, or other useful aides. He built 'The Speech' from the bricks of his reading and experience, decorating it with stories clipped out of local newspapers or popular national magazines such as *Reader's Digest*. Most of his speeches were chock full of numbers, for Reagan rarely met a statistic he didn't like, but they were also sprinkled with anecdotes that relieved the strain of so much statistical material. The anecdotes were carefully tested; Reagan listened to his audiences and relentlessly discarded lines that didn't draw a laugh. He had an ear for the oddball item that made familiar points sound new.[23]

Reagan's first political speech as a GE employee—to the school organization in Schenectady—even created minor national headlines. In a brief story in the *Miami News*, the paper reported on the presentation in which Reagan had noted that "professional patriots" were a threat to American schools because they pushed a regimental form of education. Reagan also reminded the audience of the importance of "our basic democratic principles" in fighting Communist infiltration of American life.[24]

Whether he walked a factory floor, spoke to a local civic group, or met with a local reporter, Reagan charmed those he met with his easy manner and earnest, skilled delivery of GE's message. "The guy's deadly," columnist Milton R. Bass wrote in the *Berkshire Evening Eagle* after Reagan's April 1955 visit to the GE plant in Pittsfield, Massachusetts. "He's also the best invention GE has turned out in years."[25] Recalled John Callahan, who headed GE's Conference Board for the International Union of Electrical Workers: "He came in and left 'em swooning."[26] After interviewing Reagan during his visit to the GE plant in Decatur, Illinois, staff writer Joyce Thompson of the *Decatur Daily Review* was captivated. She declared him "a pleasant, unaffected and extremely accommodating Midwesterner," adding, "Ronald Reagan is just a plain likable, easy-going guy who shows no sign of the temperament often displayed by other stars."[27]

Back at company headquarters, GE officials delighted in Reagan's performance. "Ronald Reagan is a far more valuable property today than he was one year ago," BBD&O, the ad firm that produced *General Electric Theater* and paid Reagan, concluded in an internal audience promotion memo in May 1955. "His weekly appearances on the program, his personal appearance tours and the newspaper publicity he has received . . . all help make him a more attractive subject for newspaper stories."[28] In a lengthy January 1955 article in *Broadcasting* magazine, writer Marjorie Thomas wrote that company officials were pleased with Reagan. "What would appear to be a most happy selection is that of Ronald Reagan as program supervisor-host," she wrote. The show's executive producer told Thomas: "Ronnie's position in relation to the client agency is about as carefully thought out as anything I have ever seen. There is nothing ad lib in this whole operation and the incredible thing is that so far, nothing has been fouled up."[29]

Dunckel recalled Reagan still adhered to his liberal ideology on their train rides together, but he added, "His politics were in the process of change." Dunckel, who was a conservative Republican, recalled: "Whenever he tried to defend New Dealism, or what was passing for it at the time, we would have some rather spirited arguments."[30] Ed Langley, a GE public relations executive who sometimes traveled with Reagan in the late 1950s, recalled a spat Reagan had with George Dalen, a former FBI agent who sometimes escorted Reagan on his plant tours. "We were on the

Blue Ridge Parkway and Dalen said something unkind about Eleanor Roosevelt. It really got Reagan going. He was a great admirer of hers. . . . Over the years Reagan did move pretty well over to conservatism, but he was never passive about it. He would argue. He had to be persuaded."[31]

Reagan later recognized how well eight years at GE—frenetic road trips filled with small talk, handshakes, interviews, speeches, and press conferences—prepared him for his political career. "Looking back now," he wrote after he left the White House, "I realize it wasn't a bad apprenticeship for someone who'd someday enter public life—although, believe me, that was the farthest thing from my mind in those days."[32]

Perhaps most important to Reagan's eventual political career was the training the GE years gave him in the art of political speechmaking. On the road for GE, he learned to read an audience, relate to individuals and large crowds, and test his arguments and punchlines. Reagan's years on the road—as he honed the craft of politics in a low-risk environment—would prove invaluable. "Had he never been forced to reach out to the employees at GE," his longtime aide and image maker Michael Deaver observed, "he might well have foundered when he finally got into politics. Instead, he had to learn to connect, and his newly found focus on the audience was critical to his success."[33]

7

He Had That Little Computer Up There

Reagan had expected General Electric officials to object when his speeches veered into politics. On his first GE tour, Reagan recalled, he "stood there kind of waiting to see if they were going to try to hand me a canned speech. I knew there was going to be a confrontation if they did, because I wouldn't make somebody else's speech."[1] He recalled: "With all that I had heard about the timidity of sponsors, I was somewhat surprised that General Electric delivered me as often as possible to the mashed potato circuit, and never suggested in any way what I should talk about. Nor did they ever indicate I was singing the wrong song and should switch tunes."[2]

Already a voracious reader, Reagan was even more determined to learn about a wide range of issues as he prepared for speaking engagements. Now that he worked for GE, much of his reading came from the desk of Lemuel Ricketts Boulware, the balding, round-faced vice president of GE Labor and Community Relations. A native Kentuckian and a graduate of the University of Wisconsin, the dapper Boulware had taken over labor relations at GE in 1947, the year after a violent nine-week strike by 100,000 members of the United Electrical Workers (UEW).[3] The strike was especially ugly at GE plants in Pennsylvania, Connecticut, and New Jersey, where club-wielding police had attacked striking workers. In the wake of the unrest, GE officials were shocked when community leaders in those cities overwhelmingly sided with union members. The strike was a public relations disaster for the company, as the union forced GE to give workers a wage increase that was twice the company's initial offer. The bitterness of workers toward the company alarmed GE officials.[4] As historian Kim Phillips-Fein observed:

> The deeper threat of organized labor went far beyond dollars and cents. If workers believed that they owed their benefits to the time they spent on the picket line, why would they respect the authority of the boss? Business conservatives also worried about the political mobilization of their workers which seemed implicit in the model of industrial unionism. They feared that unions would turn workers out to the polls to press for higher Social Security benefits, more public spending, and an expanded welfare state. These meant higher taxes for business, of course, but they were also dangerous for a different reason: they implied the potential economic independence of the worker from his job.[5]

The strike also got Boulware his new job. As GE officials fretted about the frightening social and political forces unleashed by the UEW action, they realized that Boulware, who directed labor relations at several GE subsidiaries, had been doing something right. None of the 16,000 employees in his subsidiaries had walked a picket line in 1946. In his new companywide position, Boulware set about fashioning the creative approach that virtually eliminated labor unrest among the company's workers.[6]

As he wrote in 1969, looking back on his early days at GE: "There had been a dearth of education about the great good that private business had accomplished in providing more and better products at more attractive prices than would have been possible from government-owned-and-operated production and distribution. Second, the public had gained an erroneous impression from the brute, crook and exploiter charge hurled so relentlessly by the enemies of business through direct and conveniently available indirect channels." Boulware said GE president Charles E. Wilson and other company leaders told him GE "simply had to correct the ridiculous situation where—despite the best of intentions and the best practices known—the company was distrusted and disapproved of by employees and neighbors in some very important matters."[7] Boulware recalled that "every improvement in employee welfare was getting to be regarded as something which we had greedily and viciously resisted, and which had had to be *forced* out of us *unwillingly*." He strived to change GE's image to that of a "good employer," dedicated to "doing right voluntarily." Boulware approached his new duties with the belief that employees often lacked "full information" about GE's mission and their role in it. Implicit in this philosophy, however, was disrupting the unions' power and avoiding labor unrest and debilitating strikes. In time Boulware's strategy worked. As one scholar who studied his influence on GE observed: "Almost alone in American industry, GE employees were declining to give their union officials an automatic strike vote to use as a bargaining club in negotiation, and were even refusing to authorize strikes."[8]

Labor leaders in the broader union world hated Boulware's tactics. His aim was to short-circuit collective bargaining by communicating directly with rank-and-file union members, not their elected representatives. Boulware argued GE should offer its employees a generous and fair offer, hold fast, and withdraw parts of the proposal as punishment if the union rejected the company's terms. In 1969 the National Labor Relations Board would declare "Boulwarism" illegal and a violation of the duty to negotiate labor agreements in good faith.[9]

Boulware was probably among the GE executives who selected Reagan for his new role as goodwill ambassador. Whatever the case, Reagan became an important part of Boulware's campaign to fight what he called "antibusiness propaganda." As one GE executive who worked with him in the 1950s observed, Reagan "was joining a company so obsessed with conservatism that it was not unlike the [radically conservative] John Birch Society."[10] And in his speeches in far-flung cities and towns, on *General Electric Theater*—and in commercials he later filmed for the company—Reagan would embody the brand of public and employee relations that Boulware imagined when he took his job in 1947.

Boulware once insisted he and Reagan met only once for about ten minutes in GE's New York office. In fact, he knew Reagan better than that. He had first met Reagan's future wife, Nancy Davis, in Phoenix in 1950, and he and Reagan corresponded into the late 1980s.[11] But Reagan did not need to communicate directly with Boulware to absorb and reflect his thinking. "He was interested very much in our employee-relations philosophy, Boulwarism," Earl Dunckel recalled, "because we were out there talking to people who were affected by it. He wanted to know what it was and all about it, because they [the employees] know about it. He didn't want to be at a loss to discuss it."[12] Sometimes a GE employee would ask Reagan, "What do you think of this business of General Electric telling our union to take it or leave it?" Dunckel said Reagan would reply: "When I was heading up a union, I recognized that there always came a time when you were at the make or break point and where it had to be one way or another. All the argumenting, all the discussion had taken place. We had passed that stage. Now it was, 'Am I going to accept your plan? Are you going to accept my plan? Are you going to go on from here, or is this going to remain a deadlock?' That's essentially what take it or leave it amounts to."[13] If Dunckel's recollection was accurate, Reagan forgot to mention that GE's negotiating strategy was all about avoiding the "argumenting" with its take-it-or-leave-it offer.

In a sense, Reagan, the former union leader, had signed up to help Boulware disarm and undermine his company's unions. Whether Reagan fully realized this is unclear. Given his dire financial straits, he may not have bothered to question how much Boulware and GE would use him to undercut the company's union representatives. Reagan was a canny negotiator of many contracts for an actors' union affiliated with the American Federation of Labor (AFL). He would only have been ignorant of the strategy Boulware and GE used in negotiating with organized labor if he had resolved not to inquire. Regardless, his role as an agent of Boulwarism would expand gradually as he became a larger part of the GE organization and saw himself not merely as a television host but as one of the corporation's public faces.

Even before Reagan arrived, Boulware had developed innovative ways to communicate with GE's employees and erode the influence and effectiveness of the company's unions. "Employees were inundated with messages," recalled Edward Langley, who then worked in public relations for GE. "They even found them stuffed in their pay envelopes: The evils of big government, big unions, the 'something for nothing attitude.'"[14] As Boulware told a group of GE employee relations managers in 1952, "So far as I am concerned, our whole objective in employee, union, and community relations is to fill each GE job—of every kind and at whatever level—with a person of suitable initial endowments and then to get and keep that employee informed, trained, directed, inspired, measured and promoted or otherwise rewarded in such a manner that he will be able to do right, want to do right, and actually do right by his and our mutual best interests at work and away from home."[15]

Langley recalled that GE employed more than one hundred writers by the early 1950s to produce its publications. Each Friday, workers received a company newspaper, *Works News*, with a mix of local plant news and company developments aimed at blue-collar workers. Other publications included *General Electric Review* (mostly for the company's engineers), *Employee Relations News Letter* (originally distributed to employee supervisors but expanded to a wide variety of non-GE "thought leaders"), and *Monogram* (a slick magazine with GE news that sometimes reported on Reagan's plant visits).[16]

GE dubbed its plant foremen "job salesmen" who, in addition to supervising workers, were expected to educate them on the company's virtues.[17] The company placed full-page ads in local newspapers to communicate these and other company values to workers and others in the community. In one such nationwide advertisement in May 1949, GE stated: "In good times and bad General Electric tries honestly to pay what is right for a fair day's work. And we believe an honest day's work is made up of the *full* interest, care and skill of the General Electric employee in addition to what is regarded as a reasonable output of effort according to modern standards."[18] In August 1952, another advertisement touted the twenty-one "dividends" of a GE job, which included "Guaranteed Retirement Income of $125 a Month—and Up!" and "Up to $300 in Loans Available."[19]

The company publications Reagan read on long train rides included *Works News* and the *Supervisor's Guide to General Electric Job Information,* a 120-page manual sent to each of GE's 15,000 supervisors that offered answers to virtually every question a disgruntled or union-influenced employee might ask. "General Electric's policy," the *Guide* said, "is to pay what is right in the particular community—all things considered—for the skill, care, effort, and working conditions involved in comparable jobs under similar circumstances." Reagan also read from the five-volume encyclopedia of company philosophy—the "Blue Books"— published by GE's diminutive president, Ralph Cordiner. Reagan likely purchased other books recommended by Boulware for the GE employees' book clubs that met periodically in workers' homes.

Boulware obsessed over educating GE supervisors and workers about economics and urged them to read books that provided a remedial education in that discipline. "Economics will help our employees understand their vital and immediate interest in customers, tools, inflation, taxes, savings, risk, and profits," Boulware said in 1952, "[and] will perhaps even encourage individual employees to go on from simple economic education to moral reawakening and political sophistication so that he will not only know what is the right thing to do . . . but will also be politically sophisticated to the point that demagogs in and out of unions and politics can't sell him gold bricks in the name of sound economics and social progress." The books Boulware recommended to GE employees in the early and mid-1950s included *Economics in One Lesson,* by Henry Hazlitt; *How You Really Earn Your Living: Every Man's Guide to American Economics,* by Lewis Haney; and *The Road Ahead,* by John T. Flynn.[20] Reagan, who majored in economics in college, almost certainly read these books.

In 1946 Hazlitt, then an economics and finance reporter for the *New York Times,* produced a short, simple, and accessible book with pointed attacks on government spending, agriculture subsidies, minimum wage laws, and labor unions. The book was particularly useful to Boulware's employee education efforts. Judging by Reagan's eventual conversion to conservatism, Hazlitt's philosophy and other simplistic attacks on big government and New Deal economic policy apparently influenced his thinking. "We are driven to the conclusion that unions, though they may for a time be able to secure an increase in money wages for their members, partly at the expense of employers, *do not, in the long run and for the whole body of workers, increase real wages at all* [emphasis Hazlitt]." Elsewhere in his book, Hazlitt's attacks on the progressive income tax surely resonated with Reagan. "People begin to ask themselves," Hazlitt wrote, "why they should work six, eight or ten months of the entire year for the government, and only six, four or two months for themselves and their families." Taxation and government spending, the author argued, "create the very problem of unemployment" that the "government spenders" say they wish to resolve.[21] (In 1981, speaking to the Conservative Political Action Committee in Washington, Reagan would praise Hazlitt as one of the "intellectual leaders" who "shaped so much of our thoughts.")[22]

A professor of economics at New York University, Lewis Haney (born in Reagan's college town of Eureka, Illinois, in 1882) wrote his economics primer in a simplistic, question-and-answer style. His philosophy was one of hostility to virtually every federal government role in the economy. With vehemence, he attacked deficit spending by government to stimulate the economy. "The plain fact is that this compensatory spending scheme is merely a device for pump priming to be turned on and off at the while of some government official and subject to his weaknesses," Haney wrote in *How You Really Earn Your Living* in 1952. He attacked organized labor and the "social planners" who passed federal laws guaranteeing collective bargaining for having "gone too far in giving monopoly power to the leaders of organized labor." He disparaged the Social Security system for the way it "penalize[d] thrift" and diminished "our ability to care for those who are really in need." He opposed federal legislation to provide health insurance. "The proposal for uniform medical service controlled by government has been, and is, pushed by those who believe in some form of Socialism," he wrote.[23]

In 1948 John T. Flynn, a journalist who was among the founders of the isolationist America First Committee in 1940, published *The Road Ahead*. Flynn had opposed American intervention in the Second World War and was a vocal critic of President Franklin Roosevelt's foreign and domestic policies. He said he wrote his book "to describe the road along which this country is traveling to its destruction." Flynn saw British-style socialism as a threat to American democracy and the Democratic Party as its willing accomplice. "The struggle for socialism has moved to an entirely different battleground under a wholly new war plan," Flynn wrote. "Up to now it has carried on its struggle inside the Democratic Party, with the result that the Democratic Party is now at its mercy in precisely the same manner as the British Liberal Party came to be the prisoner of the British Fabian movement."[24] Boulware admired Flynn's book so much that he sent a copy to every GE supervisor.[25]

Reagan read more than the books Boulware suggested. In his study of Reagan's intellectual life, historian David T. Byrne argued that *Witness*—a 1952 book by Whittaker Chambers, a *Time* magazine writer and editor and a former Communist—had "the most important intellectual influence" on Reagan during the early to mid-1950s.[26] Chambers's story of his life as a Communist and his disillusionment with the party was a best seller and has endured as a classic of the Cold War era. In 1984 at Eureka College, Reagan called Chambers's story "one of the most vivid events of my time, an event whose meaning is echoed in today's disenchantment with Communism." Reagan would recall that Chambers had "marked the beginning of his personal journey away from Communism." (As president, Reagan would award the Medal of Freedom to Chambers posthumously in 1984.)[27]

In addition to the books read during his early GE years, Reagan continued reading the other periodicals and newspapers to which he had always subscribed. To those, he added in 1955 an influential new conservative magazine, *National Review*, founded by William F. Buckley Jr.[28] "I'd be lost without *National Review*," Reagan would tell Buckley in a letter in 1962.[29]

"He was a great reader and an omnivorous reader," Dunckel recalled about Reagan. "He had that little computer up there that saved everything he read or heard."[30] In his speeches, Reagan did not mention the names of books, newspapers, or magazines he had read. But there is much evidence of Reagan's voracious reading habits. Friends and colleagues from his early Hollywood days attested to it, as did his traveling companions on his GE tours. In 1965, when Reagan was testing the waters for a possible run for California governor, journalist Lee Edwards tagged along for several days. "I asked him which books had had the most impact on his political thinking," Edwards recalled. "He hesitated, saying, well, he didn't want to single out any one particular book. Then he said, 'Well, of course there's *The Federalist* and *The Law.*' I'm hard-pressed to think of another political figure who would provide those same titles." Edwards reported he was "able to confirm [Reagan's] political tastes that same day when we visited his home in Pacific Palisades, and there in his library, dog-eared and annotated, were *The Law* by Frederic Bastiat, *Witness* by Whittaker Chambers, and *Economics in One Lesson* by Henry Hazlitt."[31] Edwards said he believed Reagan had read closely many of the books he owned. "I began pulling the books out of the shelves and looking at them. They were dog-eared. They were annotated. They were smudged by his fingers, and so forth. This was a man who had read hundreds of books."[32]

Reagan insisted he spoke only for himself in his many speeches on tour for GE, but he did admit to toeing the company line occasionally. One GE public relations executive later described Reagan's role at GE as "a sort of roguish shop steward, giving the managers mild needles while advancing company thoughts directed at productivity."[33] Asked about his message on GE tours, Reagan told Hedda Hopper in 1956: "I don't like that reading [a speech] business—you lose something. Then I made a deal with my sponsors. Now I choose my own words after they've given me the general idea of what they want conveyed."[34] But it is difficult to imagine Reagan was immune to the well-organized and pervasive pro-business propaganda of the company, which had recently rescued him from his financial travails. "Boulware's obvious strategy was to bypass the worker's elected representatives, the United Electrical Workers, in order to reach out directly to employees and convince them, as well as the public at large, that they shared common interests with GE," business historian James Hoopes observed. "It would have been surprising if he had not spotted the potential for reaching GE's nationwide workforce with the new medium of television." In other words, Boulware saw *General Electric Theater* and its new host as important and malleable tools in GE's propaganda efforts.[35]

Before long, Reagan's speeches bore the distinctive marks of Boulware's and GE's influence. "Those GE tours," Reagan later wrote, "became almost a postgraduate course in political science for me. I was seeing how government really operated and affected people in America, not how it was taught in school." That education, he said, involved better understanding the evils of big government. "From hundreds of people in every part of the country, I heard complaints about how the ever-expanding federal government was encroaching on liberties we'd always taken for granted. I heard it so often that after a while I became convinced that some of our fundamental freedoms were in jeopardy because of the emergence of a *permanent government* never envisioned by the framers of the Constitution." Primed by Boulware, Hazlitt, Haney, and others, Reagan did his own research and began including in his speeches examples of big-government abuse he had uncovered.[36] "The experience must stand as the greatest accidental political training program ever," wrote Edward Langley, a GE public relations executive who would accompany Reagan on his plant tours in the late 1950s. "It changed him. It would have changed Jane Fonda to Margaret Thatcher."[37]

IN THE EARLY YEARS of his GE tenure, Reagan regaled audiences with Hollywood stories—including his struggle against Communists—and a defense of the morals and values of the actors and others employed in his industry. Since 1949, in addition to his SAG presidency, he had chaired the 35,000-member Motion Picture Industry Council (MPIC), created that year by nine major labor, actor, and industry management organizations to fight unflattering portrayals of Hollywood morality.[38] As the *Daily Review* of Decatur, Illinois, reported on the star's October 12, 1955, visit: "The luncheon talk included discussion of show business and its problems including Communist attempts to infiltrate the movie industry. He also said that charges that Hollywood is an immoral city are untrue. He pointed out that the Hollywood divorce rate is below average for the nation, and that many Hollywood personalities give freely of their time and money to welfare projects."[39]

The following March in Vermont, Reagan spoke to three hundred members of the South Burlington Parent Teacher Association. As the local paper reported, he urged "PTA members to think of Hollywood citizens as 'just the same kind of people you are— with the same problems and the same worries.'" He told them 1 percent of those living in the Los Angeles area worked in the movie industry, but they were responsible for 12 percent of charitable contributions. Reagan also claimed that the Hollywood divorce rate was 29.9 percent compared with a 40 percent national average.[40]

Reagan had defended Hollywood in his early speeches because it was his job as president of the Screen Actors Guild and as MPIC chairman. In the beginning, he was likely responding to an onslaught of criticism of perceived movie-industry immorality that culminated in 1947, two years before his divorce from Jane Wyman. In February 1947 three prominent religious leaders— Monsignor Fulton J. Sheen, Dr. Harry Emerson Fosdick, and Dr. Sidney Goldstein—had published an impassioned column attacking Hollywood in *Motion Picture Magazine*. "At present the rate in Los Angeles is five divorces out of every six marriages," the three claimed. "If Hollywood stars are going to accept the homage that goes with stardom, then they must also accept the moral responsibility that goes with that homage."[41]

Soon the Motion Picture Research Society began targeting stars it considered examples of immoral behavior. Hollywood columnist Erskine Johnson labeled the campaign "a new witch hunt." In a December 1951 column, Johnson touted a 1947 survey of 1,235 readers of the *Hollywood Reporter* that put the film industry's divorce rate in 1947 at 29.9 percent, compared with what it claimed was a national rate of 40 percent.[42] In a column that summer, Hedda Hopper warned: "The heat's being turned on our Hollywood stars by members of the motion picture research society, to which thousands of people all over the country belong. They inform me that they intend to censor the actions of our stars even more strongly than does the [Catholic Church's] Legion of Decency."[43]

Reagan called his defense of the movie industry a "bare-boned little speech" that was his "basic Hollywood speech." In a 1989 book of selected speeches, he included his June 21, 1951, address to the Kiwanis International Convention in St. Louis. It likely was an early version of the standard talk Reagan would deliver in his early days of speaking for GE. (Transcripts and news reports about Reagan's speeches in the early 1950s are rare.) In that 1951 speech, Reagan shared a slew of statistics about Hollywood workers: "Seventy percent of them are high-school graduates or better, as against the national average of twenty-eight percent. Seventy-nine percent of the people in my industry are married; seventy percent to their first husband or wife; seventy percent of them have children; sixty-one percent of them are regular members and attendants at the churches of Hollywood." Reagan also told the audience that the 29.9 percent Hollywood divorce rate was ten points lower than the national average, an assertion he would repeat in speeches until at least December 1958.[44]

Reagan did not cite his source for the Hollywood divorce rate—he rarely gave audiences the source for any of his assertions—but it was almost certainly the 1947 *Hollywood Reporter* survey. And those figures, even in 1947, were inaccurate. They were wildly so when Reagan shared them with audiences in 1951 and later. According to statistics published in 1954 by the U.S. Department of Health, Education, and Welfare (HEW), the "crude divorce rate" in 1951—the number of divorces per 1,000 persons in the United States—was 2.5 (or 0.25 percent), meaning that if Reagan's percentage for Hollywood was correct, the movie industry's divorce rate was much higher, not lower, than the national average. While there are no federal statistics for the movie industry divorce rate in that period, the crude divorce rate for California in 1950 was 3.7 (or 0.37 percent), higher than the national rate.[45]

By 1951, however, the national divorce rate was dramatically lower than it had been in the postwar years. "The year 1950 was the fourth consecutive year in which divorces declined," HEW said in its 1954 report. "The bulk of the decrease from the 1946 peak of 610,000 divorces occurred in 1947 and 1948."[46] Put another way, the national "crude divorce rate" in 1947 had been 3.4. But by 1951, it was 2.5 percent, a steep drop. In 1955, when Reagan claimed the national divorce rate was 40 percent, it had declined again to a crude rate of 2.3 (or 0.23 percent).[47]

Reagan may not have had access to data from HEW or the Public Health Service, but newspaper reports about these data were plentiful at the time. For example, the Associated Press reported that "the [national] divorce rate dropped to a seven-year low."[48] Newspapers around the country carried the same story. Another story by the New York Times News Service in December 1954 reported, "A divorce rate down more than 40 percent from the 1946 peak was estimated" by U.S. government officials. "The spectacular eight-year decline in divorce rates has claimed little attention compared to the public stir on the subject when divorces were highest [in 1946]."[49] The following year, the *Times* reported a slight five-year rise in the U.S. divorce rate.[50]

As a leader and spokesperson for the movie industry—and as a performer whose livelihood might be at risk in a morals crusade aimed at divorced actors—Reagan's spirited defense of Hollywood was understandable and justified. It is more difficult to justify Reagan's continued reliance on statistics that were quickly outdated. Regardless of the *Hollywood Reporter*'s information, more-reliable data on divorce rates could be found in many libraries, as could news reports about that data. Reagan's advocacy of the movie business suggests an admirable urge to defend his industry, his friends, and his neighbors. That he did so for years by touting stale and inaccurate statistics showed a careless attitude about the facts. It also demonstrated that once a compelling story or statistic found its way into Reagan's basic speech, it would not soon disappear or change.

What would change by the late fifties was the emphasis Reagan placed on defending Hollywood. "As the years went on," he recalled in his 1965 memoir, "my speeches underwent a kind of evolution, reflecting not only my changing philosophy but also the swiftly rising tide of collectivism that threatens to inundate what remains of our free economy. I don't believe it was all just a case of my becoming belatedly aware of something that already existed; the last decade has seen a quickening tempo in our government's race toward the controlled society."[51] Twenty-five years later, Reagan reflected again on his speeches during the late fifties: "As time went on, the portion of my speech about government began to grow longer and I began to shorten the Hollywood part. Pretty soon, it became basically a warning to people about the threat of government. Finally, the Hollywood part just got lost and I was out there beating the bushes for private enterprise."[52]

8

Ronald Reagan, Businessman

A s his GE touring neared its second full year, Reagan sprinkled more politics into speeches and interviews. In Providence, Rhode Island, in March 1956, he held one of the most political of events—a press conference—and attacked government censorship of films. "I just can't imagine a whole generation being raised under a system in which they are told what they can see and hear without them being conditioned to being told eventually what they can read," he told reporters at the Sheraton-Biltmore Hotel.[1] By year's end, Reagan's travel and his growing outspokenness would prompt Hollywood columnist Hal Humphrey to observe: "For the past two years Ronald Reagan has traveled more miles and made more speeches than a politician. Reagan isn't running for anything, but it is part of his job [with GE] to make friends with the sponsor's employees and sell Hollywood as a hamlet with a beat."[2]

While he often discussed public affairs in his speeches of the early 1950s, Reagan had rarely veered into partisan politics. But almost from the beginning of his speechmaking, Reagan had made Communism—as well as the political censorship he claimed the government and others wanted to impose on the film industry—central topics of most of his talks. And in most of his early speeches, he cast Hollywood as the heroic defender of the nation's democratic values.

In his 1951 speech to the Kiwanis International Convention in St. Louis, for example, Reagan claimed Hollywood-produced images of American life and affluence were "holding back the flood of propaganda from the other side of the Iron Curtain." Several years later, in speeches during his travels for GE, he would often repeat this line: "We are most proud of the great tribute that was paid to us by the Kremlin in Moscow, when recently it said, 'The worst enemy of the people, the worst tool of degenerate capitalism that must be destroyed is the motion picture screen of Hollywood, California.'"[3] It is not clear where Reagan found the quote he attributed to the Kremlin. No news story in any major paper in the United States from 1945 through 1960 contained these words credited to the Soviet government. But the sentiment was probably authentic. In May 1947 a Soviet writer commenting in an official Communist Party magazine had attacked the American motion picture industry. He said Hollywood-produced films that "propagate the famous 'American way of life' give a distorted, sweetened picture of life in the United States and advertise American capitalists as noble, wealthy persons who should be imitated and obeyed."[4]

Reagan often began his diatribes with a review of his heroic struggle against the Communists in Hollywood in the 1940s. "They failed to take over the industry and today the Kremlin says Hollywood is a potent weapon against Communism," Reagan announced at a dinner hosted by the Greater Troy Chamber of Commerce in Troy, New York, in April 1955. (He also toured the GE plant in nearby Waterford.) The movie industry's image had been distorted by reporters, he said, "some of whom lack journalistic integrity." Reagan argued Hollywood was more like small-town America than most people knew. "We believe in freedom of speech and the press and we believe that when there is evil doings in our community, we look upon it with repugnance as you do." Reagan concluded, "I have long believed that the ills of the world could be cured by its people not talking about each other but talking to each other."[5]

Reagan still charmed his audiences with anodyne Hollywood stories. As he traveled the country speaking for GE, however, he soon discovered that his strong language about Communism resonated with audiences. And his anti-Communist rhetoric and his warnings about Russian aggression became even more pungent. "Let's say to Russia, 'We're going to win this Cold War, no matter what the cost in energy and dollars—even blood, if necessary,'" he told a dinner audience in Coshocton, Ohio, in late October 1956. "We'll believe what you say about peaceful co-existence when you permit East and West Germany to be reunited, when you permit North and South Korea to again become one nation. But until you do, we are going to keep a loaded gun pointed at you."[6]

As he moved about the country, Reagan's speeches became more political, and some of the journalists who covered him recognized that fact. In March 1957, a reporter for the *Trenton Evening Times*—after the actor's visit to the city—described Reagan in terms befitting an elected official, not a film star. "Ronald Reagan simply likes people," the anonymous journalist wrote. "But performing for millions of them on television each week just doesn't satisfy him. He also likes to get around the country in person, talking and shaking hands with the public as much as possible."[7]

As his speeches resonated with audiences, Reagan beefed up his talks with another issue that made them even more political: an attack on the federal income tax. He deplored the tax rate levied on actors and other high earners (the marginal top rate on regular income in 1955 was 91 percent). In an interview with Hedda Hopper in February 1956, Reagan complained the disintegrating studio system, in which actors had worked on contract only for one studio, hurt him and other high earners. "One reason why actors have gone on their own is because their studios wouldn't help meet the tax problems," he said. "Industry handled that for their executives."[8] The following year, in Hendersonville, North Carolina, Reagan attacked the federal income tax code as "immoral and unfair" and claimed that "the middle class is being taxed out of existence." Soon it became his familiar refrain. He thundered about high tax rates imposed on wealthy film stars. "If you make any dough at all, they take away 91 percent of it," he complained. And Reagan extrapolated it to apply to the rest of the population. Current tax law, he said, "is against a man earning a living for himself."[9]

The only problem with Reagan's complaint was the 91 percent tax rate applied only to taxable income over $200,000. In 1956 the median income in the United States was $3,400 and income of that amount would have been taxed at a 20 percent rate.[10] Regardless, Reagan blamed the Soviet Union and the U.S. government's response to Communist infiltration of Hollywood for the movie industry's high tax rate. "We now have documented proof that Red infiltration of Hollywood was under direct orders of the Kremlin—to be carried out by a hard core of Communist organizers," Reagan told students at the Eureka College commencement in June 1957. (He did not say what the documentation was.)

When fighting the Communists in Hollywood, Reagan explained, "We had allowed misconceptions about ourselves to grow in the public mind and thus had become a target for those people who seek to regulate and interfere." Because of this, the film industry suffered from "discriminatory taxation, needless government harassment, and political censorship." Reagan was indignant over what he regarded as the federal government's refusal to recognize that well-paid actors and others in the film industry labored under circumstances that merited favorable tax treatment. "There is not one provision in the income tax code that recognizes the special expense of entertainers for the conduct of their careers."[11] (Reagan's animosity toward the U.S. tax system may have been born in 1952 when the IRS demanded of him $21,000 in back taxes. The government had calculated what Reagan owed, based on movie income he deferred when he entered the Army, a year when he was in a lower, 88 percent marginal tax bracket. Reagan disputed the bill but paid it. A year later, he won an appeal and the IRS refunded him the money.)[12]

In his 1957 Eureka College speech, Reagan also complained about what he saw as an alarming trend of state and local governments censoring Hollywood. He claimed two hundred U.S. cities and eleven state governments "have taken it upon themselves to censor movies," meaning, "These governments are not telling us what we can hear and see—they're telling you, the public."[13] Reagan was correct about the widespread local and state censorship of films. He did not mention another form of strict censorship of movie content: the industry, through the Motion Picture Association of America's (MPAA) Picture Production Code, told movie producers what they could not include in their movies, including portrayals of suicide and sex. Some in Hollywood and the American Civil Liberties Union protested in April 1957 when the MPAA relaxed its rules but still encouraged outside groups to advise the film industry about which content to censor.[14]

For years, Reagan had defended the freedom of producers and directors to create their own standards. He argued in 1955 at a congressional field hearing in Los Angeles, "the right of the movie industry to express itself is tied in with free speech, free thought, and the free press." To Tennessee Democratic senator Estes Kefauver, who used his subcommittee to investigate sex and violence in the film industry, Reagan had said, "In all crime and violence pictures, crime never pays; right always triumphs."[15]

Although he disliked the censorship some imposed on Hollywood, Reagan saw income taxes as a greater threat. In January 1958 he took his argument to the U.S. House and its Ways and Means Committee, claiming high taxes had killed "the American dream that anyone can become rich." In his testimony Reagan presented himself as a spokesperson for both sides of the movie industry, labor and management. And he repeated the well-worn and well-tested lines he had delivered to after-dinner audiences for months. "He knew his lines so well," a United Press reporter observed, "that he had to glance only occasionally at his 15-page script."[16]

"We believe the schedule of surtaxes in the personal income tax structure is unrealistic, confiscatory, and contrary to the principles of free enterprise," Reagan told the committee in his formal statement. He argued that actors and others in the film industry were freelancers who worked in a "feast-or-famine" system that taxed them mercilessly in the years they earned a good wage. The movie industry, Reagan argued, deserved preferential tax treatment because of its role in showing the world the real America. "They see our freedoms," he explained, adding this familiar refrain: "I do not think anyone could challenge the statement that the American motion picture has probably been the greatest salesman on the world market for American goods and material of all types. The best proof I think we can give of the impact on the world of the American motion picture is the attempt a few years ago of the Communist Party to capture our industry. They objected to this American story being told on the screens of the world." Reagan's solution to the perceived overtaxation of the industry was to abolish the progressive tax system. He proposed replacing it with a flat percentage tax for everyone based on biblical tithing principles.[17]

As his indignation about the reach and growth of government rose, Reagan continued to dispense stories of government abuse. He spouted a variety of statistics that strengthened his case among audiences eager to accept his warnings about the dangers of government to individual liberty. "There is a government employee for each seventh man in this room," he told two hundred Chamber of Commerce members in Jefferson City, Missouri, in May 1958. "The thing has become so complex that between the uniformed chief of the Army and the president there are nineteen civilians. In the Navy there are eleven and in the Air Force, eight."[18] Reagan's assertion about the ratio of government workers to citizens was wrong. According to U.S. Census information then available, federal, state, and local governments employed just over eight million people. The U.S. population in 1957 was an estimated 170 million, meaning there was one government employee for every twenty-one citizens, not every seven. The military chain of command concerns Reagan had mentioned, however, were real. As Reagan spoke, Congress was considering a bill to reform the Pentagon's command structure. It would pass the Department of Defense Reorganization Act of 1958 in July.[19]

As part of his jeremiad against big government, Reagan also attacked government assistance programs. He did this often at the local United Way and Community Chest fund-raisers that featured him as a keynote speaker. In October 1958 Reagan told a crowd at a United Way dinner in Binghamton, New York, that the Russians "want things like this [the United Fund] to fail."

Reagan explained this was because "they think government should do it all . . . they don't want poverty erased . . . they don't want brotherhood. Where democracy works, they have nothing to sell."[20] At a United Chest and Red Cross event in Elmira, New York, the next day, Reagan informed audience members that their fund-raising campaign was "essential to the fight against Communism because wherever there is a symbol of democracy, Communists are against it." The stakes in Elmira were even higher than that, Reagan said. "Because of the list of industries right here in Elmira, this city ranks high on the Communist infiltration attempt." Elmira was a city of about fifty thousand situated near the Pennsylvania border in Upstate New York and boasted a half-dozen manufacturing plants. Reagan did not say how he obtained information about the Communists' designs on the city or why Communist officials would find the city more tempting than others with similar plants.[21]

It did not matter that Reagan's assertions might be wrong or that he had no special ability to surmise the attitude of the Kremlin toward local charitable organizations in the United States. Reagan's sunny demeanor and the ease with which he delivered his well-rehearsed lines landed powerfully among the business and social elites in dozens of small towns and large cities each year. "He speaks with sincerity in describing the evils of socialism and he bid fair to get carried away with a denunciation of taxes at a press conference here yesterday afternoon," a staff writer for the *Shreveport Times* wrote in December 1958, after Reagan's appearance there. "But his face is so familiar from 50 movies which brought him celluloid fame and—more lately—from General Electric's Sunday night television show. It's like listening to your next door neighbor campaigning for less bureaucracy and lower taxes."[22] Reagan's speech so charmed the locals in Shreveport that a radio station twice broadcast his remarks, "more or less by popular demand," the *Times* reported.[23]

"He came in the role of Ronald Reagan, Businessman, rather than as Ronald Reagan, Movie and Television Star," the Abilene, Texas, newspaper reported after the actor's visit in April 1959. "But experience in the latter certainly helped him get across the ideas of the former." Reagan "came preaching the cause of free enterprise" and "preached his sermon well. He is a fellow of dignity, but seemingly without affectation. He sounds like he means what he's saying. And he is free with the grin he has made famous before cameras since the late 1930s. And, what he says—particularly his off-the-cuff answers to questions put by interviewers—shows an amazing knowledge of both governmental and business affairs. It's obvious he is no mere movie glamour boy—even though he did show up at the interview wearing flaming red wool sox."[24]

In a letter to Vice President Richard Nixon in June 1959, Reagan gushed about audiences' response to his speeches. Nixon had first written to Reagan, applauding him after reading a transcript of the actor's speech "Business, Ballots, and Bureaus," which Reagan had delivered to General Electric executives in New York that spring. "During the last year particularly," Reagan wrote, "I have been amazed at the reaction to this talk. Audiences are actually militant in their expression that 'something must be done.'" Reagan told Nixon he was "convinced there is a groundswell of economic conservatism building up which could reverse the entire tide of present day 'statism.' As a matter of fact, we seem to be in one of those rare moments when the American people with that wisdom which is the strength of democracy are ready to say 'enough.' Such a wave of feeling marked the end of the 'Capone era.' Prohibition was ended the same way with people (even those who opposed drinking) deciding the wrong method had been tried."[25] Reagan did not seem to care he was addressing the vice president to a president who had presided over this alleged tide of "statism." Nor did it matter to him he had compared the Eisenhower era to Mafia rule and Prohibition.

Not every listener or local reporter applauded Reagan as the supremely knowledgeable expert on government he claimed to be. Hollywood columnist Hal Humphrey wrote in July 1960 about a meeting with Reagan that summer. "If you happen to say something to Reagan about any of these 'socialistic' trends, it is like punching a button on an I.B.M. machine," Humphrey wrote. "He spews forth an avalanche of statistics which add up to the grimmest of catastrophes for all of us." He noted Reagan had recently resigned as SAG president after becoming a producer for *General Electric Theater* (he had become Guild president briefly in late 1959 to lead a brief strike and negotiate a new actors' deal with studios). Humphrey asked him about his plans for the show. "Although I can't report the lowdown on 'G.E. Theater,' which Reagan will continue to host this fall," Humphrey wrote, "I can tell you that social security is a fraud perpetrated against the people to lull them into thinking they are getting something for nothing." After listening to Reagan expound on assorted topics— the Tennessee Valley Authority, federal school aid, the growth of government—Humphrey wrote: "If any of you have opposing thoughts on any of those subjects, I suggest you take them up with Reagan. He has all the facts and figures." Humphrey wryly observed, "I think I can understand how the Screen Actors Guild got its settlement out of the movie producers. Reagan must have talked them into submission and then buried them with figures."[26]

By the late 1950s and early 1960s, Reagan saw himself, first, as a professional political critic and, second, as an actor. Almost gone were the spirited defenses of Hollywood. He replaced them with speeches consisting of wide-ranging attacks on a metastasizing federal government that threatened to diminish free enterprise and individual liberty. Reagan's views on the issues mostly remained on the pages of local newspapers that reported on— almost always with favor—his speeches to civic clubs and other organizations during visits to cities and towns with GE plants. But as he became less an actor and more a politician—although without portfolio—Reagan's pronouncements increasingly made news. In September 1959, for example, Soviet premier Nikita Khrushchev visited Hollywood and met with some of the town's biggest stars, including Jack Benny, Frank Sinatra, James Stewart, Bob Hope, Zsa Zsa Gabor, Kirk Douglas, Gary Cooper, and Dinah Shore. Reagan boycotted the event, as did Bing Crosby, Ward Bond, and Adolphe Menjou. Although he was not alone in his protest, Reagan received most of the national attention for the boycott and for his statements attacking Khrushchev. "The State Department put the motion picture industry in an untenable position," Reagan told United Press International. "This luncheon with its obvious publicity implications increases the risk that the movie industry is extending the hand of friendship to this man and approving what he stands for."[27] Reagan's public contempt for the warm Hollywood welcome granted Khrushchev, one entertainment columnist reported, "brought him stacks of approving letters from all over the U.S.A."[28]

General Electric's top executives did not seem to mind Reagan's political outspokenness. Many years later Reagan would tell a friend, "I've always remembered GE *Theater* and Ralph Cordiner for the very fact that in all those years of speaking at the various engagements they set up, they never once told me anything I should or should not say nor did they even suggest a subject. My speeches were totally my own."[29] But Earl Dunckel recalled that the free rein the company gave Reagan—including his espousal of conservative and anti-Communist philosophy—did not please everyone at GE. This was especially true among those Dunckel called "a liberal element" in management. "I spent a lot of time defending Ron up until the point when he flatly asked [CEO] Ralph Cordiner, 'Is what I'm saying doing your company damage?'" Dunckel said Cordiner told Reagan, "You say what you believe."[30]

Reagan posed his question to Cordiner in June 1960 in response to a public flare-up over what Reagan said about the Tennessee Valley Authority (TVA) in a May 4, 1960, speech in Cleveland. The TVA, Reagan told his audience, was a prime example of government waste and "an independent business in competition with private industry, which it can undersell because of its tax-free status." Unfortunately for Reagan, the TVA was a large generator of electric power in the region and one of General Electric's largest customers. The TVA spent millions each year for electric turbines and other equipment that the corporation produced. TVA officials took offense.

"We're a customer, a very good customer, of General Electric," the TVA chairman told the *St. Louis Post-Dispatch* in June when news reports about Reagan's remarks reached him. "In our opinion it is a wrongful thing for anyone to attack his customer." GE officials did not abandon or criticize Reagan. A company spokesperson told the press that the actor was free to "attack anyone he feels like." But the company tried to distance itself from Reagan's opinions about its prominent customer. "We don't write Reagan's stuff," the GE official said. "We don't attempt to review it in advance or even afterward unless some question comes up."[31]

Reagan later said GE's defense of his freedom of speech weighed on him. "Suddenly, realization dawned," he wrote. "There wouldn't be a word. Ralph Cordiner meant what he said [about giving Reagan free rein] and was prepared to back those words with $50,000,000 worth of business. Now the responsibility was mine. Who was I to embarrass the company, just because I had carte blanche to speak my mind?"

Reagan said he phoned Cordiner, who told him not to worry about the tempest. Reagan replied that he despaired at the thought of GE workers losing their jobs "because he had defended my right to speak." Cordiner did not take the opening Reagan created to urge him to squelch his TVA criticism. "Mr. Cordiner," Reagan finally volunteered, "what would you say if I said I could make my speech just as effective without mentioning TVA?" Reagan remembered a long pause before Cordiner replied, "Well, it would make my job easier." Reagan said that dropping the language from his speeches "was no problem. You can reach out blindfolded and grab a hundred examples of overgrown government."[32] After 1962, when Reagan no longer worked for GE, he resumed his attacks on the TVA.

9

He Used to Be a Liberal

A recurring question about Reagan from the mid-1950s onward is: How did this once-committed liberal evolve into a staunch conservative? Had he truly embraced liberal policies, as he claimed? Or was it, as Garry Wills suggested, that "Reagan had to undergo no profound conversion to become a right-wing spokesman by this stage of his career. He had been a believer in the Communist conspiracy as a domestic threat, especially in the labor unions, since 1947. . . . In moving among business leaders and polishing the punch lines that brought their warmest response, it took no special effort to sympathize with their grumblings about government regulation, high taxes, and interference with the 'private sector.' Insurance executives loved it when he told them social security could be voluntary."

Put another way, Reagan was not a liberal who underwent a sudden postwar conversion to conservatism. Nor was he a bold visionary who saw the promise and power of conservatism before most of his contemporaries. Instead, he was a struggling actor in search of a new stage and a new career. His conversion to conservative politics was not especially surprising if one accepts Wills's view that Reagan "was always by temperament a company man."[1]

Reagan's wide travels over eight years would take him to many small and medium-sized towns. It is difficult to imagine him pitching to small-town audiences the liberalism he had embraced in Hollywood. This is not to suggest Reagan's abhorrence of Communism was not genuine. It was. But most liberal Democrats despised Communism as much as Republicans in the 1950s. If there was a consensus in American politics in that era, it was the necessity of opposing Communism at every turn.

It is more likely that Reagan drifted away from his liberal roots simply because he wanted to please the business-backing, economically conservative audiences to whom he spoke from 1954 onward. "What turned Reagan from liberal Democrat to conservative Republican," said Edward Langley, a GE public relations executive, who traveled with Reagan in the late 1950s, "was his deep immersion into working middle-class America and its frequently primordial views." Langley argued Reagan's exposure to his audiences and GE workers changed him. Reagan, he said, "was a consummate crowd-pleaser who loved the applause and the interplay with his listeners. Eventually, from whatever mixture of performing instinct and new conviction, he started taking his audiences' opinions for his own, and telling them what they wanted to hear." Reagan was not persuading his audiences to embrace conservativism. They already had. It was, rather, that his audiences persuaded Reagan to abandon liberalism. One day on the road, Langley said, Reagan told him, "When I was in Hollywood making pictures, I always believed that Hollywood and the politicians never understood John Doe American. The tours convinced me I was right."[2]

Among the changes Reagan's new party identification sparked in him was a complete reassessment of Richard Nixon, whom he claimed he had never admired. In 1960, Nixon was the Republican nominee for president running against Democratic senator John F. Kennedy of Massachusetts. "I think you might be wrong about Nixon," GE president Ralph Cordiner told Reagan. Cordiner said he had recently heard Nixon speak to a business group that had been skeptical about the vice president. "Nixon had convinced them he was a solid citizen," Reagan recalled. "I was such a fan of Ralph Cordiner by then that I decided to re-evaluate some of the things that the liberals (including me) had been saying about Nixon. Realizing after that that he wasn't the villain I'd thought him to be, I volunteered to campaign for him against Kennedy." Reagan said when he told Nixon he planned to register as a Republican to work for him, the vice president said "I'd be more effective if I campaigned as a Democrat, and so I agreed not to change my party affiliation until after the election."[3] Reagan's close friend Walter Annenberg was another ardent Nixon supporter. He had no doubt shared his views with Reagan. Most of Reagan's social circle also backed Nixon.

Based on the three warm letters Reagan wrote to Nixon in 1959 and 1960, however, it is difficult to accept Reagan's story about his sudden embrace of the vice president. The influence of Cordiner, Annenberg, and others may have been influential, but Reagan had other reasons to support Nixon over Kennedy. He suspected the Massachusetts senator was soft on Communism, especially compared with Nixon, who had rocketed into national prominence in 1947 by battling Communists.[4] In September 1959, after Nixon had debated the merits of democracy versus Communism with Soviet premier Nikita Khrushchev during a June visit to Moscow, Reagan wrote Nixon a warm letter of congratulations. When Nixon won the Republican nomination in July 1960, Reagan wrote to Nixon again and confessed a long-standing distrust of Kennedy's liberalism. "He leaves little doubt that his idea of the 'challenging new world' is one in which the federal government will grow bigger and do more and of course spend more," Reagan told Nixon. In the same letter, he added: "One last thought—shouldn't someone tag Mr. Kennedy's *bold new imaginative* program with its proper age? Under the tousled boyish haircut is still old Karl Marx—first launched a century ago. There is nothing new in the idea of a government being Big Brother to us all. Hitler called his 'State Socialism' and way before him was 'benevolent monarchy.'"[5]

Once Reagan decided to help Nixon, he was all in, more so than some other conservatives who doubted Nixon's conservative credentials, especially after the vice president cut a deal in July with New York's liberal Republican governor, Nelson Rockefeller, to water down the party's platform. Nixon believed he needed Rockefeller's support to win the nomination. But Goldwater and other conservatives were furious that he would compromise with their party's liberal leader. Goldwater called Nixon a "two-fisted four-square liar" and labeled his agreement with Rockefeller the "Munich of the Republican Party." Reagan appeared untroubled by Nixon's pragmatic compromise. Goldwater and other conservatives would eventually support Nixon, but not with Reagan's intensity.[6]

Nixon was enthusiastic about Reagan's offer of help, telling staff to "use him as a speaker whenever possible. He *used* to be a liberal."[7] Reagan later claimed Kennedy's father, Joseph Kennedy (who had been prominent in the movie industry in the 1920s), tried to persuade him to support his son, but he demurred. "Although I agreed at Nixon's request not to register as a Republican," Reagan wrote later, "I was really no longer a Democrat by 1960."[8] In public appearances, Reagan began calling himself a "turncoat Democrat."[9] That fall, by one account, he made more than two hundred speeches for Nixon.[10]

While no longer a movie actor, Reagan hosted and appeared in occasional episodes of *General Electric Theater* (over eight seasons he would act in thirty-five) and made other television appearances. He had not made a movie since 1957 and would not make another until 1964. His 1957 film was *Hellcats of the Navy*, co-starring his wife, Nancy Davis. Among the television shows on which Reagan made appearances as an actor in this period were *The DuPont Show with June Allyson (CBS)* in 1960, *Zane Grey Theater (CBS)* and *The Dick Powell Show (NBC)*, both in 1961, and *Wagon Train (NBC)* in 1963. He also appeared twice as host for an NBC anthology series, *Startime*, in 1960.[11]

Meanwhile, his speeches took on a growing tone of alarm over what he saw as the uncontrolled encroachment of government into most facets of American social and economic life. Speaking to the Mississippi Manufacturers Association in Jackson in October 1960—in the homestretch of the presidential contest—Reagan warned that the federal government was becoming a socialistic behemoth. "We are faced with a collection of internal powers and bureaucratic institutions against which the individual citizen is absolutely helpless," Reagan said. "This power, under whatever name or ideology, is the very essence of totalitarianism." Reagan had been decrying high tax rates since the mid-1950s. He now equated them not only with big government but also with creeping socialism. "We must recognize," he said, "that socialism through taxation may be slower, but it arrives at the same end as outright nationalization of industry."[12]

FEW OF REAGAN'S SPEECH texts are available from this period (he favored notes on index cards and rarely spoke from a script). Most published collections of Reagan's speeches start with his October 1964 speech for Republican presidential nominee Barry Goldwater. Reagan included only one text from the 1950s (remarks at the Kiwanis International Convention in St. Louis in June 1951) in a collection he published in 1989. Reagan's 1952 commencement address to William Woods College is part of his presidential papers. His address at Eureka College in June 1957, a brief rewrite of his standard "stump" speech, is available online. A 1983 anthology of Reagan speeches included one from 1961.[13]

This leaves a wide gap of Reagan's rhetoric filled partly by newspaper stories of his visits to dozens of cities and towns during his GE tours and for other occasions. These accounts, while essential in gauging Reagan's changing rhetoric, capture a small part of what he said. What is clear, however, is that most applause lines, once they found their way into a Reagan speech, did not vanish. Reagan told the same stories about Communism in Hollywood, government waste and abuse, and encroaching federal control to audiences for years.

What is also clear from news stories about Reagan's speeches and interviews from 1957 through 1964 is that his messages followed the same arc: He began with a brief discussion of Communist influence in Hollywood. He warned about renewed Soviet-backed Communist activity in the United States. And then he issued a series of dire warnings about the country's descent into socialism and totalitarianism because of a big, growing, and wasteful government apparatus. The static structure of Reagan's speeches means that studying the earliest texts (those not filled with Hollywood stories) are windows into Reagan's mind and his rhetoric from the mid-fifties onward.

Two speeches from this period, before John F. Kennedy became president, are particularly useful in understanding Reagan in the late 1950s and early 1960s. The first was a speech Reagan titled, "Business, Ballots, and Bureaus," which he delivered in May 1959 to a gathering of General Electric executives at the Waldorf-Astoria Hotel in New York. Reagan's warning about the dangers the country faced bordered on the apocalyptic. He shared an unsubstantiated quote credited to Soviet leader Nikita Khrushchev: "In fifteen years there won't be a cold war. Your country is becoming so socialistic that in fifteen years the causes for conflict between our two countries will have disappeared." To that, Reagan responded: "Can we dismiss such statements as mere bombast? Most of us can remember back when our main contact with the federal government was to go to the Post Office and buy a stamp. Today there is hardly a phase of our daily living that doesn't feel the stultifying hand of government regulation and interference."

He attacked the Social Security system. "It was never intended to supplant private savings, pension plans or insurance, but was to provide a foundation upon which security could be achieved." He condemned encroaching federal control of education, the increase in foreign aid, and federal regulation of farm prices.

Except for Communism, nothing outraged Reagan more than the progressive federal income tax, and he linked it to the Soviet Union's effort to undermine the United States. "This entire theory of progressive tax was spawned by Karl Marx more than 100 years ago," Reagan told the GE executives. "He gave it as the necessary basis for a socialist state. Karl Marx said that the way to impose statism on a people, socialism on a country, was to tax the middle class out of existence."[14]

Another early Reagan speech for which the full text survives is from his appearance before the Phoenix, Arizona, Chamber of Commerce on March 30, 1961. The Phoenix speech was so popular that a local radio station broadcast a recording of it the following month. And the local Sunnyslope chapter of the Anti-Communism Movement played a tape recording of the speech at its April 21 meeting.[15] The comparison with Reagan's

1959 speech is revealing. The themes were similar. But by 1961 Reagan expanded and filled out his arguments with more than a dozen new examples of waste, fraud, abuse, and stupidity by members of Congress and federal bureaucrats. Reagan had often warned about the threat of Communism, attacked the federal tax system, and assailed the growth and scope of government. He had done so in a country governed by a Republican president he had enthusiastically supported in 1952 and 1956. By 1961, however, a Democrat was president. In this new political environment, Reagan's criticism of the federal government became more urgent, vivid, and forceful.

As he had in 1959, Reagan was still quoting Khrushchev to warn of the Soviets' malevolent designs. The quote, however, changed. This time he told the audience the Soviet leader said: "We can't expect the American people to jump from Capitalism to Communism, but we can assist their elected leaders in giving them small doses of Socialism, until they awaken one day to find they have Communism." (It is not clear where Reagan found this quote, although it circulated widely at the time. No such statement by Khrushchev is found in any contemporaneous press account or in his papers. In 1962 the Library of Congress, responding to an inquiry about the purported quote by Khrushchev, told Congressman Morris K. Udall of Arizona: "We have searched the Legislative Reference Service files, checked all the standard reference works on quotations by Khrushchev, and consulted with the Slavic division of the Library of Congress, the Department of State, and the U.S. Information Agency, in an attempt to determine the authenticity of this quotation. From none of these sources were we able to produce evidence that Khrushchev actually made such a statement.")[16]

Regardless of the accuracy of the quote, Reagan embraced the sentiment as authentic. "They've appealed not to the worst but to the best in us, to our sense of fair play, our willingness to compromise," he said. "And compromise is a noble thing when it involves two people of diametrically opposed views, willing to meet in some middle ground where they can coexist together. But compromise in the field of legislation has been developed into a technique of foot-in-the-door legislation." With that, the rest of Reagan's speech was a breathless recitation of outrageous examples of a government run amuck. In every case, Reagan was ready with a crowd-tested example designed to persuade and enrage.

He began with health care. "Traditionally," he said, "one of the easiest first steps in imposing statism on a people has been government paid medicine. It is the easiest to present as a humanitarian project." To prove his point about the danger that universal health care posed to American freedom, Reagan shared these statistics: "In the last decade, 127 million Americans have come under the protection of some form of private medical or hospital insurance. This includes some two-thirds of the people of Social Security age, seventy percent of the total population. And if the same rate continues, by 1970, the coverage will amount to ninety percent of our population. As nearly as we can determine, the real problem concerns about ten percent of our senior citizens who have medical needs and who do not have the means to finance them."

Reagan claimed the federal government had used federal support to exert control over local school systems. "We are told we must, on a crash basis, build sixty thousand classrooms a year for the next ten years," Reagan said, referring to Kennedy's call in February to build six hundred thousand new classrooms in the next ten years. "But they forget to tell us we've been building for the last five years sixty-eight thousand classrooms a year and if we continue at that rate, by 1970, we will have a surplus of classroom space for this country." To Reagan, federal money to build classrooms and pay teachers meant only one thing: "The aim, the aim alone, is federal control." Again Reagan zeroed in, with special fervor, on federal income taxes. He declared, "There is no moral justification of the progressive tax," and then offered a shocking example:

> Take a man with a gross income of $3,500 per year and a wife and two children. When he is finished paying the tax collectors, federal, state and local and all those hidden and indirect taxes

at the end of the year, he will find the tax collector's share of his gross $3,500 is $1,059. Now some people tell us the answer to his problem is to soak those of a higher income even more. But how much leeway is left? If the government, tomorrow, started confiscating all income above $6,000, all income, the increased revenue wouldn't pay the interest on the national debt. No nation in history has ever survived a tax burden that amounted to one-third of its people's earnings. Today, thirty-one cents out of every dollar earned in the United States goes to the tax collector. And of that thirty-one cents, twenty-three cents goes to the federal government, leaving eight cents for the federal, county and the local community to divide up between itself. No wonder we have to turn to government and ask for federal aid in all of our projects. But wouldn't it make a lot more sense to keep some of that money here in the local community to begin with, instead of then routing it through that puzzle palace on the Potomac where it's returned to us, minus a sizable carrying charge?[17]

Reagan's numbers on taxes did not square with reality. According to a 2008 study by the Congressional Research Service, the average individual tax burden (including state and local taxes) in 1960 was about 14 percent of income. Another study put the average federal, state, and local tax rate for a married couple with two children at about 16 percent.[18] Reagan may have simply imagined that everyone's tax rate was as high as his. But his income put him in the top 1 percent of taxpayers. He likely found his information not after independent research but in *The Conscience of a Conservative*, a best-selling book published the previous year by Barry Goldwater. In his book, Goldwater's language is much like Reagan's: "Here is an indication of how taxation currently infringes on our freedom. A family man earning $4,500 a year works, on the average, twenty-two days a month. Taxes, visible and invisible, take approximately 32% of his earnings. This means that one-third, or seven whole days, of his monthly labor goes for taxes. The average American is therefore working one-third of the time for government: a third of what he produces is not available for his own use but is confiscated and used by others who have not earned it."[19]

Throughout his entertainment and political careers, Reagan showed a remarkable talent for discussing statistics with vivid, memorable language. In his 1961 Phoenix speech, when describing the dangers of out-of-control government spending, he conjured a mental image for his audience: "If I had here in my hand a four-inch stack of thousand-dollar bills, I'd be a millionaire. But if we had in front of us the national debt, piled up in thousand-dollar bills, the pile would be more than eighteen miles high. And this is only the part that shows above the surface like an iceberg." Reagan did not use his stories and statistics only to inform and persuade. He often used his speeches to issue a call to action, as he did in Phoenix:

> Write to your congressman and demand a tax reform [bill] immediately which will reduce the percentage of the national income the government is taking in taxes. Write to your congressman and tell him you want an end to deficit spending, that you want the same control over the federal government's right to borrow that we exert here at the local community and at the state level. Tell him further, with an eye on our children, that you want as a part of the annual budget a regular payment on that national debt. And if your congressman is one who writes back and says he, too, is for economy, but we must reduce government spending before we reduce taxes, you write back and tell him this is a dishonest theory.

Reagan launched his peroration to the Phoenix Chamber with a stirring condemnation of the perils of the creeping socialism that he argued was subsuming American democracy:

> Today, with no one using the term socialism to describe encroaching control, we find one out of seven of the workforce on the public payroll. In fifteen years, a fifty percent increase in public employees has been matched by a 170 percent increase in their payroll. One-fourth of our people [are] now entitled to government-paid medical care, socialized medicine if you

please. One-fifth of our industry [is] owned and operated by government. [Virginia] Senator [Harry] Byrd has estimated that today forty million American citizens receive some form of direct cash payment from the federal government. We have a tax system that, in direct contravention to the Constitution, is not designed solely to raise revenue, but is openly and admittedly used to regulate and control the economy and to level the earnings of our citizens, aiming again at that mediocrity which is the utopian dream of the socialist. . . .

We can't just out-wait it and hope by not looking that it will go away. Wars like this one end in victory or defeat. One of the foremost authorities on Communism in the world today, a former medical missionary, has said that we have ten years. Not ten years in which to make a decision. We have ten years to decide the verdict because within this decade, the world will become either all free or all slave. Our Founding Fathers, here in this country, brought about the only true revolution that has ever taken place in man's history. Every other revolution simply exchanged one set of rulers for another set of rulers. But only here did that little band of men, so advanced beyond their time that the world has never seen their like since, evolve the idea that you and I have within ourselves the God-given right and the ability to determine our own destiny. But freedom is never more than one generation away from extinction. We didn't pass it on to our children in the bloodstream. The only way they can inherit the freedom we have known is if we fight for it, protect it, defend it, and then hand it to them with the well-thought lessons of how they in their lifetime must do the same. And if you and I don't do this, then you and I may well spend our sunset years telling our children and our children's children what it once was like in America when men were free.[20]

To Reagan and his friends, this oration became known as "The Speech," his standard, forty-minute attack on Communism and socialism. Reagan's speech in May 1961 in Chicago to the Illinois Manufacturers' Costs Association was almost identical to what he told his Phoenix audience in March, as was his speech in November of that year in Los Angeles to the employees of Forest Lawn.[21]

As significant as Reagan's message was the method he had honed for writing and delivering his speeches. He used no speechwriter or researcher. The information he scooped up along the way and fed into his speeches came from the news articles, speeches, and reports he encountered. "He was always going through newspapers and magazines and clipping out little anecdotes or statistics that caught his eye and helped him make a point," Nancy Reagan recalled.[22]

Although a Reagan speech might be the same as what he told an audience the day before or the previous month, he did not use a printed text. Most surviving transcripts of Reagan's speeches in this era are not his. A journalist, or the organization to which he spoke, transcribed them. Reagan spoke from a stack of notecards on which he had written, in his legible but distinctive handwriting, a unique shorthand of a phrase or fact that prompted a sentence or paragraph he had memorized. "I stew around in my own mind on the basis of what I want to say and what it is that I believe needs saying," Reagan said in 1966 of his speech-writing process, "and then I sit down in front of a stack of three-by-five cards, and I start putting it together in my mind, and as I do I write 'cue' lines on those cards. I don't actually write a speech."[23]

In his 1990 memoir Reagan explained, "I've always believed that you cannot hold an audience by *reading* a speech, but when you're giving three or four or more talks a day, as I was, it's difficult to memorize every word you wanted to say."[24] The card system not only helped Reagan organize his thoughts and provided prompts along the way; it also allowed his speeches to evolve. When he wanted to replace one anecdote with another, he did not rewrite his speech but added or replaced a card. If a story did not produce the reaction he hoped from an audience, he jettisoned the card and replaced it with another—and perhaps one or two more—until he settled on the right story to make his point.

"If you opened up the second drawer" of Reagan's desk in his bedroom, "there were piles and piles of these cards, wrapped in rubber bands," his son Michael recalled.[25] "Clearly, legibility was a high priority to him," wrote historian Douglas Brinkley, who edited a book of Reagan's speech notes. "Sometimes he uses an asterisk or makes a hearty underline for emphasis. Shorthand is often the order of the day. The reader gets the impression that Reagan is a redwood tree and these are the decorations of his own philosophy, the ammunition he will need to survive the hustings ahead."[26] For example, one card in Reagan's papers (probably from his 1966 California governor's campaign) contains the following phrases and prompts in Reagan's hand, printed in block letters with a black felt-tip pen:

MANY—EXPRESSED—CONCERN
—RECENT CAMPAIGNS—
ABOUT PT. MODERN ADV.—
PLAYED—DETERM. OUTCOME.

HAVE EVIDENCED FEAR
THAT VENAL FORCES—
CHECKBOOK HEAVY—PRIN. LITE—
PCKG—CAND. LIKE SOAP—
SELL HIM TO VOTERS COMPLETE
WITH THEME CONG & SLOGAN

WHY SOME PEOPLE EVEN
GONE SO FAR—SUGGEST—THE
MONSTERS—MAD AVE.—COULD
TURN—MAGIC LOOSE
& PERSUADE—PEOPLE VOTE FOR
SOME PUB. FIG.—LK SAY—ACTOR.[27]

Reagan's ability to feign extemporization is a characteristic of many actors. Like other actors, Reagan could memorize facts, figures, and phrases. His special gift was expounding for several minutes, using one fact as a springboard. "Ronald actually had a photographic memory that's pretty phenomenal," his brother, Neil, told biographer Lou Cannon in 1968, adding, "When it came time for a test, he could take a book and in about a quick hour thumb through that book and photograph those pages and write a good test." Reagan, Neil added, "uses the same method now. He writes three or four lines on a card and each will be ten minutes of speech."[28]

Robert Gilbert, a labor lawyer who tried to prepare Reagan during the actor's visit to New York in 1949 on SAG business, recalled Reagan refused the detailed briefing he offered. "Brief me in the cab," Reagan told him. Gilbert protested such a discussion would be inadequate, but Reagan insisted. "So I briefed him in the cab," Gilbert said. "He made a two-hour speech based on a fifteen-minute briefing—and it was fabulous. This guy could absorb what he was told and regurgitate it. He was *very* glib and articulate—even if he didn't understand it."[29]

If Reagan's preparation was distinctive, so was his delivery. Because he was not reading a text, he could look at his audience for most of his talk. He never strode to the lectern clutching a folder or a stack of papers. He arrived empty-handed and fished the small set of cards from his suit pocket. To see his cards, while also keeping eye contact with his audience, Reagan usually removed one contact lens, which gave him long- and short-range vision during the speech.

And he wanted to see his audiences. "He would always direct me to avoid dimming the lights when he spoke," recalled Michael Deaver, the aide who joined Reagan's staff when he became governor of California. "Many politicians prefer a darker setting, using the spotlight as a way to focus on them and freeing the audience to settle into their chairs and remain distant and comfortable. Reagan was just the opposite. He wanted the audience to have the same amount of ownership in the event as he did. . . . He liked to see into their eyes, to gauge the effectiveness of his words and movements."[30]

Reagan's impressive voice was another effective tool. It was strong, resonant, and crackled with emotion and modulated along the way to evoke whatever response he desired. As reporter Roger Rosenblatt wrote for *Time* in 1981 before Reagan's inauguration as president:

> The voice goes perfectly with the body. No President since Kennedy has had a voice at once so distinctive and beguiling.

It too recedes at the right moments, turning mellow at points of intensity. When it wishes to be most persuasive, it hovers barely above a whisper so as to win you over by intimacy, if not by substance. This is style, but not sham. Reagan believes everything he says, no matter how often he has said it, or if he has said it in the same words every time. He likes his voice, treats it like a guest. He makes you part of the hospitality.[31]

While his skilled, polished presentation was essential for the success of "The Speech," it was Reagan's rhetoric—his message—that was the difference and made him a popular conservative voice in the early 1960s. Historian Jonathan Darman wrote:

The men and women in Reagan's crowds were eager to hear Reagan's story, for he was offering them a kind of clarity that was otherwise in short supply. The official pronouncements from Washington in the early Cold War were full of frustrating ambiguity. The Soviets were the enemy, of course, but the pragmatists in power counseled that that enemy should be confronted only when strategically necessary. Where the officials dwelled on qualification and complexity, Reagan's message was refreshingly unconditional: America must either vanquish the Soviet threat or perish from the earth.[32]

10

Operation Coffeecup

Reagan's higher profile as a popular conservative speaker prompted the chair of California's Republican State Central Committee to promote him as a possible governor. "I think he would make a great candidate," John Krehbiel said at a press conference in Sacramento in January 1961. Reagan demurred. "I'm very honored that people would feel I could be a candidate for such a high office," he told a reporter, "but I said I would not be a candidate. It would represent too much of a change in my way of living and what I'm trying to do."[1]

Reagan would eventually train his eyes on California politics. For now, however, he focused on playing a larger role in national affairs, including fighting what he and other conservatives considered "socialized medicine." In Congress, calls intensified for what would become, in 1965, the federal Medicare system, a program that provided health insurance to most Americans sixty-five and older. A generation earlier, Presidents Franklin Roosevelt and Harry Truman had failed to pass legislation guaranteeing health insurance to older and poor Americans. With Kennedy in the White House, the decades-old cause gained renewed energy. Answering Kennedy's request for legislation, in 1961 Representative Cecil King of California and Senator Clinton Anderson of New Mexico, both Democrats, introduced a bill to levy a 0.25 percent tax on most wage earners to fund hospital and nursing home care for fourteen million Social Security recipients.[2]

To fight the bill, the American Medical Association launched Women Help American Medicine (WHAM), a campaign led by the association's Women's Auxiliary, made up of doctors' wives. Part of WHAM involved educating the public about the dangers of "socialized medicine." WHAM also sponsored a clandestine component, Operation Coffeecup, to influence Congress by persuading citizens to flood members with personal letters opposing the King-Anderson bill. The centerpiece of Operation Coffeecup was a ten-minute talk by Reagan about the bill and its dangers entitled, "RONALD REAGAN speaks out against SOCIALIZED MEDICINE." The AMA recorded and transferred Reagan's talk to 33.3 RPM vinyl phonograph records. And in April 1961 WHAM distributed records to auxiliary members in almost every county in the nation.

The record arrived in a jacket adorned with Reagan's photo. Inside were instructions for using the recording to its greatest effect. WHAM told recipients to invite friends and neighbors for coffee to hear Reagan's talk and encourage them—on the spot—to write personal letters to their members of Congress, stating their objections to the bill. "Make letter-writing easy," the instructions said. "Provide guests with stationery, pens and stamped envelopes. Don't accept an 'I'll do it tomorrow' reply—urge each woman to write her letters while she's in your house—and in the mood!" The AMA encouraged the women to write the letters "in her own words" so it would not alert members of Congress to the campaign.[3] Text on the jacket's sleeve told recipients to share this message with guests: "Reagan volunteered to make this record because of his own strong personal conviction. He was not paid to do so." Listeners were not told, however, that Reagan's father-in-law, Loyal Davis, was one of the nation's most prominent surgeons, the chair of the Board of Regents of the American College of Surgeons, and a fierce opponent of the bill.

Reagan's talk was an expansion of the "socialized medicine" portion of his basic speech. (The report in the *Arizona Republic* of his March 1961 Chamber of Commerce speech in Phoenix was headlined, "Reagan Lashes State Medicine.")[4] This time he added details about the King-Anderson bill. He also included remarks tailored to frighten the doctors' wives into believing their husbands would lose their livelihoods at the hands of a tyrannical federal government. He suggested the government would dragoon doctors into a new federal physician corps and ship them off to some distant city.

The words would have been familiar to anyone who had heard Reagan speak in recent years. It was his tone and inflection that changed. Reagan knew he was not speaking to five hundred people in a banquet hall. About a dozen women in each setting would hear his words as they sipped coffee in a living room while staring at a record player. He did not need to project but, rather, to emote. The message called for an intimate voice, and Reagan delivered. Listeners might have known this as a radio voice. Reagan, the talented former radio announcer, delivered his well-practiced lines with strategic pauses that made it appear he was speaking without a text, pausing occasionally as if gathering his thoughts. Reagan knew nothing if not how to size up an audience. "I learned in radio in Des Moines long ago," he told an interviewer in 1957, "if you memorize your message and then visualize a small group like one in a cigar store instead of thousands who are listening in, you don't sound like you are making a speech. Instead, it's like you are having an informal talk."[5] Reagan's recording began without fanfare or formal introduction:

> Back in 1927, an American socialist, Norman Thomas, six times candidate for president on the Socialist Party ticket, said the American people would never vote for socialism. But he said under the name of liberalism the American people will adopt every fragment of the socialist program.
>
> There are many ways in which our government has invaded the precincts of private citizens, the method of earning a living. Our government is in business to the extent of owning more than 19,000 businesses covering forty-seven different lines of activity. This amounts to a fifth of the total industrial capacity of the United States. But at the moment, I would like to talk about another way, because this threat is with us and, at the

moment, is more imminent. One of the traditional methods of imposing statism or socialism on people has been by way of medicine.

Reagan had been careless with his assertions. No such quote by Thomas has been discovered.[6] More important, he conflated socialism with Communism. This was a dubious assertion that anyone who studied the American Communist movement would have understood but which, thanks to years of indoctrination by Reagan and other anti-Communists, many listeners might have accepted. Reagan's rhetorical sleight of hand was effective, wrote Jeffrey St. Onge, a communication studies scholar who analyzed Reagan's recording. He argued Reagan had voiced "a microcosm of the AMA's larger argumentation—fictionalizing a seemingly coherent viewpoint of a seemingly coherent socialist enemy. This quote gave a face to the enemy—collectivism—and positioned it as a real and imminent threat to the United States."[7] More likely to scare the wives of doctors, however, was Reagan's next warning. He predicted a dystopian future in which a socialist-inspired law would deprive their husbands and their husbands' patients of their personal liberties:

Now, in our country under our free enterprise system, we have seen medicine reach the greatest heights that it has in any country in the world. Today, the relationship between patient and doctor in this country is something to be envied any place. The privacy, the care that is given to a person, the right to choose a doctor, the right to go from one doctor to the other.

But let's also look from the other side, at the freedom the doctor loses. A doctor would be reluctant to say this. Well, like you, I am only a patient, so I can say it in his behalf. The doctor begins to lose freedoms. It's like telling a lie, and one leads to another. First, you decide that the doctor can have so many patients. They are equally divided among the various doctors by the government. But then the doctors aren't equally divided geographically, so a doctor decides he wants to practice in one town and the government has to say to him you can't live in that town, they already have enough doctors. You have to go someplace else. And from here it is only a short step to dictating where he will go. This is a freedom that I wonder whether any of us have the right to take from any human being.

I know how I'd feel, if you my fellow citizens decided that, to be an actor, I had to become a government employee and work in a national theater.

Take it into your own occupation or that of your husband, all of us can see what happens—once you establish the precedent that the government can determine a man's working place and his working methods, determine his employment. From here it is a short step to all the rest of socialism, to determining his pay and pretty soon your son won't decide when he's in school, where he will go or what they will do for a living. He will wait for the government to tell him where he will go to work and what he will do.

In this country of ours took place the greatest revolution that has ever taken place in world's history. The only true revolution. Every other revolution simply exchanged one set of rulers for another. But here for the first time in all the thousands of years of man's relation to man, a little group of the men, the founding fathers—for the first time—established the idea that you and I had within ourselves the God-given right and ability to determine our own destiny.

Reagan closed his talk with a familiar tactic: He urged listeners to write, repeatedly, to their representatives in Congress. And he used lines that any audience member at a recent Reagan speech would have recognized: "If you don't [write letters], this program I promise you will pass just as surely as the sun will come up tomorrow and behind it will come other federal programs that will invade every area of freedom as we have known it in this country. Until, one day, as Norman Thomas said, we will awake to find that we have socialism. And if you don't do this, and if I don't do it, one of these days you and I are going to spend our sunset years telling our children and our children's children, what it once was like in America when men were free."[8]

The AMA could not keep Operation Coffeecup a secret for

long. In June, syndicated columnist Drew Pearson reported the Reagan-AMA campaign had "caused such a deluge of mail to swamp Congress that congressmen want to postpone action on the medical aid bill until 1962. What they don't know, of course, is that Ron Reagan is behind the mail; also that the American Medical Association is paying for it."[9] Reagan's recording was not confined to the living rooms of doctors' homes. Actress Rosemary DeCamp, who worked with Reagan in two films in the 1940s, credited her "disillusionment" with him in the early 1960s to hearing "the endless repetitions of his recorded voice in my doctor's waiting room. He told us Medicare would sweep this country into bankruptcy [and] by all means stop the King-Anderson bill which would provide funds for the sick, the elderly, and the disadvantaged." DeCamp said she thought, "This couldn't be the same man who had fought for the workers in our union!"[10]

Although the AMA's campaign to stop Medicare would fail with the bill's passage in 1965, Reagan and the other opponents allied with the doctors' organization succeeded in the short term. The Senate would narrowly reject the legislation in June 1962, and the proposal would also fall short in Congress in 1963 and 1964.[11] As Pearson's column suggested, Reagan's involvement—despite its eventual disclosure—was helpful in stopping Medicare's momentum. In a 1963 survey of U.S. senators, two-thirds of the respondents reported the volume of their mail on the health insurance issue was much higher than mail on other issues of comparable public interest. Political scientist Max J. Skidmore, who uncovered the details about Operation Coffeecup for a 1989 academic journal article, concluded that Reagan's record and the organized effort to stimulate mail to Congress "without question increased the number of letters considerably." Furthermore, Skidmore wrote, "The senators' responses [to the survey] suggested that Operation Coffeecup succeeded in appearing spontaneous, as indeed it should have given the conditions that it established."[12]

As his Operation Coffeecup recording and other speeches from the late 1950s and early 1960s showed, Reagan was a wellspring of facts, anecdotes, and quotes. He condemned the spread of Communism and encroaching socialism (including "socialized medicine"). He railed against censorship, misguided agriculture policy, oppressive taxation, and bureaucratic overreach. And he heaped scorn on government waste and abuse and creeping federal control of education. In the dozens of articles by local and national publications that quoted his warnings about these and other dangers, however, no journalist checked or questioned Reagan's many assertions. Typical was this report in the *Daily Nonpareil* in Council Bluffs, Iowa, on November 17, 1961. It was headlined, "Reagan Warns 300 at Chamber Banquet . . . Americans Are Slowly Losing Their Freedom through Federal Controls":

Through federal control of business, agriculture and institutions, Americans are losing their freedom on the installment plan.

Ronald Reagan, a TV personality, gave this warning to more than 300 persons attending the annual Chamber of Commerce banquet Thursday evening at Hotel Chieftain.

"There are prominent Americans who hate Communists but not communism," Reagan said.

"They feel that if we move our economy to the left—toward socialism, we won't antagonize Russia and create an international catastrophe," he said.

"These people who support more and more federal control feel they are guided by humanitarian ideas and they think they are doing the right thing, but individual liberty and our free enterprise system is the only way to stop communism." . . .

"Federal agencies spend $35 million a year to better egg production methods and then turn around and buy up 12 million dollars of eggs to hold the price level."

Reagan said the federal government owns more than 1,000 businesses of 47 varieties which compete against private businesses. "Yet the federal government can go far below the competitive price and suffer a loss. That loss is made up in taxes." . . .

Reagan said many federal taxes are hidden. "Taxes account for one-half of your telephone bill, one-half of the price of a loaf of bread, and a quarter of the price of a new car."[13]

Beguiled by Reagan's charm and sunny disposition, as well as his authority and confidence, the journalists covering him wrote glowing stories about his visits and repeated his many assertions. These local papers—many of whom counted General Electric among their largest advertisers—may also have perceived some subtle, implicit pressure to report on Reagan and his company with favor. Occasionally a newspaper might publish an editorial challenging something Reagan said or a reader might complain or challenge him in a letter to the editor. But such instances were rare.

The closest thing to a published rebuke or fact check of a Reagan speech in a local or regional newspaper came in October 1961 after his late-September appearances in Portland. He had attacked President Kennedy's policies in two speeches given prominent play in the statewide paper, the *Oregonian*. As in other papers, the *Oregonian*'s story about Reagan's rhetoric was respectful and credulous. The reporter wrote, "A conservative Republican, Reagan is an outspoken authority on Communist encroachment."[14] In response, Blaine Whipple, executive secretary of the Oregon Democratic Party, delivered a rebuttal on a local radio station. The *Oregonian* covered the speech in which Whipple said Reagan's speeches were "in many instances extremely partisan attacks against the program and policies of the Kennedy administration and the Democratic Congress." If Whipple questioned any of Reagan's factual assertions, the newspaper did not report them.[15]

In 1961 a television program checked Reagan's speech "Losing Freedom by Installments" and noted that seven of his forty factual assertions were false. In response, a writer for the *Iowa Farm Bureau News* rushed to his defense. "So when you think perhaps Reagan was wrong seven times," Bob McMann wrote, "he was right thirty-three times and that amounts to a lot of those freedoms we are losing by installments."[16]

Even as his speeches became pungent and pointed and his assertions more controversial, Reagan escaped criticism for his words and scrutiny of those assertions. This was likely because national journalists still regarded him as an actor and TV personality who spoke out on political issues. These political journalists had little or no reason for concern over what an actor might have said to the La Crosse, Wisconsin, Chamber of Commerce or even the American Bankers Association. His views on politics did not interest them.

To local journalists, however, Reagan was a genuine movie star who hosted one of the most-watched shows on television. Reagan might have spoken about trout fishing or automotive repair and received the same worshipful reports in the local papers that dutifully covered his appearances. To these local audiences, and the journalists who covered his speeches to them, Reagan was a knowledgeable, principled patriot. He persuaded them not only that he cared about the nation's drift toward Communism but also that he knew how to fight the evil forces that threatened to destroy their freedoms.

Reagan did not warn vaguely about the nation's problems. He offered specifics about the dastardly programs, wrapped in memorable, accessible anecdotes. Reagan also constantly refined his standard speech and memorized it. His delivery was flawless. He left the impression he was not a man speaking from a prepared text but, rather, a person of substance and stature who understood the issues intimately and believed deeply in his cause. In short, at every stop, Reagan staged a virtuoso political performance. In a few years he would become a potent national political force and the most prominent political leader in one of the nation's most populated states. He might have been performing off the national stage, but he was moving more confidently and directly toward a political career than any political journalist understood in 1962. A major American political figure's career was coming into its own in the years before 1964, and because few noticed or cared, Reagan was free to say whatever he wanted without scrutiny or criticism.

FIG. 1. Young Ronald Reagan (second from right) with his parents, Jack and Nelle Reagan, and his older brother, Neil, in 1916. Ronald Reagan Presidential Library.

FIG. 2. Reagan's first experience in show business came as a sports announcer in Davenport, Iowa, at woc radio and, later, in Des Moines, as the voice of the Chicago Cubs and White Sox at wHO radio. Ronald Reagan Presidential Library.

FIG. 3. (*opposite top*) Reagan won critical acclaim for his portrayal of Drake McHugh in the 1942 film *Kings Row*. Everett Collection Inc./Alamy.

FIG. 4. (*opposite bottom*) Reagan and his first wife, actress Jane Wyman, with their children, Maureen and Michael. They married in 1940 and divorced in 1949. Alamy.

FIG. 5. (*above*) Reagan played military officers in many of his movies, including *Desperate Journey*, which he made in 1942 with Errol Flynn and Arthur Kennedy. Everett Collection Inc./Alamy.

FIG. 6. Reagan spent most of World War II working as a personnel officer and narrator of propaganda films at the First Motion Picture Unit of the Army Air Corps in Culver City, California. Ronald Reagan Presidential Library.

FIG. 7. While in the Army during World War II, Reagan starred in a patriotic musical by Irving Berlin—1943's *This Is the Army*—while on loan to Warner Bros. George Murphy, a future Republican U.S. senator from California (beside Reagan), played his father. Alamy.

FIG. 8. As president of the Screen Actors Guild, Reagan testified about Communism in Hollywood before the House Un-American Activities Committee in Washington in October 1947. Ronald Reagan Presidential Library.

FIG. 9. Reagan, standing, at a 1950 meeting of the Screen Actors Guild. Seated, from left to right, are actors Jane Wyman, Henry Fonda, Boris Karloff, and Gene Kelly. Walter Olesky/Alamy.

Fig. 10. Reagan and Nancy in
1953 on the set of her movie
Donovan's Brain. Ronald
Reagan Presidential Library.

FIG. 11. *Chicago Tribune* ad in September 1954 announcing the premiere of Reagan's new show, *General Electric Theater*.

Fig. 12. Reagan in a publicity photo for *General Electric Theater*, the hit CBS television show he hosted, and occasionally acted in, from 1954 to 1962. Ronald Reagan Presidential Library.

Fig. 13. General Electric president Ralph Cordiner hired Reagan to host *General Electric Theater* and to serve as a company spokesman. Cordiner was later national finance chair for Barry Goldwater's 1964 presidential campaign. General Electric.

FIG. 14. Reagan with company employees during a visit to a General Electric plant in Danville, Illinois, in October 1955. Ronald Reagan Presidential Library.

FIG. 15. Reagan also appeared in television and newspaper advertisements for company products, including this ad in March 1961 in the *Tampa Tribune.*

FIG. 16. Reagan speaks to workers at a General Electric plant in Danville, Illinois, in October 1955. Ronald Reagan Presidential Library.

FIG. 17. Reagan and Nancy in their "Home of the Future," built by General Electric. The company stocked the home with the latest electrical wonders and featured the house in GE advertising. John Springer Collection/ CORBIS/Corbis via Getty Images.

FIG. 18. An advertisement in the White Plains (NY) *Journal News* in November 1961 for Fred Schwarz's "California School of Anti-Communism," broadcast on TV stations in California and New York. Reagan was one of many Hollywood entertainers who spoke.

FIG. 19. Album cover for Reagan's 1961 recording for Operation Coffeecup, the campaign by the American Medical Association to stop Congress from enacting Medicare. Wikimedia Commons.

FIG. 20. (*opposite top*) Reagan on the set of his last movie, *The Killers*, which he began filming in November 1963 with Norman Fell and Angie Dickinson. Everett Collection Inc./Alamy.

FIG. 21. (*opposite bottom*) Republican senator Barry Goldwater appears in New Hampshire in March 1964 after his loss in that state's presidential primary. RBM Vintage Images/Alamy.

FIG. 22. (*opposite top*) Reagan at the 1964 Republican National Convention in San Francisco. He attended as an alternate delegate for Arizona senator Barry Goldwater. Everett Collection Inc./Alamy.

FIG. 23. (*opposite bottom*) Reagan appears with Republican Party presidential nominee Barry Goldwater in Los Angeles in 1964. He served as California co-chair of Goldwater's presidential campaign and stumped for him across the state. Wikimedia Commons.

FIG. 24. A newspaper ad on October 31, 1964, announces reruns of televised speeches for Barry Goldwater by Reagan and actor John Wayne. Appleton (WI) *Post-Crescent.*

Figs. 25 and 26. Screenshots of Reagan's nationally televised speech, aired on NBC on October 27, 1964, on behalf of Barry Goldwater's presidential campaign. Screenshot from Ronald Reagan Foundation, https://www.youtube.com/watch?v=qXBswFfh6AY.

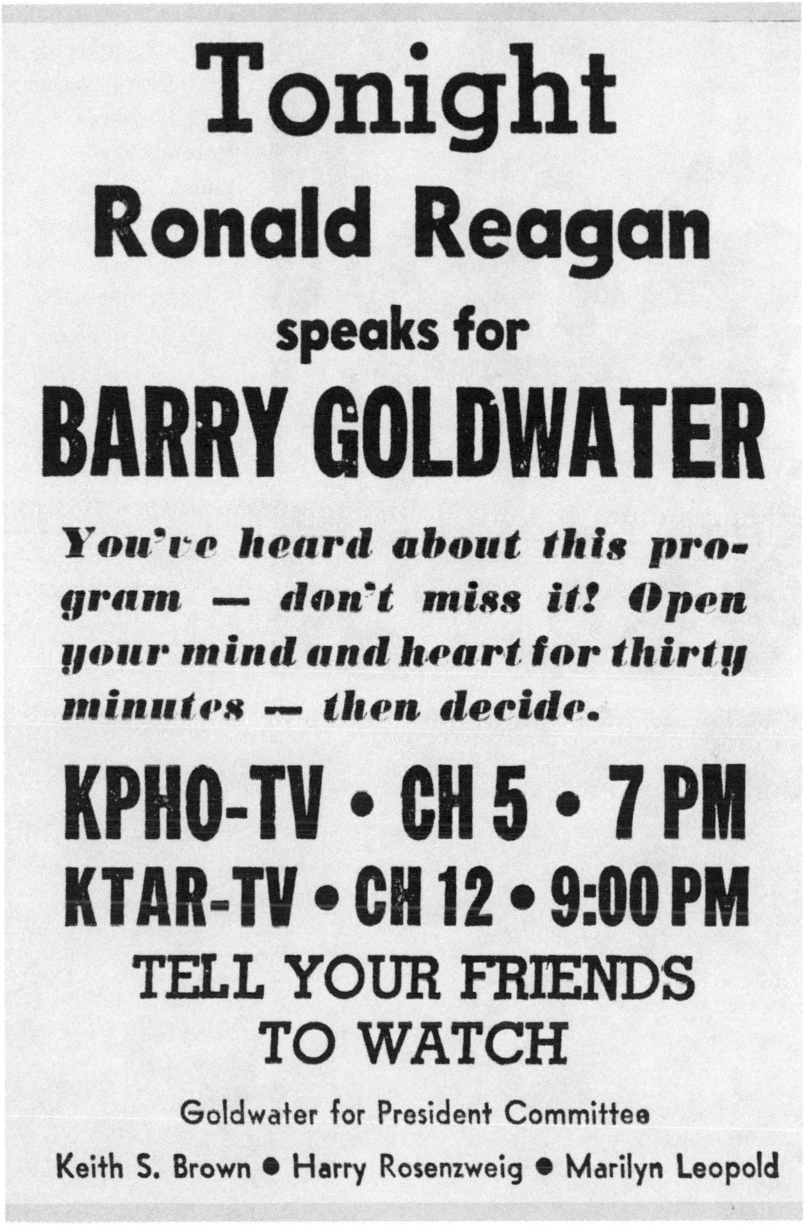

FIG. 27. A newspaper ad in the *Arizona Republic* announcing a rerun of Reagan's televised speech for Republican presidential nominee Barry Goldwater on November 2, 1964. Similar ads ran in newspapers across the country.

FIG. 28. Reagan and Nancy celebrate his election as governor of California in November 1966. Ronald Reagan Presidential Library.

FIG. 29. Reagan waves to delegates after President Gerald Ford invited his former rival to deliver the closing speech at the 1976 Republican National Convention in Kansas City. Gerald Ford Presidential Library.

11

Of Course, Bobby Kennedy Is Behind It

I n July 1961 Reagan sounded the alarm about what he claimed
was a new Communist campaign to capture the movie
industry. "The Communists in Hollywood laid off after the
failure of the big industry strike in 1947, which they hatched
and spawned," he told a breakfast crowd at Hollywood's Brown
Derby. "But now they are renewing in the spirit of [Vladimir]
Lenin's maxim of two steps forward and one backward." While
he opposed its ideology for years, Reagan had once argued for
tolerating the Communist Party. He now viewed it as a mortal
threat to American democracy that should be outlawed. "There is
a confusion over whether the Communist Party is just in political
disagreement with us," he said. "That's not the case. It is loyal to
a foreign power aimed at our destruction."[1]

In speeches of the early 1960s—and as late as 1985—Reagan
shared a statement he said Lenin had made in 1923. He claimed
the Communist revolutionary had boasted the Soviets would
conquer Eastern Europe, organize Asia, take on the United States,
and "that last bastion of Capitalism will not have to be taken. It
will fall into our outstretched hands like an over-ripe fruit."[2] As
was often the case, Reagan had engaged in sloppy research for
the purported quote. He may have plucked this one from the
1959 *Blue Book of the John Birch Society*, in which its Far-Right
founder, Robert Welch, wrongly credited the statement to Lenin.[3]

Regardless of the quote's accuracy, Reagan's apprehension seemed to be a reaction to the public reappearance in Hollywood of screenwriter Dalton Trumbo the year before. In 1960, the former Communist was no longer on the Hollywood blacklist, and he earned credit for writing the screenplays for the popular movies *Exodus* and *Spartacus*. Reagan saw Trumbo's rehabilitation as a reassertion of the Communist influence he believed he and his SAG compatriots had long ago quashed. In April 1960 *Playboy* published an article by Trumbo in which he had attacked the blacklist as a witch hunt. When Hugh Hefner, the magazine's publisher, heard that the article irked Reagan, he wrote to him and defended his decision to publish Trumbo. "The gag of censorship, the intimidation of blacklisting, the attempt of any kind to quiet a voice with which you or I may not be in total agreement, is the first step toward tyranny, and is precisely what this country is fighting against and what all totalitarian nations, Communist Russia included, have always stood for."

Reagan waited almost two months to reply, and when he did, he composed a six-page, handwritten defense of his role in the anti-Communist movement. "How can I make you understand," he wrote to Hefner, "that my feeling now is not prejudice born of this struggle but is realization supported by incontrovertible evidence that the American Communist is in truth a member of a 'Russian American Bund' owing his first allegiance to a foreign power?" Reagan closed his argument with this appeal:

> I, like you, will defend the right of any American to openly practice and preach any political philosophy from monarchy to anarchy. But this is not the case with regard to the communist. He is bound by party discipline to *deny* he is a communist so that he can by subversion and stealth *impose* on an unwilling people the rule of the International Communist Party which is in fact the government of Soviet Russia. I say to you that any man still or now a member of the "party" was a man who looked upon the death of American soldiers in Korea as a victory for his side. For proof of this I refer to some of the ex-communists who fled the party at that time and for that

reason, including some of Mr. Trumbo's companions of the "Unfriendly 10."

Hollywood has *no blacklist.* Hollywood does have a list handed to it by millions of "moviegoers" who have said, "We don't want and will not pay to see pictures made by or with these people we consider traitors." On this list were many names of people we in Hollywood felt were wrongly suspect. I personally served on a committee that succeeded in clearing these people. Today any person who feels he is a victim of discrimination because of his political beliefs can avail himself of machinery to solve this problem.[4]

Reagan made at least one inaccurate assertion in his letter to Hefner: regardless of their views on the political leanings of screenwriters, many U.S. moviegoers were eager to see *Spartacus,* the second most popular film of 1960, and *Exodus,* the ninth-rated movie that year.

REAGAN'S ATTACKS ON COMMUNISM pleased conservative audiences, but his prominent role in stopping what he and other conservatives called "socialized medicine" made him a larger celebrity in the political world. Reagan was not merely an entertaining after-dinner speaker; his recorded words had produced a deluge of mail that helped prevent—for a few years, at least—passage of legislation he and other conservatives despised. In recent years, audiences around the country had known him as a film and TV star who spoke about political issues and Communism in Hollywood. Anyone who examined him more closely would have recognized he had become a dynamic, conservative voice in his own right as he crisscrossed the country warning about Communism and the unchecked growth of big government.

While doctors' wives continued playing his record to their friends and neighbors, Reagan searched for new audiences with whom to share his anti-Communist alarm. In the summer of 1960, he latched onto the conservative crusade of an Australian physician turned preacher and anti-Communist proselytizer, Fred Schwarz. The forty-eight-year-old Schwarz belonged to a growing movement of anti-Communist Christians that included Reverend Billy Graham, leader of the Billy Graham Evangelistic Association; J. Vernon McGee of the Church of the Open Door in Los Angeles; Bob Wells of the Central Baptist Church in Orange County, California; and Billy James Hargis, leader of the radio and television ministry *Christian Crusade*, from which he preached his weekly anti-Communist message to followers on 500 radio stations and 250 television stations.

In 1958 Schwarz's organization, the Christian Anti-Communist Crusade, had launched a series of weeklong seminars that featured lectures and film screenings, usually lasting from 8:30 a.m. to 10:00 p.m. each day. "Faculty" members for what he dubbed his "School for Anti-Communism" included prominent speakers like Connecticut Democratic senator Thomas Dodd, Minnesota Republican congressman Walter Judd, and former FBI counterspy Herbert Philbrick. "The school will be aimed at giving information on the mind, morals, motives, and methods of Communism," Schwarz had said in announcing a five-day school in Philadelphia in November 1960. "The imminent dangers of Communism are much greater than most people realize."[5]

In the beginning, at least, Schwarz's schools were popular and well attended. This was especially true in Southern California in the late 1950s and early 1960s, a hotbed of conservative activism and anti-Communist fervor. Schwarz staged his first Greater Los Angeles School of Anti-Communism in November, several weeks before the Philadelphia school. Six hundred locals signed up for the five-day curriculum, held at the Biltmore Hotel.[6] When he brought the school back to Los Angeles in August 1961, named the "Southern California School of Anti-Communism," the response was overwhelming. More than 17,000 people signed up to attend the five-day event in the 15,700-seat Los Angeles Memorial Sports Arena. Those left standing outside—a crowd estimated to be as large as 5,000—listened to the speeches over a loudspeaker. Richfield Oil Corporation paid to broadcast, live, the school's proceedings for four days from 7:30 p.m. to 10 p.m. on a local television station.[7] Later a Times-Mirror Broadcasting executive told Walter Judd the ratings for the broadcast had far exceeded the company's expectations: "For instance, we had special audience surveys made on Wednesday and Thursday night and on both nights the anti-Communism program topped everything on the air including major network entertainment programs."[8]

Among the speakers were Schwarz, Philbrick (who was also that night's master of ceremonies), Dodd, and a slew of Hollywood conservatives, including Roy Rogers, Dale Evans, John Wayne, and Lee Childs. Reagan was a featured speaker on August 30, relying on his familiar themes about welfare and encroaching government: "Those advocates of the welfare state fail to realize our loss is just as great if it happens on the installment plan."[9] Reagan told the crowd that America's youth were a prime audience for the Communists. "You're a target," he told the assembly's young people. "Communists will appeal to your rebellious nature . . . they will make you feel your patriotism is hollow. Then they will fill up the vacuum with their philosophy." After Reagan's short, well-received presentation, singer Pat Boone entertained the crowd with several songs. Boone then said to wild applause, "I don't want to live in a Communist United States. I would rather see my four girls shot and die as little girls who have faith in God than leave them to die some years later as godless, faithless, soulless Communists."[10]

In his study of Schwarz's movement, historian Hubert Villeneuve noted the profound impact of the school's message in Southern California:

> In the following months, popular anti-Communism manifested itself to an unprecedented level in Southern California. Civic clubs organized patriotic rallies in record numbers, businessmen invited anticommunist speakers to address their chambers of commerce luncheon talks. Suburbanites showed anticommunist films in their churches and joined anticommunist organizations. Conservative housewives formed anti-Red study groups in their kitchens and living rooms. Bill Becker, West Coast correspondent for the *New York Times*, wrote that conservatism "is marching in double-time in Southern California to the twin strains of anticommunism and

pro-Americanism." For years, this grassroots anticommunist activity had been a common feature all across America, and especially in the Southwest, where anticommunist sentiment was strong. However, in late 1961, South California saw the upsurge of a popular anti-Communism which expressed a particularly conservative, anti-collectivist and nationalist outlook. Some observers had considered that the demise of Senator Joe McCarthy in the mid-1950s had led to a decline in anticommunist grassroots activity throughout the nation. Clearly, they were wrong.[11]

In October Reagan reprised his presentation with an array of politicians and movie stars—including Judd, Dodd, Schwarz, and actors Wayne, James Stewart, and Walter Brennan—at a nighttime rally at the Hollywood Bowl. Sponsored by Schwarz's organization, the event drew a crowd of 15,000. Schwarz called it "Hollywood's Answer to Communism," a production that thirty-three television stations in a six-state region carried live that night. A tape of the program also aired on WPIX-TV in New York City on November 2.[12]

Schwarz's anti-Communism crusade revealed and stoked the fears many Americans had about Communism. His operation also highlighted the potential for a profitable career as an anti-Communist clarion. In this realm Reagan was a relatively minor player, traveling what he often called "the mashed potato circuit," warning about the dangers of big government and creeping socialism. Schwarz, to whom Reagan occasionally attached his star in 1961, was earning big money with his schools. The *St. Louis Post-Dispatch* reported in July 1962 that Schwarz's total annual receipts from the sale of literature and admission from meetings and schools in 1961 had been $1.27 million. This was up dramatically from $364,000 the year before, according to audited reports by the Crusade.[13] (It is not clear what, if anything, Schwarz paid Reagan for his appearances.)

With popularity came protest. When Schwarz and his school arrived in Seattle in February 1962, a hostile collection of ministers and rabbis greeted them. "It is not enough to be anti-Communist," the group of twenty-one said in a prepared statement. "Hitler was anti-Communist; so was Mussolini. Each rose to power under the guise of saving his land from the threat of Communism. Each made the same appeal to hysteria and hatred. Each proclaimed himself and his followers the only true patriots and labeled all who dared dissent as subversives in league with enemies of the state."[14]

In several of his syndicated columns in February 1961, George Sokolsky, who also led the American Jewish League against Communism, attacked Schwarz and other anti-Communist leaders. Some of them, he said, were "thieves who move in on any movement to enrich themselves. They are opportunists who find a way of living on other men's enthusiasms and fears." In another column, Sokolsky ridiculed Schwarz, John Birch Society members, and those he called "Extreme Rightists" for "shouting, yelling, booing, mass-meetings, the raising of enormous funds—these are not the means for saving the world from the terrorism of revolution."[15]

As popular as the anti-Communist movement was in Southern California, its appeal proved limited. A school Schwarz held in New York's Madison Square Garden in July attracted a small audience and a group of vocal protesters.[16] In Akron, Ohio, in October 1962, his anti-Communism school drew only fifty people.[17]

Reagan's association with Schwarz was fleeting. But it showed the difficulty of sustaining a large movement with outsized ambitions that put it in conflict with other anti-Communist groups. Those included Jewish anti-Communist organizations that believed Schwarz's movement relied too heavily on Christian religious appeals. Reagan was among the crusaders who usually left religion out of his messages. His talks contained only perfunctory references to God. This may be why Reagan's appeal, if not broader than Schwarz's, would prove longer lasting. His message was not just anti-Communism but also contained warnings about the growth of government and the welfare state. When he did discuss Communism, he spoke not only of its ideology but the threat the Soviet Union posed to individual liberty and American peace and security. More important to Reagan was that he understood his audience and his own limitations. For now, at least, he would continue speaking to the groups that had been applauding him for the past eight years.

Despite Reagan's relative moderation—at least, compared with Schwarz, Hargis, and the John Birchers—the first two years of Kennedy's presidency pushed him further to the right. By February 1962 his rhetoric took on a darker, starker tone. "We are in a great war," he told an audience of 1,200 at a Republican-sponsored Lincoln Day Dinner in Tucson. "This is a war begun a hundred years ago by Karl Marx, and the enemy is doing fine without having to use conventional weapons." Reagan warned of the consequences of the federal government growth. "Strengthening the power of the central government," he said, "is a factor common to Socialism, Communism, and Liberalism." In his speech, Reagan also praised the person many conservatives hoped would be the Republican Party's next presidential nominee, the state's junior senator, Barry Goldwater. Referring to a water dispute between Arizona and California, Reagan told the audience, "We will give up on the water if you will let your junior senator belong to the nation."[18]

That year Reagan joined the boards of several far-right organizations, including Young Americans for Freedom. Reagan supported Republican California congressman John Rousselot, a prominent member of the John Birch Society. Although other conservatives like Richard Nixon avoided the radical politician, Reagan delivered the keynote address at a fund-raising dinner for Rousselot in August 1962. In his speech he attacked the Kennedy administration for believing "the old-fashioned idea of individuality is inadequate in modern day problems and seeks to establish government control and direction of the economy and society."[19]

Reagan rejected suggestions his rhetoric had become more partisan. "It's a curious thing," he would write a few years later. "I talked on this theme of big government during six years of the Eisenhower administration and was accepted as presenting a nonpartisan viewpoint. The same speech delivered *after* Jan. 20,

1961, brought down thunders of wrath on my mind, the charge that my speech was a partisan political attack, an expression of my right-wing extremism." Reagan said the criticism from the Left caused him "to realize that a great many so-called liberals aren't liberals—they will defend to the death your right to agree with them."[20]

Reagan also took his fight against Communism in Hollywood to *General Electric Theater*. He produced two episodes based on the 1960 book by author Marion Miller, *I Was a Spy*, in which the suburban California homemaker described her five years inside the Communist Party as an FBI double agent. In these episodes, Reagan was not only the host but played Miller's husband, Paul, who had also worked as a double agent. "I've wanted to do an anti-Communist story for a long time, but the right one never came along," he told the *Detroit Free Press* in March 1962. The paper's reporter suggested Reagan's interest in these new episodes was also a response to the show's declining ratings. *General Electric Theater* had finished twentieth for the 1960–61 season and would drop from the top thirty for the 1961–62 season. The show was now in its eighth season, and the reporter speculated it suffered because of the success of the hit western *Bonanza*, which aired at the same time on NBC. "It's the seven-year itch," Reagan explained. "We feel it's about time we reviewed what we are doing. So far no decision has been made beyond the fact the sponsor wants to continue a half-hour anthology series." Reagan did not mention *Bonanza*, instead blaming the poor ratings on GE having vetoed turning the show into an hourlong broadcast. "It is a tremendous problem," Reagan said, "to find good half-hour scripts."[21]

In March 1962 General Electric dropped Reagan's show from its fall lineup. The decision came only a month after a federal grand jury subpoenaed Reagan to ask him about his role in the 1952 blanket waiver that had allowed MCA and Revue to produce television programming, including *General Electric Theater*, and hire Reagan as its host. Coming so soon after his testimony led Reagan and others to assume GE canceled the show as a damage-control move. In July the grand jury indicted MCA for various antitrust violations, one of which related to the 1952 waiver. The indictment named SAG as a coconspirator. MCA settled the case (dumping its lucrative talent agency business), and the Justice Department dropped the charges.[22] Reagan, however, believed his support for Richard Nixon in the 1960 presidential election had prompted the U.S. Justice Department, led by Robert Kennedy, to hound him, GE, and MCA-Revue. Many years later, Reagan would tell biographer Lou Cannon that a GE official called in early 1962, asking him to tone down his political speeches and focus on selling GE products. Reagan said he angrily rejected the request and told the unnamed executive, "There's no way that I could go out now to an audience that is expecting the type of thing I've been doing for the last eight years and suddenly stand up and start selling them electric toasters. You'd suffer, and so would I. I can't do that."

Reagan claimed that after the executive continued pushing him to squelch his political rhetoric, he finally replied, "That's it. If it's the speeches, then you only have one choice. Either I don't do the speeches at all for you, or we don't do the program; you get somebody else." Within two days, Reagan said, GE canceled his show.[23] He was fifty-one and, for the first time since the mid-1950s, unemployed.

In his book *Governor Reagan*, Lou Cannon wrote of GE executives' concerns about the ratings and the damage *Bonanza* did to their show's audience. As early as 1961—and again in early 1962—executives of GE, CBS, and BBD&O met to discuss the show's future. Although GE wanted to keep its Sunday night spot on CBS, all parties agreed the show needed a new format. Reagan "refused," one of the GE executives involved in the discussion recalled. "He wanted the TV exposure, since acting was still his profession." At an impasse with Reagan over the show's future, GE fired him and replaced his show that fall with an anthology series airing at 9:30 p.m. on Sundays. The show—*General Electric True*, starring Jack Webb and based on stories published in *True* magazine—aired for one season.[24]

Reagan's daughter Patti, then nine, recalled dinner conversations about the Kennedy administration's imagined anger at Reagan for his political activism, including his attacks on

Kennedy's proposed health care program. "We're on our way to a controlled society," she said her father complained one night after General Electric fired him. "The government is trying to control everything. And Robert Kennedy is behind this attack on me."

"He is?" Patti asked. "Why would he want you fired?"

"Because I'm speaking out against the Kennedy administration and the road they're trying to lead us down."

"*Of course*, Bobby Kennedy is behind it," Patti said her mother, Nancy, chimed in. "It's obvious."[25]

In his postpresidential memoir, Reagan claimed the Kennedy administration assigned cabinet members to travel to the cities where Reagan spoke to drown or oppose his antigovernment message. "In the television business," he wrote, "we used to call that 'counter programming,' an effort to knock out the competition with a rival show. I don't have any proof they planned it that way, but I don't think it was coincidental."[26] A review of news accounts of Reagan's appearances during this period revealed no instance of a Kennedy cabinet member following him, at least none that local papers covered.

Ralph Cordiner, the former General Electric CEO and later its board chair, downplayed the notion GE fired Reagan over his political activism. "We had many letters from irate customers," Cordiner said in May 1963, "but our view was that he had a right to say what he liked, as an individual." Cordiner also tried to smooth over the unpleasantness of Reagan's dismissal, explaining, "We mutually decided eight years is a long time."[27] More likely than a political conspiracy to undermine Reagan hatched in the Kennedy White House was the indisputable fact of the show's poor ratings. Viewership was down considerably, something Reagan admitted publicly at the time. "We were never told that [the show was canceled because of Reagan's political activism]," Bill Clotworthy, the BBD&O executive who was script supervisor of the show for about seven years, said in 2004. "We were always under the impression . . . that it was *Bonanza* that killed the show. It just wasn't viable anymore."[28] Later Reagan said, "Our half-hour, black-and-white, was up against an hour color program [*Bonanza*] with four permanent stars, plus a weekly guest star, all wrapped in a budget several millions of dollars greater than ours."[29]

Without the routine of his show and travel for GE, Reagan took time off from giving speeches. Daughter Patti recalled he went most days to his nearby ranch.[30] Reagan also helped his friend Loyd Wright, the former president of the American Bar Association, who was challenging the reelection of California Republican senator Thomas Kuchel, the U.S. Senate minority whip. That Wright had been Jane Wyman's lawyer in her divorce suit against Reagan in 1948 did not end their friendship. Reagan enlisted in February as Wright's campaign chair.[31]

Another Republican challenger to Kuchel, Republican Howard Jarvis, tried using Reagan's liberal past against Wright, noting the actor had only recently switched parties and "for years" had been listed on the letterhead of the United World Federalists. In a statement blasting Jarvis, Wright defended Reagan, noting his vigorous support of Richard Nixon in 1960. "Furthermore," he added, "Ronald Reagan has been espousing through every medium available the conservative cause to stop the Fabian Socialists in this country from squandering the people's hard-earned tax money and the drift toward the welfare state."[32]

Although he no longer traveled for GE, Reagan appeared on *General Electric Theater* reruns through the summer. And in cities and towns across America, women still gathered around record players to sip coffee while he attacked "socialized medicine."[33] But Reagan was out of work. He would continue looking for movie and television acting opportunities, but those would be rare. Younger Hollywood stars had supplanted him. His was an earlier, black-and-white era. Even his television show had been broadcast in black-and-white, despite the popularity of color television and the ironic fact that GE produced color televisions (CBS's reluctance to broadcast in color reportedly annoyed GE executives). Earnings from eight years hosting a popular show, combined with his producer income, had made him wealthy and financially secure. Still he wanted cash flow as well as the adulation of the audiences he had entertained and motivated for so long. "I'm out of a job," he told William F. Buckley Jr. in June.

"Even though the GE *Theater* continues on through the summer (reruns) I've been sans income for a time and will continue until I'm rediscovered."[34] He began offering his stump speech for a fee.[35] "More and more, in these years," Garry Wills observed, "he lived to deliver The Speech. It had become his mission in life. He sought occasions to issue his warning, and audiences were so moved that the performance became a famous one. The public relations adjunct to his plant tours had now become the center of his life."[36]

12

Have You Reregistered as a Republican Yet?

Through April 1962 Reagan was busy. His speeches attracted more attention, thanks to citizens and businesses who paid to broadcast his remarks on television and radio stations. In Tucson, the Pima County Republican Committee bought time to play Reagan's speech "Losing Freedom . . . by Installments" on a radio station in late February.[1] About the same time, a radio station in La Grande, Oregon, announced in a newspaper ad it would air the speech "by popular demand."[2] A few days later, KWKH radio in Shreveport, Louisiana, broadcast—"by popular request"—a speech Reagan had delivered to the Tyler, Texas, Chamber of Commerce.[3] When Reagan spoke in early March to the Amarillo, Texas, Chamber of Commerce, a television station and its affiliate radio station carried his address live.[4]

After Reagan spoke to an audience of 10,000 in Dallas in March 1962, the Lone Star Steel Company played "Ronald Reagan's now famous speech, 'What Price Freedom,'" on television and radio stations in the region, including on a Texarkana, Texas, radio station and a nearby Shreveport television station. The company also published excerpts from Reagan's speech in weekly newspaper advertisements and reported the response was "overwhelming."[5] In her syndicated Hollywood column, Louella Parsons (like Reagan, she grew up in Dixon, Illinois) claimed Reagan's crowd in Dallas was larger than those John F.

Kennedy and Richard Nixon had attracted during their recent visits to the state.[6]

Audiences did not need Reagan's presence or voice to enjoy his speeches. In January, in Port Angeles, Washington, members of the Rotary Club listened as the program chairman read the text of a speech Reagan had delivered the previous October in San Francisco.[7] Other groups that gathered to hear recordings of Reagan's speeches included the Seymour, Indiana, Kiwanis Club (in mid-January) and the Minnesota Chapter of the Daughters of Founders and Patriots of America in Minneapolis (in March).[8]

After taking the summer off, Reagan roared back into politics in the fall of 1962, backing Nixon in his ill-fated race for California governor against the incumbent Democrat, Pat Brown. During September and October, Reagan appeared on Nixon's behalf in places like Redlands, Oakland, San Bernardino, Santa Clarita, San Diego, San Rafael, Santa Rosa, and Los Angeles.[9] As he had in 1960, Nixon suggested that Reagan should campaign for him as a Democrat. Reagan did so until he appeared one day at a fund-raising event near his home in Pacific Palisades. Reagan recalled a woman stood up in the middle of his speech to ask, "Have you reregistered as a Republican yet?"

"Well, no, I haven't yet, but I intend to," Reagan replied.

"I'm the registrar," Reagan said the woman announced, as she marched down the center aisle and laid a registration form before him.

"I signed it and became a Republican," Reagan recalled, "then said to the audience, 'Now, where was I?'"[10]

On October 9, Reagan shared a platform with Governor Brown at the California Real Estate Association's annual convention in Oakland, condemning high taxes and warning about Communist subversion of the federal government. "I think it is time you and I recognized there can be no security tonight any place in the free world if there is not fiscal and economic stability within the United States."[11]

In the days before the November 6 statewide elections, Reagan delivered the first of two speeches on television stations around California, endorsing the Republican ticket. In the first, he joined the Republican nominee for attorney general, Tom Coakley, to discuss what one newspaper advertisement described as "the need for a change in the state's highest legal office."[12] In the broadcast for Nixon, aired statewide on Sunday, November 4, Reagan delivered his standby speech that included some California-specific language. To his standard lines about government spending, Reagan added, "Under the Brown administration, spending has gone up forty-seven percent and we've increased the number of state employees by thirty percent. We have the highest per capita tax in the history of California, the highest per capita tax of all the fifty states and for that we have the highest crime rate per capita in all of the nation." He did not mention Nixon until the broadcast's final two minutes. "We can be represented by a governor who needs no introduction in meetings of the highest of the world's leaders," Reagan said. "Can you possibly believe that a man like Dwight David Eisenhower, whose love of country is beyond question, could have been closely associated with Richard Nixon as he was for eight years and now recommend him for high office, as he is doing, if he did not believe him worthy to serve?"[13]

HE HAD NO TELEVISION show and had not made a movie in years, yet Reagan still saw himself as an actor or TV personality. Others, however, noticed a change in his public profile and priorities. *New York Times* reporter Homer Bigart, in an October 1962 story about the John Birch Society, noted Reagan's support for Bircher congressman John Rousselot and described Reagan as "a film star who has emerged as a right-wing oracle."[14]

Oracle or not, Reagan had no immediate plans to quit the entertainment business. On New Year's Day 1963, he joined former Miss America Bess Myerson to host—for the second year in a row—the CBS television broadcast of the Tournament of Roses Parade and Pageant from Pasadena.[15] In February the fifty-two-year-old Reagan told a reporter he had signed a movie contract with Universal International. "I like the timing of this move," he said. "Somehow, instinctively, I think this is smarter than trying to look for another long run on television."[16] There were no immediate movie deals. For 1963, his only dramatic acting credit would be a guest appearance on the NBC television western drama series *Wagon Train*.[17]

Americans would see him that year as the narrator or host of four documentaries. The first was a ninety-minute film, *The Truth about Communism*, by filmmaker Sid O. Fields, who had produced two earlier movies on the same topic. "The film presents a dramatic collection of newsreel and still shots that cover a number of events in USSR history over the past 30 years," reported one newspaper promoting the movie.[18] Another newspaper told readers the documentary featured "film smuggled from behind the iron curtain."[19] Civic clubs and other organizations in several cities presented the film to their members and the public, including the Greater Los Angeles Press Club and the Santa Monica Junior Chamber of Commerce.[20] Whenever the film's promoter could find local sponsors, the Reagan-narrated documentary appeared on television stations. In 1963, it aired in Los Angeles; Tucson and Phoenix, Arizona; Dayton and Cincinnati, Ohio; St. Louis, Missouri; Eau Claire, Wisconsin; and Richmond, Indiana.[21]

Reagan also narrated and hosted a twenty-seven-minute film, *The Ultimate Weapon: The Minds of Free Men*. The William Volker Fund produced the movie, based on a 1956 book and lectures by retired Army major William Mayer. The author argued that American prisoners during the Korean conflict had succumbed to Communist brainwashing because of low morals and soft American living. The film was a dramatization of the imagined experience of a group of U.S. prisoners of war brainwashed by their Chinese captors in the early 1950s.[22] "The Communists found some support for their charge that we're passive, uncommitted to a definite system, sometimes opportunistic, self-seeking," Reagan said in the film. "Our prisoners were part of ourselves. What they did or failed to do reflects on our acts, our failings. What must be understood is that these failings can undo freedoms dearly purchased: Isolate the individual even as he becomes submerged in the mass. Erode our political and economic and social system as effectively as any shooting war."

As narrator, Reagan blamed those "who seek more and more relief from government to solve the problems of life," thereby hastening the spread of Communist ideology in the United States. "Our enemies are largely within ourselves."[23] The mysterious Film Consultants of California distributed the documentary to libraries and other organizations with a discussion guide. It was meant primarily for political, civic, and other community groups (although it aired on a Chicago television station the night of January 1, 1963). For example, in March 1963, members of the Uniontown, Pennsylvania, Business and Professional Women's Club viewed the film at its monthly meeting. That month, the Santa Rosa, California, Lioness Club did the same. In Pensacola, Florida, in May, a Mormon church invited the public to view the film in its chapel.[24]

Reagan narrated another thirty-minute documentary that year, *The Welfare State*, sponsored by the Church League of America. One Illinois Republican group that showed the film at its July meeting described it as "an excellent documentary on the hazardous state of affairs which the liberal administrations have led our country over the past 30 years." Other civic and political organizations—in places like Long Beach, California, Hartford, Connecticut, and Harlingen, Texas—showed the film to all who cared to watch.[25] In his fourth documentary of 1963, Reagan narrated an eighteen-minute antilittering film, *Heritage of Splendor*, produced by the Keep America Beautiful organization and financed by the Richfield Oil Corporation. "The litter problem seems to get worse," Reagan said in the film. "Sadly and ironically, because of scientific advances and new improvements in modern living, trash only becomes trash after it first serves a useful purpose. It becomes litter only after people thoughtlessly discard it." Producers sent the film to state and local antilittering and beautification organizations for showings.[26]

In other towns, copies of Reagan's standard political speech continued to circulate. In Iowa, for example, the *Mt. Pleasant News* ran a story in March, "Reagan Speech Available Here," in which the town's Junior Chamber of Commerce urged groups to use the film for their meetings. "Mr. Reagan is a very high powered speaker," the story reported.[27] In his national newspaper column in April 1963, Harry T. Everingham—one of the leaders of a far-right, anti-Communist organization, We the People—praised Reagan as "one of the bravest opponents of socialism in America." And he offered a printed copy of a Reagan speech to anyone who sent him ten cents and a self-addressed stamped envelope.[28]

Reagan kept up a busy speaking schedule through the late spring, early summer, and fall of 1963. In April, he appeared in Dixon, where he gave 1,200 people at the Dixon High School gym a rendition of his now-famous antigovernment speech, "What Price Freedom." To his friends and former neighbors, he declared, "Our salvation lies in chaining down government to certain, specific, constitutional functions. The Constitution is still our contract."[29]

The following day in nearby Mount Morris, Illinois, Reagan spoke at ceremonies dedicating the Mount Morris Freedom Bell (now the Illinois Freedom Bell) in the town's Kabla Square. "The reason we're losing the cold war is that too many people refuse to believe we're in it," Reagan told the gathering. "I believe in the Peace Corps and things like that, but I think we'd be a lot farther ahead if we sent a regiment of Marines around the world and let them parade through the hostile areas." Before pulling the rope to sound the bell, Reagan reeled off one of his most popular and moving lines, a feature of almost all his speeches: "If we don't protect our freedom, we'll spend our sunset years telling our children and our children's children what it was like in this country when we were free."[30]

In Arkansas City, Kansas, later that week, Reagan addressed a crowd at the town's auditorium-gymnasium, telling them the world was "faced with a choice between totalitarianism and freedom." Referring to the threat of nuclear war—this was seven months after the October 1962 Cuban Missile Crisis—Reagan quoted Lenin. He asserted the Russian Communist leader had once said, "If it should become necessary to kill three-quarters of all the people in the world, it would be worth it if the remaining one-quarter were Communist." (Lenin wanted a worldwide Communist revolution. However, the quote, attributed to him by anti-Communist activists in the 1950s and 1960s, is not in any of his published writings or speeches.) "We have come to a time for choosing," Reagan said, "and we should recognize that two contrary philosophies divide us. Either we believe in our traditional freedom with constitutional limits in the power of government, or we abandon the American Revolution and confess someone in a far distant capital can plan for us better than we can."[31]

REAGAN'S RISE AS A popular and strong conservative voice coincided with a wave of anger among conservatives toward the East Coast moderates and liberals who they believed dominated their party. Conservatives viewed these leaders as having presided over a decade of appeasement of liberal Democrats. But their dissent gained little traction because the party's leader, Dwight Eisenhower, towered over the GOP for most of the fifties. Eisenhower had joined his party shortly before he ran for president in 1952. Politically he had been a blank slate until he became a politician. Only those on the outer reaches of the Far Right anti-Communist wing of the Republican Party, however, doubted his patriotism or his judgment on military and national security matters. Among those doubters had been the late Wisconsin Republican senator Joseph McCarthy. His reckless allegations about Communist influence in the State Department and elsewhere repulsed Eisenhower, especially after McCarthy, in 1952, questioned the patriotism of Gen. George C. Marshall, Eisenhower's mentor and close friend.

Despite uneasy relations with the ultra, anti-Communist Right, most Americans never questioned Eisenhower's loyalty to his country. But John Birch Society founder Robert Welch did, calling Eisenhower "a dedicated, conscious agent of the Communist conspiracy."[32] The charge was absurd. Eisenhower was a lifelong patriot and undisputed war hero. Nixon was a darling of anti-Communists. Conservatives respected Eisenhower's sometimes bellicose secretary of state, John Foster Dulles, who belonged to the East Coast establishment but had championed a hard line against the Soviet Union and Communist China. Nonetheless, some conservatives lamented Eisenhower's passivity on military affairs. He had wound down the Korean conflict and accepted Communist control of the northern half of the Korean Peninsula, a decision that angered many conservatives. And he was in no hurry to plunge the nation into another conflict in Indochina, no matter how much anti-Communist hard-liners in Congress and in his administration pushed him.

Eisenhower's relationship with conservatives over domestic issues was also troubled. In 1956 he had accepted an expansion of the Social Security system that many on the Right, like Reagan, regarded as a shocking enlargement of the welfare state. Other conservatives believed Eisenhower was lukewarm about cutting federal spending. Often unable to work with leaders of his own party, especially in the Senate, the president sometimes consulted and compromised with Majority Leader Lyndon Johnson, a Democrat. Eisenhower had appointed former California governor Earl Warren as chief justice of the Supreme Court, a decision he regretted.[33] After the unanimous landmark 1954 *Brown v. Board of Education* civil rights decision, Warren's liberalism persuaded many conservatives the president was not a reliable member of their movement.

Perhaps the Republican in Congress most distressed about Eisenhower was Barry Goldwater, the flinty Arizona senator and hero of the beleaguered conservative movement. Once a strong supporter of Eisenhower, Goldwater had also supported Joseph McCarthy, about whom he once said, "I couldn't approve of some of the charges McCarthy was making, but there was a tremendous amount of evidence to support his allegations."[34] In 1954, when Eisenhower proposed federal assistance for those struggling to afford health insurance, Goldwater attacked the plan as a "dime-store New Deal." Goldwater broke again with Eisenhower in 1957 over the president's proposed 1958 federal budget. In a Senate speech, the senator called the $71.8 billion budget, which he considered wasteful, "a betrayal of the people's trust." He charged Eisenhower's administration "was demonstrating tendencies to bow to the siren song of socialism." Robert Alan Goldberg, author of a 1995 biography of Goldwater, saw the speech, along with Goldwater's other acts of dissent that year, as "the rallying cry for a generation of conservatives and made him a national figure."[35]

By 1963 Goldwater was the undisputed leader of the conservative movement. His 1960 book, *Conscience of a Conservative*, was an enormous success. As a prominent conservative writer of the time remarked, the book was a "powerful testimony, if anybody had been listening, to the tremendous thirst for a statement of conservative principles at a certain level of the literate population of the country in the early 1960s."[36] Goldwater had long been a neighbor to Reagan's in-laws, Loyal and Edith Davis, in Phoenix's fashionable Biltmore Estates neighborhood.[37] Reagan and Goldwater became friends in the early 1950s, although Goldwater later suggested Reagan's liberalism in that decade was, at first, an obstacle to their relationship: "He was so far to the Left, he wouldn't talk to me. In fact, he called me a black fascist bastard one day."[38] Such a remark by Reagan (unless made in jest) is almost impossible to square with everything known about his personality and manner. And Reagan was not much of a liberal by 1952, the year he had enthusiastically supported Eisenhower for president.

Whatever may have occurred during their first few meetings, by the late 1950s and early 1960s, Reagan and Goldwater were friends and political allies. Reagan had been listening to Goldwater—and to other rumblings of a conservative uprising—for years. Although he never directly criticized Eisenhower, as did Goldwater, almost every speech Reagan had given over the past decade was about the growth of government. And his warnings about the threat of domestic Communism—until 1961, at least—had been an implicit criticism of Eisenhower's leadership. As well as any political leader in the country, and far better than most, Reagan understood the mood of the movement Goldwater led and which would one day be his to lead. Reagan revered Goldwater as a person and a potential president. He also admired Goldwater's book, which "contained a lot of the same points I'd been making in my speeches."[39]

In an April 1963 speech to the American Citizens Forum in Omaha, he had endorsed Goldwater for the 1964 Republican Party presidential nomination. The only problem was Goldwater had not announced his candidacy. And while many in the movement wanted him to run and were plotting to draft him, the senator was unenthusiastic about the idea. Unlike some of his supporters, Goldwater understood the difficulty of defeating a glamorous, popular Democratic incumbent like John F. Kennedy. To the audience in Omaha, Reagan noted Goldwater "is being very cautious," which did not begin to describe the senator's reluctance to run. He characterized Goldwater's attitude toward the race as, "Let's not play the homecoming game until we have a fair chance of winning."[40] Although he admired Goldwater and backed him for president, Reagan did not appear to trumpet Goldwater to many audiences that spring. Or, if he did, journalists covering his speeches regarded the endorsement as unremarkable.

FROM MID- TO LATE 1963, Reagan limited his speaking engagements, but not because he was losing his fervor for preaching anti-Communism and small government. Instead, he still clung to faint hopes of reviving his acting career. In October, when a Republican organization in suburban New Orleans invited him to speak in December, he begged off. He explained he was under contract to Universal Studios for a movie but did not know when filming might begin. Because he would not fly, Reagan said he could not spare "several days round trip" by train to Louisiana. "It was my hope," he explained in his letter, "that by this time I would be scheduled for a picture and could count on accepting invitations such as yours prior to its starting date or immediately following production."[41]

On November 23, 1963, the day after Kennedy's assassination, Reagan began filming what would be the last movie of his acting career. It was a remake of a 1946 film, *The Killers*, a violent tale based loosely on a short story by Ernest Hemingway. It was the first time he played a villain. Despite an impressive cast that included Lee Marvin and Angie Dickinson, the movie—first intended for television—proved too intense for broadcast. The producers would release it in theaters the following summer. And it would flop.[42] "It's one I try to forget," Reagan would tell the *Saturday Evening Post* in 1974. "I had no faith in the story."[43]

True to form, during the filming, Reagan spent much of his

155

downtime reading. He did not attempt to talk politics with Dick-inson, who had been friends with Kennedy. "You weren't about to talk politics when this man had just been murdered—and most of us were Democrats," Dickinson said. "But Ronnie was always studying on the set. He was knee-deep in all this political stuff."[44]

REAGAN AND THE CREW wrapped up filming in early January 1964, about the time Goldwater announced he would seek the Republican presidential nomination. Even before Kennedy's assassination, Goldwater had finally warmed to running. The Arizona Republican said he and Kennedy had discussed—should Goldwater win the GOP nomination—a plan to barnstorm the country together and debate the issues. With Kennedy dead, however, Goldwater knew the American people would not turn the new president, Lyndon Johnson, out of office. And he understood, "barring a political miracle, I'd lose the race against Lyndon Johnson. The American people would not accept three different presidents in little more than a year, and the certain conservative-liberal fight for control of the GOP would leave the party on the ropes in the national election campaign."[45]

Maybe Goldwater decided to run because he loathed Johnson and considered him "treacherous" and a "hypocrite." Even so, he briefly considered calling off the campaign. But friends and top supporters persuaded him he had no choice but to plunge ahead. "Alright, goddam it," he said finally, "I'll go." Over the next ten months, his ambivalence would show. Goldwater would wage a lackluster campaign. While he would capture the imagination of conservatives hungry for a repudiation of Eisenhower's moder-ation and Kennedy-Johnson liberalism, Goldwater would never find a way to expand his appeal. "He ran like a man who didn't expect to win," said one good friend, Republican senator John Tower of Texas, "and that had an awful psychological drag on the campaign."[46]

Reagan was one supporter who did not seem to understand his candidate was just going through the motions. In the coming months, he would not only give his all to Goldwater's campaign; his advocacy for the Arizonan's candidacy would propel Reagan into prominence that was greater and longer lasting than Goldwater's. Reagan would sign up to help Goldwater win the White House. And, in losing, Goldwater's campaign would give Reagan his first stepping-stone to stratospheric political renown and the beginnings of a political career that would take him all the way to the White House.

GOLDWATER HOBBLED FROM HIS Scottsdale, Arizona, home on Friday, January 3, 1964, to finally announce his candidacy for the White House. On crutches—his right foot encased in a plaster cast after bone-spur surgery—Goldwater stood at a lectern on his flagstone patio.[47] "I was once asked what kind of Republican I was," Goldwater told the gathering. "I replied that I was not a 'me-too' Republican. That still holds. I will not change my beliefs to win votes. I will offer a choice, not an echo. This will not be an engagement of personalities. It will be an engagement of principles." He added, "I've always stood for government that is limited and balanced and against the ever-increasing concentrations of authority in Washington. I've always stood for individual responsibility and against regimentation. I believe we must now make a choice in this land and not continue drifting endlessly down and down for a time when all of us, our lives, our property, our hopes, and even our prayers will become just cogs in a vast government machine."[48]

Few supporters were more excited by this statement and about Goldwater's candidacy than Reagan. By early 1964 he had been promoting the Arizonan for more than a year and was eager to join his friend's campaign. First, however, Reagan had to finish the memoir—*Where's the Rest of Me?*—he was writing with Hollywood ghostwriter Richard C. Hubler, scheduled for publication in 1965. With its deeply personal reflections on his small-town upbringing, his struggles against Communism, and ruminations on a range of political issues, the book's appearance suggests Reagan was already preparing for a career in politics as early as 1963 or 1964. Once done with the memoir, Reagan poured his energies into Goldwater's campaign, focusing on helping him win the all-important California Republican primary that June.

Neither Goldwater nor his campaign, however, had thought to formally recruit Reagan or offer him useful work in California. Volunteering was Reagan's idea. And when he enlisted, he did not contact Goldwater but, instead, wandered into the candidate's San Francisco headquarters while in the city one day in the spring of 1964. Approaching the first person he saw—Kay Valory, the California Speakers Bureau chair for the Goldwater campaign—Reagan introduced himself and volunteered to help. Valory phoned Goldwater's national headquarters and asked officials in Washington to let her sign up Reagan for duty.[49] They did. (In 1966, Reagan would appoint Valory cochair of his northern California gubernatorial campaign committee. After he became governor, he appointed her to several state positions.)

IN EARLY 1964 CONSERVATIVES were rising within a divided Republican Party, but they were not yet a majority. They were, as Eugene Patterson, editor of the *Atlanta Constitution*, observed, a "federation of the fed up." These conservatives, a *Time* magazine reporter added, "are fed up with the portents of economic, social, and moral decay they see across the U.S., particularly in its crime-infested cities. They are fed up with big government and big spending, with a bland foreign policy and with America's failure to use its power abroad."[50]

Conservatives were also angry that a large, powerful bloc of moderates and East Coast liberals still dominated their party apparatus, and in places like New York, liberal Republicans ran the party's machinery. It was not just that liberals controlled a significant faction of the party; many regarded them as the GOP's real strength. With Johnson the overwhelming favorite to win the Democratic Party's nomination, some observers argued that the Republicans' only chance of victory was in nominating a liberal Republican who might attract liberals and moderates outside the South. They believed Johnson was a regional candidate with limited appeal. And they thought he might be vulnerable against a liberal like New York governor Nelson Rockefeller or one of the unannounced, potential candidates who coyly remained on the sidelines, waiting for Goldwater, Rockefeller, or both to falter.

Those included Nixon, Pennsylvania governor William Scranton, and Michigan governor George Romney. The array of Republican candidates—and potential candidates—in 1964 showed the extent to which the GOP still saw itself as a moderate-to-liberal party: Rockefeller, Scranton, Romney, Maine senator Margaret Chase Smith, and Henry Cabot Lodge (the former Massachusetts senator who was Nixon's 1960 running mate and now served as Johnson's ambassador to South Vietnam).[51]

Goldwater was the only true conservative in the field, which gave him a clear advantage that some fearful liberals and moderates recognized as a threat to their dominance. In an editorial the day after he announced his candidacy, the *New York Times* noted Goldwater's growing popularity among conservatives. "Since [Ohio senator] Robert A. Taft was defeated by General Eisenhower in 1952, no ranking Republican has spoken for the conservatives with anything like the vigor or appeal that Mr. Goldwater has displayed," the *Times* said.[52] A national poll of Republicans conducted by the Associated Press in November 1963 confirmed Goldwater's popularity. In the survey he enjoyed an overwhelming lead among the potential GOP candidates.[53] Goldwater was not just the lone conservative in the race; he was also the most popular conservative politician in the country after his years of campaigning in dozens of cities for Republican candidates. And those conservatives believed their time had arrived. "There were many right-wingers, rank-and-file Republicans, party leaders, businessmen, and others who shared [Goldwater's] belief that true conservatism had never really received a fair test at the polls in the modern political era," a *New York Times* history of the 1964 race noted. "To them, the Eastern liberal establishment that had captured the Republican party twenty years before was again trying to lead it to defeat."[54]

There was little evidence that a liberal or conservative Republican leading a divided and disorganized Republican Party could beat Johnson. Early polls put the president ahead of Goldwater by 55 percentage points and beating Rockefeller by 57 points.[55] Goldwater entertained no notion he could win. "I didn't want to run for the presidency," he later wrote. "That's God's truth. . . .

It's also true that I knew, and said privately from the start, that I would lose to President Johnson." But before he could lose the general election, he had to win his party's nomination. If Goldwater and his aides believed the early polls and thought the sledding to the Republican convention might be easy, their experience in the first primary state, New Hampshire, disabused them. "The New Hampshire primary was a lesson in how not to run a campaign," Goldwater later admitted.[56]

Goldwater's propensity for gaffes only compounded the disorganization in his campaign. When a reporter asked him about the Social Security system, Goldwater suggested several changes, including making it "flexible and voluntary."[57] Speaking to *Life* magazine in January, he offered the controversial idea of sharing nuclear weapons with NATO allies: "All NATO forces stationed in Europe, regardless of nationality, should be equipped with, and trained in the use of, nuclear weapons, particularly of the so-called battlefield or tactical variety."[58]

His campaign's disorganization and his undisciplined encounters with the press tripped up Goldwater. He finished second in New Hampshire, losing to Lodge—who won a write-in campaign despite having shown no enthusiasm for the race—and edging out Rockefeller, who finished a point behind. Goldwater and Rockefeller quickly emerged as the only legitimate contenders for the nomination, while Scranton, Nixon, and Romney waited in the wings in hopes that Rockefeller's candidacy might fade or die. Goldwater, meanwhile, benefited almost everywhere from the division between liberals and moderates, winning the unified support and votes of conservatives while Rockefeller, Lodge, and others split the remaining ballots. Even after Goldwater's loss in Oregon in May (he finished third behind Rockefeller and Lodge), he was on the verge of winning enough delegates to capture the nomination. As it soon became clear, the winner of California's eighty-six delegates would have a majority of delegates or at least the momentum to ensure victory at the party's July convention in San Francisco.

Luckily for Goldwater, this decisive primary was in a state well suited for his politics. "Goldwater had been in and out of

[California] probably more than he had in Arizona, giving speeches for the party, for fundraisers, etc.," recalled Stuart Spencer, a consultant who worked for Rockefeller in 1964 (and would help manage Reagan's gubernatorial campaign in 1966).[59] Between 1958 and 1964, Goldwater had delivered about five hundred speeches to audiences in California.[60]

Those who understood California politics knew that in some regions, especially Southern California, the state was ripe for Goldwater's brand of conservatism. "Goldwater's politics resonated among a powerful group of regional businessmen—and their strong backing of his campaign, in turn, helped to generate his grassroots support," historian Lisa McGirr wrote in her history of the American Right. Nowhere was this more pronounced than in Orange County, a fast-growing Los Angeles suburb, home to enthusiastic Goldwater backers like Walter Knott of Knott's Berry Farm and founder of the California Free Enterprise Association. Knott and a group of prominent business leaders backed Goldwater with their money and time. They also funded the wide distribution of his book *Conscience of a Conservative* and other far-right publications. Those included John Stormer's warnings about alleged disloyalty in the U.S. State Department, *None Dare Call It Treason*, and conservative activist Phyllis Schlafly's best-selling *A Choice Not an Echo*. One prominent Goldwater supporter in Orange County recalled, "There was literature coming out in every way. Hard-cover books to soft-cover books, tracts, one-page sheets. You couldn't imagine the stack. . . . It was incredible."[61] As historian Jonathan Darman wrote in his account of the 1964 race:

> The wise people in Washington hadn't seen the California that Reagan knew. They hadn't seen places like Orange County. In those Southern California suburbs, middle-class white refugees from the Midwest had embraced Goldwater's style of conservatism as a modern religion. There, voters needed no convincing that the Communist threat to civilization was real and that conspirators lay within their midst. There, the John Birch Society was no fringe group; it had thousands of county residents on its newsletter subscription list. There,

Phyllis Schlafly's manifesto . . . was passed around like a secret Bible speaking the one true faith in a world of heretics. There, in February 1964, Goldwater supporters set out to collect thirteen thousand signatures to get their candidate on the state's primary ballot. By the end of their first day, they already had close to three times that many. And there, the weekend before the California primary, when Reagan appeared at a rally for Goldwater, the crowd that turned out was twenty-eight thousand strong. You didn't have to look closely at the faces in that crowd to know one thing: Barry Goldwater was going to be the Republican Party's nominee in 1964.[62]

As the polls in California tightened, the race turned ugly. For months Rockefeller had painted Goldwater as an extremist. The charge became more credible in late May when Goldwater appeared on ABC's Sunday morning news show, *Issues and Answers*, and mentioned the idea of using low-yield nuclear weapons in South Vietnam to defoliate the forests to expose enemy supply lines in the U.S.-backed war in that country.[63] After his Oregon victory, Rockefeller had framed the outcome of the California primary as deciding "whether the Republican party is going to move forward in the mainstream of public life or whether it will pull off into a small eddy, pulled there by a small minority in the party."[64] Said Stuart Spencer, Rockefeller's consultant, about his candidate's scorched-earth strategy in California: "We had to destroy Barry Goldwater as a member of the human race."[65]

13

Which One Was the Candidate?

Fortunate for Goldwater was the exquisite timing of the birth—three days before the California primary—of Governor Nelson Rockefeller's fourth son to his new, second wife, Margaretta Large Fitler Murphy Rockefeller. News of the baby created national headlines and reminded voters in California and elsewhere of the scandalous fact that the New York governor's wife, nicknamed "Happy," had surrendered custody of three of her four children when divorcing her first husband.[1]

Rockefeller's own 1962 divorce and his remarriage the following year had already caused him political headaches. Those included a press conference in late May by sixteen Protestant California pastors who declared that his divorce and remarriage "struck a serious blow" against the Christian idea of matrimony.[2] Rockefeller's campaign had once ridiculed Goldwater by posing the question, "Do you want a leader or a loner?" Rockefeller's messy personal life left the New York governor open to the counter question, which some Goldwater supporters spread: "Do you want a leader or a lover?"

Rockefeller had vast wealth, and his money allowed him to assemble the more professional campaign organization. "The local TV was saturated with arguments on behalf of the New York governor—and we had nothing," Stephen Shadegg, a Goldwater campaign staffer, recalled.[3] Goldwater had what journalist Robert

Novak described as "a plethora of militant, often fanatic workers competing with each other" to help their candidate. "There was no end to Goldwater groups at the grass roots."[4] A legion of passionate volunteers, however, did not mean a well-managed campaign. "They were unregimented and uncoordinated, yet massive," William F. Buckley Jr. wrote, adding, "Volunteers were everywhere, doing everything, indeed inventing things to do." As one Goldwater staffer said to Buckley, the campaign's volunteers "ran through the woods like a collection of firebugs."[5]

To some, Goldwater's California effort looked like a repeat of his disastrous New Hampshire campaign. Goldwater resolved he would not repeat those mistakes. In New Hampshire, he believed, his inexperienced staff served him poorly. "We flew up and down the state in random leaps that made no sense," Goldwater recalled, "sometimes spending more time in airplanes and cars than campaigning." In California, after his campaign chair scheduled twenty-four appearances in one day (including four press conferences), Goldwater balked and insisted on trimming his schedule. That included holding no more than three daily appearances, delivering speeches only to large audiences, and conducting fewer press conferences. Goldwater also relied heavily on television to broadcast his speeches throughout the state.[6] By the campaign's final days, Goldwater's advertising on radio, television, and in newspapers, particularly in the *Los Angeles Times*, would far exceed Rockefeller's.[7]

REAGAN STUMPED FOR GOLDWATER throughout California in the weeks before the primary. On March 19, serving as the emcee for a $100-per-plate dinner for Goldwater in Los Angeles, he told the Republican crowd: "I believe that Barry Goldwater offers the best opportunity we have to restore individual freedom and constitutional limits to the powers of government." In his brief speech, Reagan did what he would do several times before the campaign ended: he would outshine Goldwater. Reagan was more polished and affable, more skilled at emoting, and far better at reading crowds than Goldwater. "What did you think of the affair?" one attendee asked a friend after the dinner. The friend replied: "It was pretty good, but I think it would have been more effective if Ronald Reagan had made the main speech and Barry Goldwater had just sat there and nodded."[8] If Goldwater resented Reagan's ease before audiences, he did not betray it. The candidate and his aides appeared grateful for the actor's help. From March through the June primary, Reagan appeared with Goldwater, or on his behalf, in places like Los Angeles, Pasadena, Oakland, San Mateo, Van Nuys, San Diego, and Santa Ana.[9]

In his speeches, Reagan cast the primary's outcome in stark terms. "The issue in this election," he said in San Diego in early May, "is whether we believe in man's capacity for self-government or whether we abandon the American Revolution . . . and say an elite group far away in the capital can govern us."[10] Introducing Goldwater at a rally at Orange County's Knott's Berry Farm, a smiling Reagan reflected about two ways he might describe Goldwater to the crowd. One, he said, was as the true voice of Republicanism. Or, he mused, "Should he be introduced as a Neanderthal man, a bigot, a warmonger, looking out at us from the 19th century?" To which Charles Mohr, the *New York Times* reporter covering the event, observed: "To some hearers it seemed doubtful that such questions—televised to a large audience—were very useful to Mr. Goldwater in his struggle with [Rockefeller], even though they were intended as biting attacks on the opposition." Like Goldwater, Reagan was angry over the liberal Republican assault on Goldwater. He told the crowd the criticism was the "most vicious and venomous campaign against a candidate in our party we have ever seen."[11]

Appearing with Goldwater at a dinner at the Biltmore Hotel in Los Angeles, Reagan had warned guests about "a conspiracy in the Eastern liberal press" that wanted to "discredit a great American by creating a false image and running against that. But *they* aren't going to get away with it." Journalist Joseph Lewis noted Reagan's message was "standard Goldwater cant, but Reagan delivered it as though he had discovered a new insight: there were plotters and he was exposing them. An angry roar of approval rose from the crowd; Reagan got more applause than Goldwater, who breezed through his speech."[12]

Goldwater and Reagan were striking contrasts in style. Goldwater was often grumpy on the stump. Adoring crowds often cheered his introduction at rallies with extended chants of "We want Barry! We want Barry!" Goldwater had little appreciation or patience for such theater. He would sometimes lean into the microphone and growl, "If you'll shut up, you'll get him." Then, as writer Rick Perlstein wrote in his history of the Goldwater campaign, "he'd stick a hand in a pocket, slouch into the podium—and deliver overcooked broccoli to a crowd demanding raw meat."

Reagan, on the other hand, delighted in speaking to an audience and bending them to his will. Goldwater regarded campaigning as a chore. Reagan understood audiences came for a performance, not a lecture. At the end of one rally, Reagan, who had already spoken, mounted the podium again and brought the crowd to its feet with his closing message. After Reagan finished speaking at a fund-raising event in San Francisco—with Goldwater also in attendance—a member of the hotel's wait staff turned to a prominent Goldwater supporter and asked, "I'm confused. Which one was the candidate?"[13]

On primary day, Goldwater edged out Rockefeller to win the all-important state by 68,350 votes out of 2.1 million cast. In losing, Rockefeller carried forty-five of California's fifty-eight counties, but a massive turnout in conservative Southern California provided Goldwater the victory. In Orange and Los Angeles Counties, he outpaced Rockefeller by a combined 207,000 votes.[14] That night Reagan spoke to Goldwater's victory party at Los Angeles's Ambassador Hotel. The crowd was jubilant but still angry with Rockefeller for his pointed attacks on their candidate. "We are going to have to forget an awful lot of bitterness and that we don't want to win a convention, we want to win an election," Reagan told the crowd from the podium. "Let's start making love to Democrats." The crowd was not ready to entertain thoughts of conciliation. When Reagan mentioned that he had once worked to elect Harry Truman, some in the audience responded with hisses.[15] Reagan would later tell an interviewer, "The party was shattered and split right down the middle."[16]

The intense, heartfelt enthusiasm of Goldwater's California

supporters had been important to his success. Just as important, however, was Rockefeller's troubled personal life. As one of Goldwater's prominent supporters, journalist William Rusher, observed, "Only Rockefeller could turn motherhood into a liability."[17] After his defeat, Rockefeller withdrew and threw his support to a reluctant Scranton and urged Nixon and Eisenhower to do the same. No doubt recognizing the inevitability of Goldwater's nomination and not wanting to further split their party, the former president and his vice president remained on the sidelines and, after the convention, offered Goldwater lukewarm support.[18]

Goldwater's "juggernaut flattened the GOP moderates," *Time* observed, as supporters of the losing candidates brooded about their party's expected loss in November. Others worried about Goldwater's behavior should he win. "Can you imagine what would have happened if Goldwater had been in the White House during the Cuban missile crisis?" an aide to Michigan governor George Romney, a prominent Goldwater detractor, asked a reporter for *Time*, who wrote: "The aide thereupon touched a lighted cigarette to an inflated balloon. Pop!"[19] Romney was bitter about Goldwater's win, threatening shortly after the California primary to do "everything within my power to keep him from becoming the party's candidate."[20] Their machinations proved fruitless.

NOW THAT GOLDWATER WAS the nominee, Reagan was eager to play an even larger role in his friend's presidential campaign. He would attend the Republican convention as an alternate California delegate. He would applaud, with the rest of Goldwater's delegates, as his candidate embraced the extremist label in his acceptance speech. "I would remind you," Goldwater said to wild, sustained applause, "that extremism in the defense of liberty is no vice. And let me remind you also that moderation in the pursuit of justice is no virtue."[21] Not everyone loved the line. Nixon, seated in the hall, did not clap. An alternate delegate in the Pennsylvania delegation told a UPI reporter afterward that the nominee had "read decent Republicans out of the party and the John Birchers into it."[22] These and other harsh comments proved the gathering had been no love fest. In fact, Goldwater's convention had marked a decisive shift in the party's balance of power away from the East Coast establishment that had ruled it for decades—a shocking and disorienting development for many liberals and moderates. "This convention is historic," columnist Murray Kempton wrote, "because it is the emancipation of the serfs. . . . The serfs have seized the estate of their masters."[23]

Besides Goldwater's "extremism" line, the most memorable image of the convention came when Goldwater delegates heckled and booed as Rockefeller struggled to deliver his speech. "The Republican party is in real danger of subversion by a radical, well-financed minority," Rockefeller lectured delegates as they considered amendments to the party's platform at the convention's Wednesday session.[24] It is doubtful Reagan was among those booing Rockefeller, but he did not hide his unabashed enthusiasm for Goldwater and his message before, during, and after the contentious convention. And Reagan would enlist completely in Goldwater's fall campaign, so much so that he expected to chair Goldwater's general election effort in California.

That decision forced Reagan into a confrontation with Philip Davis, a prominent Southern California business executive and former state assemblyman, who also wanted the position. When Goldwater campaign leaders gathered in Los Angeles to decide on the California chairmanship, the meeting grew contentious. "The Davis group felt they had earned the right to run the show in California, since many of them had been among Senator Goldwater's earliest and most active supporters in that state," Clifton White, a Goldwater campaign strategist, recalled. As the meeting grew heated and the attacks on Reagan became pointed, White prepared to stand and intervene in Reagan's defense. Before he could do so, Reagan grasped his arm. "No, Clif," Reagan whispered. "This is my fight. Let me handle it." Reagan confessed he had less political experience than Davis. Then, White recalled, he "went on to offer such persuasive arguments for his involvement in the campaign that the meeting broke up in a happy compromise: Reagan and Davis would serve as Co-Chairmen for Citizens for Goldwater in California."[25] Reagan described the arrangement: "While another cochairman managed day-to-day operations of the campaign, my job was to travel around the state speaking on behalf of Barry and to help him raise campaign funds."[26]

Reagan was not the only member of his family to enlist in the Goldwater campaign. His brother, Neil, was the West Coast vice president for McCann Erickson, the advertising firm that would oversee production of Goldwater's campaign spots and television programs. Among Neil's assignments was to accompany Goldwater on the campaign's American Airlines 727. To the press on Goldwater's jet, Neil did more than promote Goldwater's candidacy. According to Lyn Nofziger, the Copley Newspapers reporter assigned to cover Goldwater's team, Neil bragged about his brother's burgeoning political ambitions. "We're going to run Ronnie against [California Republican U.S. senator] Tommy Kuchel no matter what Kuchel runs for," Nofziger, who would work for Reagan in his 1966 governor's race, recalled Neil boasting.[27]

He may have had his eyes on an office of his own (although he denied it to anyone who asked), but Reagan poured himself into the work of electing Goldwater, oblivious to the near impossibility of his candidate's election. "I covered the state of California from top to bottom," he later said.[28] Reagan told an interviewer in 1967 that he worked "full time . . . averaging about five or six appearances a day."[29]

His first major role in the California campaign came in early September at a massive rally at Dodger Stadium in Los Angeles to mark the beginning of Goldwater's general election campaign in California. The event featured one hundred "Goldwater Girls, rodeo trick rider Montie Montana and his western troupe, and a baby elephant, which rode into the stadium in a vintage Rolls Royce behind the San Fernando Valley Youth Band.[30] Reagan served as master of ceremonies, introducing retired Air Force Gen. James Doolittle, who had led the first bombing raid on Tokyo during World War II. Before turning over the microphone to Doolittle, Reagan entertained the crowd of 53,000 with jabs at Lyndon Johnson and California's Democratic governor, Pat Brown, joking, "The governor couldn't be here to welcome [Goldwater]. This is his night to tear off bumper stickers." Of Johnson, Reagan made a crack about the president's disgraced former aide, Bobby

Baker, under investigation for corruption and a frequent target of Goldwater's attacks. Johnson, Reagan said, "just wants to prove he can do for us what he did for Bobby Baker." To cheers and boisterous applause, Reagan added, Johnson "is the only man who can read *Uncle Tom's Cabin* and think Simon Legree was the hero." Reagan added a dig at Johnson's wife, Lady Bird, whose Austin television station, KTBC, was the source of much of the president's wealth. Reagan suggested that a rumor circulating in Washington was "that just before the election Lyndon is going to put the country in his wife's name."[31]

Reagan's remarks at this rally were among the most pungent comments he would utter about the presidential race. As he campaigned around California for Goldwater, he usually offered little more than warmed-over versions of the speech he had delivered to audiences across the country for the past decade. To a Goldwater event at a high school in Santa Cruz in late September, Reagan repeated his shopworn lines about Communism. "We are at war with the most-evil enemy of all time—the Communists—and we are losing that war because most Americans don't believe we are in it." Audiences and local journalists, even if they knew they were hearing a well-worn speech, did not care. As the reporter covering the event wrote, "The handsome speaker, glancing only occasionally at his notes, held the audience spellbound."[32]

At most stops on the campaign trail, Reagan shared one of his favorite applause lines. He told listeners Johnson's antipoverty programs granted an average of $4,700 for room and board for youth training camps in the federal Job Corps program, an initiative many conservatives hated. "Hell," Reagan said to raucous laughter, "we can send 'em to Harvard for $2,700!"[33] (Tuition at Harvard University in 1964 was about $1,520.)[34] As late as 1985, the first year of his second term in the White House, Reagan would repeat variations of this line. By then, Reagan claimed the cost of Job Corps training had risen to $15,200.[35] Reagan also regularly ridiculed the idea of government assistance for the poor. Another applause line that had found its way into his speech was: "There is an increasing number of Americans who can't see a fat man standing beside a thin one without automatically coming to the conclusion that the fat man got that way by taking advantage of the thin one." Reagan would repeat this line into the 1980s.[36]

"LBJ is campaigning on the slogan 'Peace and Prosperity,'" Reagan told a group of 150 students in Kentfield at the College of Marin cafeteria on October 22. "They say, 'You never had it so good.' Well, there may be peace for the rest of us, but some of you probably will be in South Vietnam soon, fighting a total war."[37] A few days later, in San Rafael, Reagan spoke to about 450 "spellbound" Goldwater supporters at the local high school. "We should say to the enemy we have no aggressive intent," Reagan said. "But we should say to him there is a point beyond which he dare not advance, because there is a price we will not pay!"[38]

Reagan's speeches in these small California towns dazzled audiences. "If Oscars were passed out for articulate spokesmen, the odds are almost certain that the 1964 winner would be a man who has never run for political office," reporter Bill Strobel wrote about Reagan in the *Oakland Tribune* on October 30. "What Reagan has to say about Goldwater, about freedom of the individual, and about constitutional government has, according to one GOP official, 'set off the most amazing response I've ever seen in any political campaign.'"[39]

Historian Matthew Dallek, who studied Reagan's early political career, wrote that his speeches for Goldwater "were popular, but to moderates and liberals, Reagan mainly deepened the impression that conservatives were anti-Communist paranoids who saw subversives under every rock." Dallek believed Reagan "came across as just one of many angry Goldwaterites on a quixotic crusade."[40] Clifton White thought such characterizations were unfair. "It became obvious to me that he was a serious, genuinely thoughtful man who bore little resemblance to the image that even then was being painted of him as a superficial actor with no real grasp of the issues confronting the country," White wrote in 1981.[41] Another campaign aide, William Middendorf, remembered Reagan in a similar way: "I called Reagan almost every day and found him willing, with great good spirit, to take on any assignment at a moment's notice." Middendorf recalled Reagan "always deliver[ed] a great message. He may have given some 100 speeches."[42]

Where Reagan deviated from his usual rhetoric was to defend Goldwater against attacks by Democrats who echoed charges by some Republicans that Goldwater was a bellicose, trigger-happy cowboy who would start a nuclear war. In April 1964 Goldwater released a policy paper that contained a proposal to give the supreme NATO commander in Europe "direct command over a NATO nuclear force, trained, ready, and equipped on European soil." The notion of a field general with unilateral authority to use nuclear weapons did not create much news until Goldwater repeated it in Cleveland in late August. There he explained the nuclear weapons he would entrust to the generals "may truly be called, and ultimately will be called, conventional weapons."[43] In an interview about the same time, Goldwater described these nuclear weapons as "very small."[44] Johnson and other Democrats pounced, using that remark and others Goldwater had made about nuclear weapons to pummel him. "For nineteen peril-filled years," Johnson told a crowd of 100,000 in Detroit on September 7, "no nation has loosed the atom [bomb] against another. To do so now is a political decision of the highest order, and it would lead us down an uncertain path of blows and counterblows whose outcome none may know." Johnson insisted that "no president of the United States can divest himself of the responsibility for such a decision."[45]

In his remarks at a Goldwater rally in San Diego on October 14, Reagan defended his friend by going on the attack. "We have been lied to by [Defense Secretary Robert] McNamara, by [Vice President Hubert] Humphrey, and by the president of the United States," Reagan said. He echoed Goldwater's argument that the bomb in question was a small, tactical weapon. And he repeated the assertion by many Goldwater supporters that thirty NATO commanders "have had the authority to drop the big bombs without the president's permission under certain circumstances."[46] A few weeks later, to an audience at a San Rafael high school, Reagan assured his listeners that Goldwater was not "a man who would recklessly send others to war."[47]

Goldwater disciples who heard Reagan's emotional warnings about Communism and out-of-control government did not know or care that Reagan delivered lines he had rehearsed so much he could reel them off like extemporaneous ruminations. Everywhere Reagan went, especially in the small towns in rural California, local papers promoted his appearances and greeted him like a major celebrity or significant political figure. "Political monologue replaced movieland dialogue at a Republican dinner at Redwood Acres last night as actor Ronald Reagan turned all guns on the Democratic Administration of President Johnson," the *Eureka Humboldt Standard* reported on October 6 after Reagan's visit to that northern California seaside city.[48] Of Reagan's early October trip to Petaluma, columnist Bill Soberanes of the *Argus-Courier* led his story thus: "Politics create some colorful situations, and there's always an extra touch of excitement when a movie actor of Ronald Reagan's stature appears on the scene." Soberanes assured readers that Reagan "did a magnificent job of eulogizing [sic] Barry Goldwater."[49] After Reagan's appearance in early October in Auburn, northeast of Sacramento, the local paper raved: "Actor Ronald Reagan, still boyish looking at 53, delighted more than 800 persons here last week by calling for a Republican sweep on election day and claiming that Barry Goldwater will halt the advance of socialism in the United States."[50]

Reagan had charmed the crowd at a major Goldwater fund-raising event in Los Angeles the week before at the Cocoanut Grove, a tropical-themed nightclub in the Ambassador Hotel. Holmes Tuttle, a prominent Southern California Ford dealer and longtime Reagan friend and admirer, had helped organize the $1,000-a-plate event (more than $8,000 in 2019 dollars) to raise money for Goldwater's campaign. A tall, balding, soft-spoken man, Tuttle had been a force in California Republican politics since 1956. That year, he had supported Eisenhower's reelection and, with good friend and drugstore magnate Justin Dart, raised money for Republican candidates while quietly asserting himself within the party. For the event's speaker, Tuttle wanted one headliner who could draw a crowd and inspire an audience. He quickly settled on Reagan. Goldwater would address the crowd by film, while the candidate's wife, Peggy, would attend but not speak.[51]

On the night of the event, before an audience of about five hundred guests—some of the most influential and wealthy

Republicans in Southern California—Reagan delivered precisely the speech Tuttle had expected. "I gave basically the same talk I'd been giving for years," Reagan later wrote, "altering it slightly so that it became a campaign speech for Barry." Reagan recalled he spoke of "the relentless expansion of the federal government, the proliferation of government bureaucrats who were taking control of American business, and criticized liberal Democrats for taking the country down the road to socialism." Reagan did not regard his twenty-minute talk as remarkable. "It was a speech, I suppose, that, with variations, I'd given hundreds of times before," he recalled.[52] However, the response from audience members, some of whom had never heard it, was overwhelming. They gave him a standing ovation. "To Ronnie it was just another speech, another audience to charm," biographer Lawrence Leamer wrote, "but it was a call to arms to the dispirited Goldwaterites, a warning against the Soviet threat, and to many a signal to rally around a new conservative champion."[53]

Watching from their table at the rear of the room were Tuttle and another friend of Reagan's, Henry Salvatori, a prominent Republican fund-raiser and founder and CEO of the Western Geophysical Company, the world's largest offshore seismic contractor. As Reagan basked in the applause, the two men glanced at each other in amazement. When the dinner was over, Tuttle said attendees swarmed him, suggesting he find a larger forum for Reagan to deliver his message. "We were swamped with requests," Tuttle said, remembering that people told him, "My God, these are the issues, these are the things that Goldwater has been missing. These are the things that we and all the people are concerned about today. He [Goldwater] has gotten himself into the position of always defending himself." One person suggested putting Reagan and his message on television. The idea made sense to Tuttle and Salvatori.[54]

After the crowd left the nightclub, they invited Reagan to drop by their table. Once seated, the group asked if he would deliver the speech on television if they could raise money for the airtime. "Sure," Reagan replied, "if you think it would do any good." As they discussed what such a program would look like, Reagan offered a shrewd idea. "If we did it, I suggested that instead of repeating my speech in front of a camera in a television studio, it might be more effective if I spoke to an audience in a setting similar to the one in which they'd heard it." Reagan understood the advantage of speaking to a live audience that would respond to his words with applause and laughter, as opposed to talking to a cold, unresponsive camera in an empty television studio.[55]

James Kilroy, a forty-two-year-old real estate developer best known as a champion yachter, had not been among those attending the Cocoanut Grove dinner. But he agreed to help raise the money to air Reagan's speech on national television after public relations executive Robert Raisbeck told him about Reagan's words and the audience's enthusiastic response. Kilroy said he traveled to Washington, where he met with Dean Burch, chairman of the Republican National Committee, and Ralph Cordiner, General Electric's former president who now served as Goldwater's national fund-raising chair. "Both Ralph and Dean bought into the concept," Kilroy later wrote, adding that to produce and air the program, the California group formed a separate "Barry Goldwater Television Committee." Kilroy said the funding plan "was simple: Henry Salvatori and I would put up 'seed money' for the filming, editing, and airtime for the first show." They expected Kilroy would end the program with a pitch for contributions "that could be put towards future shows."[56]

Kilroy's memory was faulty. In fact, Reagan's friends had created a Los Angeles–based, semiautonomous organization, "TV for Goldwater-Miller," in September, weeks before the Cocoanut Grove speech, so the idea for a televised Reagan speech did not inspire the committee. (The group, according to a report in the October 12, 1964, edition of *Broadcasting* magazine, included Salvatori, Tuttle, anti-Communist activist W. Cleon Skousen, television director Robert "Doc" Livingston, Walter Beardsley of Miles Laboratories, Patrick Frawley of Schick Safety Razor Co., Coalson Morris of Electra Motors, Atlanta business executive Thomas Callaway Jr., Los Angeles attorney Marshall McDaniel, and Walter Knott and Frank White, both of Knott's Berry Farm in Orange County.)[57]

From its California headquarters, the group sent out letters asking for funds to support producing and airing television programs on behalf of Goldwater's campaign. With the money the letters generated, the committee produced a half-hour film of a Goldwater rally at Boston's Fenway Park on September 24 and a two-hour recording of a so-called "Captive Nations Rally" on September 30 in Los Angeles. Each program ended with a fund-raising appeal. The committee sent copies to local Goldwater organizations, urging them to raise money to show its programming on television stations in their communities. The two-hour program, the committee suggested, could be the basis for local fund-raising telethons for Goldwater's campaign. "It's a sort of self-supporting spiral that never stops growing," a committee spokesperson told *Broadcasting* in early October. "Every time we get one show on the air, it brings in enough money to get us started toward the next one."[58]

More likely Kilroy's trip to Washington was about folding the newly conceived Reagan speech and others into programming the campaign and Kilroy's committee had already agreed to produce. "They wanted to have some official recognition so that they would be assigned or else [be] allowed to select certain functions that needed to be done," recalled Gardiner Johnson, then a member of the Republican National Committee from California, "and they would do it themselves without the intervention of the national committee or Goldwater committee staff."[59]

The California committee had access to large sums of money, a reality that forced the Goldwater campaign to tolerate its efforts. In mid-September, the committee reported to the Goldwater committee it would spend at least $300,000 a week for television spots for Goldwater, beginning September 16. This figure was likely eye-popping to officials in Washington. A rogue but supportive committee of California businessmen would buy as much as $1.8 million (almost $15 million in 2019 dollars) in television advertising for Goldwater (by early November it would raise and spend more than $2 million).[60] A memo by the RNC's advertising agency—after a meeting with the California committee's Raisbeck—suggested the campaign would accept the committee's help but would not cede control over its advertising. As the report noted, "The [RNC] agency stated they must control all production for such projects."[61] This was the first inkling that the relationship between the Goldwater campaign and the California committee would hit rough waters.

Kilroy and his partners next hired Raisbeck's Los Angeles firm, P.R. Counsellors, Ltd., to produce Reagan's program.[62] The price of the first network production was substantial. When it would air on NBC the night of October 27, the half-hour of airtime would cost the group $115,236. That included $22,300 to preempt the network's scheduled program hosted by David Frost, *That Was the Week That Was.*[63]

Reagan had suggested taping one of his regular speaking engagements for Goldwater in California, but the logistics of staging a network-quality production outside a studio would have been daunting.[64] Instead, Raisbeck rented an NBC studio in Burbank and created a space that would look to the television audience like a meeting hall or hotel ballroom. In front of about four hundred metal folding chairs arranged in theater style, Raisbeck designed a high stage, adorned with red-white-and-blue bunting, on which stood a large lectern outfitted with two microphones. Reagan would stand alone on this stage before a dark, draped background. On the wall to the right of where the audience would sit was a row of pleated drapes on which hung two large campaign posters featuring Goldwater's image. Raisbeck would record the program with several RCA color cameras using videotape. This included one camera on a boom that would sweep across the room and focus on Reagan, at the podium, in the program's first minute.[65]

On Monday, October 12 (probably in the evening), Reagan took the stage to applause from the audience of Goldwater supporters and Republican activists. The television audience would later hear an announcer opening the program, "The following prerecorded political program is sponsored by 'TV for Goldwater-Miller' on behalf of Barry Goldwater, Republican candidate for president of the United States. Ladies and gentlemen, we take pride in presenting a thoughtful address by Ronald Reagan."

14

A Rendezvous with Destiny

Wearing a trim, dark suit with a white shirt and white pocket square (on television, his clothing would almost disappear into the shaded background), Reagan launched into his speech. "Thank you and good evening," he began. "The sponsor has been identified, but unlike most television programs, the performer hasn't been provided with a script. As a matter of fact, I have been permitted to choose my own words and discuss my own ideas regarding the choice that we face in the next few weeks. I have spent most of my life as a Democrat. I recently have seen fit to follow another course." The statement about his party change was accurate enough. Reagan had left his former party two years earlier. But anyone who knew him or had attended one of his speeches from the mid-1950s onward would have known him as a conservative Republican. Reagan continued:

> I believe that the issues confronting us cross party lines. Now, one side in this campaign has been telling us that the issues of this election are the maintenance of peace and prosperity. The line has been used, "We've never had it so good."
>
> But I have an uncomfortable feeling that this prosperity isn't something on which we can base our hopes for the future. No nation in history has ever survived a tax burden that reached

a third of its national income. Today, thirty-seven cents out of every dollar earned in this country is the tax collector's share, and yet our government continues to spend $17 million a day more than the government takes in. We haven't balanced our budget twenty-eight out of the last thirty-four years. We've raised our debt limit three times in the last twelve months, and now our national debt is one-and-a-half times bigger than all the combined debts of all the nations of the world. We have $15 billion in gold in our treasury; we don't own an ounce. Foreign dollar claims are $27.3 billion. And we've just had announced that the dollar of 1939 will now purchase forty-five cents in its total value.

As for the peace that we would preserve, I wonder who among us would like to approach the wife or mother whose husband or son has died in South Vietnam and ask them if they think this is a peace that should be maintained indefinitely. Do they mean peace, or do they mean we just want to be left in peace? There can be no real peace while one American is dying someplace in the world for the rest of us. We're at war with the most dangerous enemy that has ever faced mankind in his long climb from the swamp to the stars, and it's been said if we lose that war, and in so doing lose this way of freedom of ours, history will record with the greatest astonishment that those who had the most to lose did the least to prevent its happening. Well, I think it's time we ask ourselves if we still know the freedoms that were intended for us by the Founding Fathers.

Not too long ago, two friends of mine were talking to a Cuban refugee, a businessman who had escaped from Castro and, in the midst of his story, one of my friends turned to the other and said, "We don't know how lucky we are." And the Cuban stopped and said, "How lucky you are? I had someplace to escape to." And in that sentence, he told us the entire story. If we lose freedom here, there's no place to escape to. This is the last stand on earth.

And this idea that government is beholden to the people, that it has no other source of power except the sovereign people, is still the newest and the most unique idea in all the long history of man's relation to man.

For the first few minutes of his speech, Reagan hurried through his words. His voice was clipped. He was stern. Despite having appeared on film and television for decades, he appeared slightly nervous. Audience members, unaccustomed to serving as props for a television production, may have been uneasy, too. That would explain why they did not respond after Reagan's early, dependable applause lines. Silence from an anxious audience appeared to throw Reagan off stride. In the speech's first minutes, he struggled to find his pace as he tried to gauge his studio audience. He knew he was also talking to the millions of viewers who would watch him and hear his words a few weeks later. He did not speak from a text, but delivered his remarks, as always, using note cards on which he had printed, in shorthand, the phrases he wanted to deliver. He had spoken these words dozens of times in the months and years before this moment:

> This is the issue of this election: whether we believe in our capacity for self-government or whether we abandon the American revolution and confess that a little intellectual elite in a far-distant capital can plan our lives for us better than we can plan them ourselves.
>
> You and I are told increasingly we have to choose between a left or right. Well I'd like to suggest there is no such thing as a left or right. There's only an up or down: man's old—old-aged dream, the ultimate in individual freedom consistent with law and order, or down to the ant heap of totalitarianism. And regardless of their sincerity, their humanitarian motives, those who would trade our freedom for security have embarked on this downward course.

Next Reagan turned to an attack on the social and economic reforms that President Lyndon Johnson had pushed through Congress earlier that year: "In this vote-harvesting time, they use terms like the 'Great Society,' or as we were told a few days ago by the President, we must accept a 'greater government activity in the affairs of the people.' But they have been a little more explicit in the past and among themselves—and all of the things that I now will quote have appeared in print. These are not Republican accusations. For example, they have voices that say 'the cold war will end through acceptance of a not undemocratic socialism.' Another voice says that the profit motive has become outmoded; it must be replaced by the incentives of the welfare state; or our traditional system of individual freedom is incapable of solving the complex problems of the twentieth century."

When he turned to farm policy, Reagan said the "Founding Fathers" knew "that outside of its legitimate functions, government does nothing as well or as economically as the private sector of the economy. Now, we have no better example of this than government's involvement in the farm economy over the last thirty years." Next came a flurry of statistics: "Since 1955, the cost of this program has nearly doubled. One-fourth of farming in America is responsible for 85 percent of the farm surplus. Three-fourths of farming is out on the free market and has known a 21 percent increase in the per capita consumption of all its produce. You see, that one-fourth of farming—that's regulated and controlled by the federal government. In the last three years we've spent $43 in the feed grain program for every bushel of corn we don't grow."

As Reagan approached eight minutes, one-third of the way into his speech, he relaxed. He was looser, more connected to the audience. He found a comfortable pace. He also delivered familiar lines on well-worn themes with barely a glance at his notes. He continued to speak about farming: "The Secretary of Agriculture asked for the right to seize farms through condemnation and resell them to other individuals. And contained in that same program was a provision that would have allowed the federal government to remove two million farmers from the soil. At the same time, there's been an increase in the Department of Agriculture employees. There's now one for every thirty farms in the United States, and still they can't tell us how sixty-six shiploads of grain headed for Austria disappeared without a trace and Billie Sol Estes never left shore."

That last line—about a Texas businessman with ties to Lyndon Johnson, convicted on federal fraud charges in 1963—sparked the first laughter and applause of the speech. Ninety seconds later, Reagan provoked more laughter with this reference to the federal Area Redevelopment Agency: "They've just declared Rice County, Kansas, a depressed area." He paused for a second, then added: "Rice County, Kansas, has two hundred oil wells, and the 14,000 people there have over $30 million on deposit in personal savings in their banks. And when the government tells you you're depressed, lie down and be depressed."

As he had done for months in his speeches, Reagan mocked the idea the government could—or should—try to alleviate hunger and poverty: "So they're going to solve all the problems of human misery through government and government planning. Well, now, if government planning and welfare had the answer—and they've had almost thirty years of it—shouldn't we expect government to read the score to us once in a while? Shouldn't they be telling us about the decline each year in the number of people needing help? The reduction in the need for public housing? But the reverse is true. Each year the need grows greater; the program grows greater. We were told four years ago that 17 million people went to bed hungry each night. Well, that was probably true. They were all on a diet."

For the first ten minutes, Reagan had lectured his audience with a rapid-fire barrage of facts. Brimming with barely concealed indignation—one historian described it as "simmering rage"—Reagan hardly smiled.[1] Now he slowed his pace and, for the first time, he gestured naturally. This, finally, was the Reagan that audiences around the country had seen and heard for years. This was the Reagan who might persuade a crowd he was speaking these words from the heart. Perhaps he relaxed because he was talking about one of his favorite topics—federal welfare policy.

Now—so now we declare "war on poverty," or "You, too, can be a Bobby Baker."[2] Now do they honestly expect us to believe that if we add $1 billion to the $45 billion we're spending, one more program to the thirty-odd we have—and remember, this new program doesn't replace any, it just duplicates existing programs—do they believe that poverty is suddenly going to disappear by magic?

Well, in all fairness I should explain there is one part of the new program that isn't duplicated. This is the youth feature. We're now going to solve the dropout problem, juvenile delinquency, by reinstituting something like the old CCC [Civilian Conservation Corps] camps and we're going to put our young people in these camps. But, again, we do some arithmetic, and we find that we're going to spend each year, just on room and board, for each young person we help $47,000 a year. We can send them to Harvard for $2,700 ! Course, don't get me wrong. I'm not suggesting Harvard is the answer to juvenile delinquency.

The audience laughed at the Harvard quip, a well-worn line he knew would provoke a reaction. He gave them another example of welfare abuse and another flurry of numbers. "But seriously, what are we doing to those we seek to help?" he asked, explaining, "Not too long ago, a judge called me here in Los Angeles. He told me of a young woman who'd come before him for a divorce. She had six children, was pregnant with her seventh. Under his questioning, she revealed her husband was a laborer earning $250 a month. She wanted a divorce to get an $8 raise. She's eligible for $330 a month in the Aid to Dependent Children Program. She got the idea from two women in her neighborhood who'd already done that very thing." (Decades later, journalists and some historians would castigate Reagan for creating a mythological "welfare queen" during his 1976 campaign for president. As this and other Reagan speeches from the 1960s show, he had peddled this myth for decades.)[3]

Reagan now waded into the most controversial portion of his program, one that would prompt Goldwater's aides in Washington to consider forbidding his California friends from broadcasting it. "Now, we're for a provision that destitution should not follow unemployment by reason of old age, and to that end we've accepted Social Security as a step toward meeting the problem,"

Reagan said. "But we're against those entrusted with this program when they practice deception regarding its fiscal shortcomings, when they charge that any criticism of the program means that we want to end payments to those people who depend on them for a livelihood." Reagan presented the standard conservative argument against compulsory Social Security: "They've called it 'insurance' to us in a hundred million pieces of literature. But then they appeared before the Supreme Court and they testified it was a welfare program. They only use the term 'insurance' to sell it to the people."

Making his case for a voluntary system, Reagan said "a young man, twenty-one years of age, working at an average salary," could purchase an insurance policy "that would guarantee $220 a month at age sixty-five. The government promises $127. He could live it up until he's thirty-one and then take out a policy that would pay more than Social Security." Reagan wondered, "How are we so lacking in business sense that we can't put this program on a sound basis, so that people who do require those payments will find they can get them when they're due, that the cupboard isn't bare? Barry Goldwater thinks we can." Then Reagan uttered the most radical argument of the speech, one that Johnson would use against Goldwater in speeches and television commercials:

At the same time, can't we introduce voluntary features that would permit a citizen who can do better on his own to be excused upon presentation of evidence that he had made provision for the non-earning years? Should we not allow a widow with children to work and not lose the benefits supposedly paid for by her deceased husband? Shouldn't you and I be allowed to declare who our beneficiaries will be under this program, which we cannot do? I think we're for telling our senior citizens that no one in this country should be denied medical care because of a lack of funds. But I think we're against forcing all citizens, regardless of need, into a compulsory government program, especially when we have such examples, as was announced last week, when France admitted that their Medicare program is now bankrupt. They've come to the end of the road.

(History would prove this an inaccurate portrayal of the French health care system. In early October, after Goldwater made the same charge, French officials issued a statement asserting that the country's health care system was financially sound.)[4]

Reagan next launched into his standard diatribe against foreign aid, unleashing more statistics. "We set out to help 19 countries," he said. "We're helping 107. We've spent $146 billion. With that money, we bought a $2 million yacht for [Ethiopian emperor] Haile Selassie. We bought dress suits for Greek undertakers, extra wives for Kenya[n] government officials. We bought a thousand TV sets for a place where they have no electricity. In the last six years, 52 nations have bought $7 billion worth of our gold, and all 52 are receiving foreign aid from this country." (Contrary to Reagan's assertion, which other conservatives also promoted, the Ethiopian ship was a converted U.S. Navy seaplane tender given to the country to serve as the flagship of its fledgling navy.)[5]

He fired another volley of figures when he turned to his standard attack on the growth and reach of the federal government. "No government ever voluntarily reduces itself in size," he declared. "So governments' programs, once launched, never disappear. Actually, a government bureau is the nearest thing to eternal life we'll ever see on this earth." The audience chuckled as he fed them even more statistics on government employment, punctuated with this anecdote: "In Chico County, Arkansas, James Weir overplanted his rice allotment. The government obtained a $17,000 judgment. And a U.S. marshal sold his 960-acre farm at auction. The government said it was necessary as a warning to others to make the system work."

Reagan had rarely mentioned Goldwater during the first twenty minutes. He did not speak the candidate's name until he explained his position on Social Security at the fifteen-minute mark. But what he said next, while not part of his standard message, was some of the most powerful and emotional language of the broadcast. "Last February 19 at the University of Minnesota, Norman Thomas, six-times candidate for president on the Socialist Party ticket, said, 'If Barry Goldwater became president, he would stop the advance of socialism in the United States.'" Reagan paused slightly before declaring, "I think that's exactly what he will do." The audience roared its approval.

After a brief assault on socialism in America, Reagan observed, "Our Democratic opponents seem unwilling to debate these issues. They want to make you and I believe that this is a contest between two men—that we're to choose just between two personalities." Now Reagan turned personal in his words about Goldwater and defended not his candidate's political philosophy but his compassion and integrity: "Well, what of this man that they would destroy—and in destroying, they would destroy that which he represents, the ideas that you and I hold dear? Is he the brash and shallow and trigger-happy man they say he is? Well, I've been privileged to know him 'when.' I knew him long before he ever dreamed of trying for high office, and I can tell you personally I've never known a man in my life I believed so incapable of doing a dishonest or dishonorable thing."

Reagan described two episodes from Goldwater's life he said showed the nominee's humanity. "This is a man who, in his own business before he entered politics, instituted a profit-sharing plan before unions had ever thought of it. He put in health and medical insurance for all his employees. He took 50 percent of the profits before taxes and set up a retirement program, a pension plan for all his employees." Reagan said Goldwater "sent monthly checks for life to an employee who was ill and couldn't work" and "he provides nursing care for the children of mothers who work in the stores. When Mexico was ravaged by the floods in the Rio Grande, he climbed in his airplane and flew medicine and supplies down there."

Then Reagan told a compelling story about Goldwater, a moving account the candidate's staff had not publicized:

An ex-GI told me how he met him. It was the week before Christmas during the Korean War, and he was at the Los Angeles airport trying to get a ride home to Arizona for Christmas. And he said that [there were] a lot of servicemen there and no seats available on the planes. And then a voice came over the loudspeaker and said, "Any men in uniform wanting a ride to

Arizona, go to runway such-and-such," and they went down there, and there was a fellow named Barry Goldwater sitting in his plane. Every day in those weeks before Christmas, all day long, he'd load up the plane, fly it to Arizona, fly them to their homes, fly back over to get another load.

Reagan told another story about Goldwater. "During the hectic split-second timing of a campaign, this is a man who took time out to sit beside an old friend who was dying of cancer." Then he arrived at the main point of his stories about his friend's decency and concern for people: he is not a warmonger, as Johnson's campaign would have you believe. "This is not a man who could carelessly send other people's sons to war. And that is the issue of this campaign that makes all the other problems I've discussed academic, unless we realize we're in a war that must be won."

That statement set up Reagan's passionate defense of Goldwater's policy of toughness against Communism and the Soviet Union. "Those who would trade our freedom for the soup kitchen of the welfare state have told us they have a utopian solution of peace without victory. They call their policy 'accommodation.' And they say if we'll only avoid any direct confrontation with the enemy, he'll forget his evil ways and learn to love us. All who oppose them are indicted as warmongers. They say we offer simple answers to complex problems. Well, perhaps there is a simple answer—not an easy answer—but simple: if you and I have the courage to tell our elected officials that we want our national policy based on what we know in our hearts is morally right."

Reagan acknowledged the risks of a confrontational military strategy. He added: "Every lesson of history tells us that the greater risk lies in appeasement, and this is the specter our well-meaning liberal friends refuse to face—that their policy of accommodation is appeasement, and it gives no choice between peace and war, only between fight or surrender. If we continue to accommodate, continue to back and retreat, eventually we have to face the final demand—the ultimatum."

Citing Nikita Khrushchev, Reagan asserted the Soviet leader had said that the United States is "retreating under the pressure of the Cold War, and someday when the time comes to deliver the final ultimatum, our surrender will be voluntary, because by that time we will have been weakened from within spiritually, morally, and economically." Khrushchev arrived at this belief, Reagan argued, after hearing American voices "pleading for 'peace at any price' or 'better Red than dead,' or as one commentator put it, he'd rather 'live on his knees than die on his feet.'" Reagan said that would only lead to war.

His dramatic language about the Soviet threat was a set-up for Reagan's final push. These were the words Reagan had used to end his speeches for years. He knew well how the studio audience—as well as the Goldwater supporters who would hear his words on television—would react to his emotional closing. Reagan launched his peroration:

> You and I know and do not believe that life is so dear and peace so sweet as to be purchased at the price of chains and slavery. If nothing in life is worth dying for, when did this begin—just in the face of this enemy? Or should Moses have told the children of Israel to live in slavery under the pharaohs? Should Christ have refused the cross? Should the patriots at Concord Bridge have thrown down their guns and refused to fire the shot heard 'round the world? The martyrs of history were not fools, and our honored dead who gave their lives to stop the advance of the Nazis didn't die in vain. Where, then, is the road to peace? Well, it's a simple answer, after all.
>
> You and I have the courage to say to our enemies, "There is a price we will not pay." There is a point beyond which they must not advance. And this—this is the meaning in the phrase of Barry Goldwater's "peace through strength." Winston Churchill said, "The destiny of man is not measured by material computations. When great forces are on the move in the world, we learn we're spirits—not animals." And he said, "There's something going on in time and space, and beyond time and space, which, whether we like it or not, spells duty."
>
> You and I have a rendezvous with destiny.

We'll preserve for our children this, the last best hope of man on earth, or we'll sentence them to take the last step into a thousand years of darkness.[6]

We will keep in mind and remember that Barry Goldwater has faith in us. He has faith that you and I have the ability and the dignity and the right to make our own decisions and determine our own destiny.

Reagan's penultimate words—"a rendezvous with destiny"—would have been familiar to anyone who had attended a Reagan speech over the past several years; those who remembered Reagan's political hero, Franklin D. Roosevelt, also would have recognized the phrase. FDR had used it near the end of his acceptance speech to the 1936 Democratic National Convention in Philadelphia: "This generation of Americans has a rendezvous with destiny."[7] Reagan had been ending his speeches with the famous line since at least the late 1950s.[8] And the words "last best hope on Earth" may have sounded familiar to some viewers, too. These words were inspired by Abraham Lincoln's annual message to Congress in December 1862: "We shall nobly save or meanly lose the last best hope of earth."[9]

As Reagan ended, the studio audience leaped to its feet in sustained applause as Reagan waved and walked off the stage and down the side steps. James Kilroy of the California team replaced him at the podium and made a brief pitch for contributions that the TV for Goldwater-Miller committee needed to air Reagan's speech on network and local broadcasts in the days before the election. "I want to ask each of you to take part in this important presidential campaign by contributing what you can to keep the Goldwater crusade on the air," Kilroy said. "Send one, ten, fifty dollars, or any amount, to TV for Goldwater-Miller, box 80, Los Angeles, 51."[10]

15

Why Didn't Goldwater Talk Like That?

Jim Kilroy said the most difficult part of preparing Reagan's television program for broadcast was persuading its star to approve a money plea at the end. "Ron and Nancy didn't like it, so we convinced him," Kilroy later said. "Nancy was the hardest to convince." Begging for money in political broadcasts would soon be common. In 1964, however, many candidates and their advisers viewed such pitches as unseemly or undignified. For example, a financial appeal after a thirty-minute Goldwater campaign film, *Conversation at Gettysburg*, featuring former President Eisenhower, might have generated considerable cash when it aired on national television in late September. Goldwater's campaign manager, however, killed the idea, which one adviser believed deprived the struggling campaign of a half million dollars.[1]

Once Reagan approved the financial appeal, Raisbeck edited the program down to exactly twenty-nine minutes. Next, he, Kilroy, and the TV for Goldwater-Miller organization tested their show by airing it on television stations in at least four California markets and on one Chicago station. Three nights later, on October 23, the speech aired at 9:30 p.m. on KCRA-TV in Sacramento and at 7 p.m. on KNBC-TV in Los Angeles. The speech also aired that night on WNBQ-TV in Chicago; the next day, on KIEM-TV in Eureka and in Oakland on KRON-TV.[2] On October 25, it aired on KEYT-TV in Santa Barbara. The audio of

Reagan's speech also aired on Sacramento radio station KFBK-AM at 8:00 p.m. on October 20.[3]

After assessing the early, positive reaction to the program, Kilroy and Raisbeck knew they had something powerful on their hands. Within hours of the program's first broadcast, viewers responded with telegrams of support to Reagan, the Goldwater campaign, and the California group. "This 30 minute speech is exciting revealing and factual and it holds the attention of the opposition," A. P. Pawluk of Pomona, California, said in a telegram to RNC chairman Dean Burch on October 25, adding, "Are you making arrangements to review and telecast nationwide the speech[?]" Helen and Lyle Randles of Los Angeles also sent a telegram to Burch after they saw the early KNBC broadcast on October 23. "We firmly believe that the whole nation should have the opportunity to hear Ronald Reagan speak on national television," they wrote. "He knows how to say what needs to be said[.] Give America a chance to hear and see him[.]"[4]

After watching the speech on local television on October 23, Margaret Barstow of Los Angeles wrote in a telegram to the Southern California Republican Party headquarters: "Ronald Reagan is the most forceful and effective speaker we have. . . . If we could have him on nationwide television this election would be won. I am sending money."[5] To Reagan, Mr. and Mrs. Robert L. Stevenson of Los Angeles wrote in a telegram: "Your speech [was the] greatest ever delivered." Mr. and Mrs. Harold Babcock of San Bernardino wired TV for Goldwater-Miller: "Talk excellent. Already won Congress. Please repeat program. . . . Sending donation."[6]

In Washington, meanwhile, Goldwater's aides learned of the California group's plan to air the speech on NBC the night of Tuesday, October 27. They did not approve. The first sign of trouble had appeared in an October 19 memorandum to the RNC from Albert Tilt of the advertising firm Erwin, Wasey, Ruthrauff & Ryan (a subsidiary of McCann Erickson, the firm hired to produce broadcast advertising for the party and the Goldwater campaign). After viewing the Reagan program, the agency concluded, "This would appear useful only in its full length as a half-hour for local use." Several days later, on October 22, another agency memo noted the purchase of airtime on NBC. "Agency questioned running of Ronald Reagan film," the memorandum reported. The writer added that, instead of Reagan's speech, the campaign should show a Goldwater rally filmed at New York's Madison Square Garden or run a repeat of a Goldwater speech that had aired on national television on October 21.[7]

The next day, another memorandum remarked, more pointedly: "The agency strongly protested the use of these funds at the expense of a last week of spots. It was noted that the moneys used by the [California] TV committee were almost totally attributable to the money pitches run by the National Committee using Box 80, Los Angeles 51; that it was strategic suicide to feature anything but the Candidate in the last week of the campaign." The memo also asserted the Reagan broadcast would be "a violation of an agreement between the agency and the TV Committee."[8]

While they opposed the thirty-minute program, Goldwater's campaign staffers were not oblivious to how Reagan could help them. As early as late September, Goldwater's advertising firm had approved and aired a sixty-second spot that Reagan recorded. In the ad, he defended Goldwater against attacks of extremism and warmongering. "I asked to speak to you because I'm mad," Reagan said, seated on a stool as he looked at the camera, arms crossed. "I've known Barry Goldwater for a long time. When I hear people say he's impulsive and such nonsense, I boil over. Believe me, if it weren't for Barry keeping those boys in Washington on their toes, do you honestly think our national defense would be as strong as it is?" Goldwater's campaign commissioned the spot to address charges Goldwater would start a war between the United States and the Soviet Union. "Do you honestly believe that Barry wants his sons and daughters involved in a war?" Reagan asked in the commercial. "Do you think he wants his wife to be a wartime mother? Of course not."[9]

Reagan's effectiveness in a sixty-second spot, however, did not mean the campaign wanted him to star in a thirty-minute national program. As late October approached, Goldwater's campaign manager, Denison Kitchel, and policy adviser William

Baroody noted the Reagan speech and the plans his California associates had for airing it on NBC. Annoyed with the California group for its impertinence in having bought national airtime on Goldwater's behalf, Kitchel and Baroody reviewed the speech transcript and demanded the California group kill its program. Reagan's discussion of Goldwater's plans for a voluntary Social Security system violated everything Baroody wanted Goldwater to communicate in the campaign's closing days.[10] And it was not only Kitchel and Baroody who wanted to spike the speech. Campaign aide William Middendorf believed the RNC's advertising agency, an early opponent of a Reagan broadcast, had encouraged the two men to oppose the program, as "this pulled their right to claim a commission of perhaps $23,000."[11] Outraged that Goldwater aides in faraway Washington were conspiring to cancel Reagan's broadcast, Walter Knott phoned Goldwater's advisers to offer them a choice: If the Goldwater campaign wished to air another program on NBC the evening of October 27, it must raise the money for it. TV for Goldwater-Miller, he said, would only pay to run Reagan's speech.[12]

Perhaps hoping to perform an end run around the California group, Kitchel and Baroody urged Goldwater to call Reagan. Goldwater phoned on Sunday, October 25, to speak with Reagan about the upcoming Tuesday evening broadcast. "He sounded uneasy and a little uncomfortable," Reagan recalled, adding that Goldwater told him his advisers suggested substituting another program for Reagan's speech. "He said they were afraid my speech, coming so close to the eve of the election, might backfire on him because of references in it to problems with the Social Security system."

Reagan protested. "Barry, I've been making the speech all over the state for quite a while and I have to tell you, it's been pretty well received, including whatever remarks I've made about Social Security. I just can't cancel the speech and give away the airtime; it's not up to me." Reagan noted the California group had raised the money for the program. "They're the only ones who could cancel or switch it." Goldwater said he would view the film and call Reagan again. After Goldwater heard the speech's audio, he asked his staff, "What the hell's wrong with that?" Goldwater called Reagan and told him to proceed.

Reagan admitted the episode rattled him. "Who was I to tell a presidential candidate what he should or shouldn't do in his campaign?" he wrote. Reagan recalled that he had seen the campaign film, *Conversation at Gettysburg*, that Baroody had suggested as a replacement for his speech and was not impressed. (The thirty-minute program was an edited version of a less-than-inspiring conversation between Goldwater and Eisenhower, filmed at the former president's home in Gettysburg, Pennsylvania.) "After Barry's second call," Reagan wrote, "I thought for a while of calling the group who had purchased the airtime and asking them to withdraw my speech. Barry's advisors had shaken my confidence a little." Then Reagan remembered the times he had given that speech and the positive response it always received. After a sleepless night, he resolved to proceed.[13]

Little did Reagan know that two of Goldwater's top aides were still unwilling to concede. Goldwater campaign aide Stephen Shadegg recalled that "as late at 5:30 on Tuesday afternoon [October 27], Kitchel and Baroody were still attempting to persuade Reagan's sponsors to cancel the showing."[14] Well sourced in the Goldwater campaign, columnists Roland Evans and Robert Novak reported, "Even after the Reagan film ran once on television, Baroody tried (unsuccessfully) to prevent it from being shown again."[15]

JUDGING BY TELEGRAMS TO Dean Burch on October 27 from viewers in the Los Angeles area—several of them from the Pacific Palisades neighborhood where Reagan lived—the California group took nothing for granted. In Burch's papers at the Arizona Historical Foundation are a dozen telegrams from October 26–27 urging the RNC chairman to air the program (or not to cancel it). The language in several of the telegrams suggests the California group may have spread the word among its supporters that Reagan's show was in jeopardy. "Keep Ronald Reagan on TV. He can reach more this way[.] No time for coffee," wrote Robert N. Cushon of Pacific Palisades.[16] Also from Pacific Palisades, Paul Smith wired Burch: "Ronald Reagan by far most effective speaker for Goldwater. Don't change plans for Tuesday telecast." Smith's wife also sent a telegram to Burch that morning, saying, "I have phoned friends all over the country to watch Reagan telecast. Please don't cancel it." Mrs. Forest Nance of Pacific Palisades told Burch in her telegram, sent the morning of October 27: "We have raised over [$]30,000 specifically for Reagan telecast and had phoned network. Calling everyone. Please do not consider cancellation."[17]

GOLDWATER'S TELEVISION ADVERTISING FOR the fall campaign was an amateurish mix of sixty-second spots and thirty-minute speeches that preempted scheduled network programming. Campaign aide J. William Middendorf believed "most of those who did watch [the thirty-minute shows] were either conservative junkies looking for a fix or Johnson campaign workers looking for fodder."[18] Unlike the sixty-second spots aired during news or entertainment programs, Goldwater's longer programs were appointment viewing. Advertised in local newspapers and in TV Guide, the campaign pitched them to a wide audience, but they attracted few viewers.[19]

There was little in the Goldwater shows that audiences might have found inspiring. "Many who tuned in out of curiosity," Middendorf said, "quickly went looking for something interesting to watch."[20] Goldwater's programs were so bad that NBC president Robert Kintner believed the Republicans' advertising may have boosted the ratings success of a new drama series on a rival network. Three times in October, the Goldwater campaign preempted NBC programming at 9:30 p.m., and Kintner believed that drove viewers to ABC, resulting in a "huge audience" for its twice weekly prime-time soap opera, Peyton Place. "You couldn't convince [the Goldwater campaign]," one advertising executive later said, "that voters' favorite entertainment shows—like Petticoat Junction—shouldn't be preempted."[21]

The production quality of Goldwater's programs was also poor. "I didn't have much experience with TV," recalled Charles Lichenstein, who produced Goldwater's television ads. (In 1983, President Reagan would appoint Lichenstein chief alternate UN delegate for the United States.) "I didn't look at it very much. I didn't even like it very much," he added. "I was an amateur in the technique of political advertising on TV."[22] That also was the opinion of Bruce Reagan (no relation to the actor), who was the state chairman for special groups for Goldwater's California campaign. "[Goldwater] TV programs up to this point have been ineffective and anemic," he wrote in a letter to Goldwater's campaign manager, Denison Kitchel, on September 30. "I have had literally hundreds of people from all parts of the state comment unfavorably on the undeniable fact that Barry's appearances have lacked punch, that they failed to name names, places, and times, that they are far too low geared."[23]

Like other Goldwater programs that fall, the prime-time broadcast of Reagan's October 27 speech was promoted in advertisements in newspapers across the country. "TONIGHT Don't miss 'A TIME FOR CHOOSING' with Ronald Reagan," read the standard advertisement of the TV for Goldwater-Miller Committee. Some papers published advance news stories about the speech. "Former Democrat Ronald Reagan will make a nation-wide television broadcast on behalf of Republican presidential candidate Barry Goldwater Tuesday night," a story in the *Oakland Tribune* reported on October 25.[24] The *Chicago Tribune* featured a prominent story about the speech headlined, "TV's Reagan Speaks Up Tonight for Barry." The story mentioned the first broadcast of the speech the previous Friday, and the writer was under the impression that Reagan's Tuesday night speech would be "a sequel" to the first broadcast in Chicago (which had been a test run).[25]

On the night of the broadcast, Reagan and Nancy watched from the home of a friend in Los Angeles. The speech aired at 9:30 p.m. (in New York and California). When it was over, Reagan said, "The others in the room said I had done well. But I was still nervous about it and, when I went to bed, I was hoping I hadn't let Barry down." Around midnight, Reagan recalled, the phone rang. It was a call from Washington, where it was 3 a.m. "The call was from a member of Barry's campaign team," Reagan said, "who told me the Goldwater-for-President campaign switchboard had been lit up constantly since the broadcast."[26]

In its first national showing, the speech was not a ratings juggernaut, but it was the most-watched television program the Republicans or Goldwater's campaign would air that fall. According to the Neilson ratings company, the October 27 show drew 4.26 million households, representing 13 percent of that hour's television audience. When TV for Goldwater-Miller aired it again on NBC the night of October 31 (before a less-remembered thirty-minute program for Goldwater hosted by actor John Wayne), it attracted 4.05 million households or 14.2 percent of the nationwide television audience.[27]

More impressive to Goldwater's campaign aides and the Republican National Committee staff was the outpouring of contributions and thousands of phone calls, letters, and telegrams that Reagan's speech produced in the days after its first showing. Reagan told one interviewer in 1967 he had received 25,000 messages about his speech.[28] Clifton White, the national director of Citizens for Goldwater-Miller, sent a telegram to Reagan the next morning: "Phones ringing round the clock here since your telecast. Our deepest thanks and congratulations for a magnificent presentation."[29]

Eisenhower was among those who watched the speech. On October 30, back in Gettysburg after a weeklong hospital stay in Washington, he called his former attorney general and political adviser, Herbert Brownell, to discuss the "fine speech by Ronald Reagan." Later that day, he spoke with another former aide, Bryce Harlow, and told him, "Reagan's speech was excellent."[30]

Average citizens sent telegrams to Reagan at his home or in care of the California group. "Just heard your speech," wrote Roy Carney of Lake Forest, Illinois, in a telegram the night of October 27. "It was thrilling [,] the best speach [sic] of the campaign[.] We are sending a check to your committee[.]" R. Bell of Brooklyn wrote to TV for Goldwater-Miller the next morning: "Greatest political speech we've heard. You are the strongest thing going for Uncle Goldie. You touched all the bases." Wrote Chester Tripp of Chicago: "[Your speech] is by far the best of the crop. Trust it can be heard again by millions within the next few days." Mrs. Bruce Willard Turner of Baltimore told the California group that Reagan's was the "most thrilling and spellbinding speech I have ever heard[.] Can't we have it again before election[?]" From Hawaii, movie director John Ford wrote, "Great Ronnie great."

Others sent telegrams to the Goldwater campaign and demanded to know how often Reagan would speak on national television. "Will he talk to women on television for Goldwater any day time?" asked Mr. and Mrs. Clifford Hood of New York City. "Does more money mean more television time than presently scheduled?" G. F. Daugherty of Cambridge, Ohio, wired the California group: "[Reagan's] speech was absolutely the best presentation of the entire campaign. Even die-hard Democrats admit its effectiveness and impact. It must be repeated between now and Tuesday [Election Day]. It made converts out of a number and caused many people to re-evaluate their thinking about the present administration."[31]

Most of Goldwater's top aides, who had opposed a washed-up actor speaking on national television for their candidate, finally grasped the impact of Reagan's words and his powerful presentation. Except for Baroody, they now endorsed the program, and they voiced strong support for the California group's plans to broadcast it several more times before Election Day.

And the financial appeal that Reagan and Nancy had worried about proved a bonanza for the California group's ability to keep showing the speech. Checks poured into the committee's Los Angeles post office box. It is not clear how much cash Reagan's speech generated for the Goldwater campaign and the California group. Reagan claimed it helped raise $8 million. In a story about the campaign's fund-raising published after the election, the *New York Times* said Reagan's speech "is reported to have brought more than $750,000 in contributions." A more credible estimate, from journalist David Broder and political scientist Stephen Hess, was about $600,000. Whatever the case, it was clear Reagan had produced an impressive amount on Goldwater's behalf, more than TV for Goldwater-Miller could spend. According to post-election reports, the committee raised $2.51 million that fall, but spent just over $2 million, leaving a $500,000 surplus.[32]

In analyzing campaign spending reports from the election,

Congressional Quarterly noted the impact of Reagan's speech on Goldwater's late fund-raising surge: "Not unimportant . . . were the direct television appeals for Goldwater campaign funds by Ronald Reagan, [actor] Raymond Massey and National Chairman Dean Burch, which brought in over 200,000 contributions of $100 or less. Just within the last six days before the election, $2,800,000 poured into the Republican campaign chest in Washington."[33] (That $2.8 million is equal to about $23 million in 2019 dollars.)

All this money allowed the California group to air Reagan's speech again on national television and in dozens of local markets around the country. In some markets, local Republican organizations paid to air the speech, which suggests TV for Goldwater-Miller had shipped copies across the country before the October 27 national showing. For example, the Winnebago (Illinois) County Women's Republican Club paid to show the speech on WREX-TV in Rockford at 6 p.m. on October 28.[34] In Davenport, Iowa, the Goldwater Volunteers of Scott County paid to show it on WQAD-TV on October 30, the next night on WHBE-TV, and on November 2, again on WQAD-TV.[35] In Lafayette, Indiana, the Tipp County Citizens for Goldwater-Miller bought time for the program on WLFI-TV on November 1. In Sheboygan, Wisconsin, on November 2, the local Republican Party organization purchased a full-page ad that included the complete transcript of the speech. In Ames, Iowa, the local Republican Party did the same. Committees and party organizations in dozens of other markets bought newspaper ads to publicize the October 31 national rebroadcast of the speech, which was a double feature of Reagan and John Wayne.[36]

The continued showings prompted even more telegrams and phone calls of praise. "Listeners are spellbound and many loyal contributors to Barry Goldwater have expressed their desire that you continue to use Mister Reagan from now through Monday night," Mr. and Mrs. Burt Ford wrote to Burch from their home in Dallas. From Atlanta, C. G. Fulton wired the Republican National Committee to say, "Repeat Ronald Reagan on national TV Monday[.] Most wonderful speech I have heard." To retired Air Force major William Pierson, who wrote a letter to the RNC on October 29, "That speech was the most convincing piece of political oratory

I have ever heard." Pierson urged the RNC to buy time "on all three networks for three consecutive evenings in order to expose as many voters as possible to that outstanding speech."[37]

In Ohio, an unnamed columnist for the *Sandusky Register* noted on October 30, "The Goldwater campaign has suffered in getting its basic message across to Americans everywhere." He complained that "countless words have been crammed down the citizens' throat" and "most of us are getting pretty sick and tired of it." However, the writer gushed, "Actor Reagan took the whole issue in perspective. It was terrific!"[38] *Chicago Tribune* reporter Larry Wolters also noted the positive response to Reagan's speech. "Citizens for Goldwater headquarters in Chicago reported yesterday," he wrote on October 31, "that more than 5,000 requests for copies of the Reagan address and for repeat presentation have been received and that more than 3,000 copies already have been sent out with other thousands still to follow."[39]

In a postelection review for a book he would publish in 1965, Goldwater aide Stephen Shadegg collected impressions from politically active friends and associates around the country. Several correspondents mentioned Reagan's speech as the campaign's highlight. "If the Ronald Reagan presentation had been used earlier and reiterated . . . the race would have been much closer," a Goldwater supporter from Lansing, Michigan, told Shadegg. A Republican activist from Defiance, Ohio, wrote: "Had the Senator been able to present his case as effective[ly] as Ronald Reagan did for him, it would have been a great help." The unfavorable comparison of Goldwater to Reagan was a recurring theme. From Denver, a correspondent told Shadegg: "[The] TV appearance of Ronald Reagan [the] last week in [the] campaign brought almost unanimous response: 'This is what we wanted to hear!' or 'Why didn't Goldwater talk like that' or 'Why isn't he [Reagan] running for president[?]'" Another writer, from Winter Park, Florida, complained about Goldwater: "The only complaint I would have about his campaign would be his speeches. When Reagan spoke everyone said, 'Why didn't [Goldwater] say it that way?'"[40]

16

The Brightest Spot of the Dreary Campaign

Although Johnson crushed Goldwater in a historic landslide that some believed spelled doom for the conservative movement, Reagan's celebrated speech had been an undeniable bright spot for conservative Republicans. The actor gave conservatives hope that their problem had been the message, not the messenger. And some journalists, columnists, and Republican Party activists now saw Reagan in a new light. He was not just another TV star who rented his glamour to a political campaign before he returned to the set. As a political person, Reagan now enjoyed stature and lasting notoriety. Even some liberals who watched his speech—their numbers had been small—swooned over Reagan's delivery.

Commentators assessing the carnage of Goldwater's defeat acknowledged Reagan's effectiveness as a Republican spokesman as well as his ubiquity. "As it turned out," a *Chicago Daily News* reporter wrote the week following the election, "Ronald Reagan appeared more frequently than Goldwater, arguing in Goldwater's behalf."[1] The public response to Reagan's speech prompted the *Garden City* (KS) *Telegram* to lament: "[T]he movie actor himself might have run a better race than the man he supported."[2] In his national column, Fulton Lewis Jr. quoted the Virginia Republican Party chair, Robert J. Corber, who said of Goldwater as a candidate: "Something is obviously wrong when the best speech of the entire campaign is produced in Hollywood by an actor who is an amateur in the field of politics." (Little did Corber know that Reagan was anything but an amateur.) Adding his own thoughts about Reagan, Lewis observed that the speech was the Republican Party's "most effective single weapon."[3] Roland Evans and Robert Novak echoed Lewis a few days later, writing in their column, "The brightest spot of the dreary campaign was a sleeper: A 30-minute televised speech by actor Ronald Reagan. . . . Even Democrats admitted it was the campaign's most effective oratory."[4] In the *New York Times*, columnist Arthur Krock said Reagan's speech was not just an effective argument for Goldwater but "perhaps" had been "the most cogent exposition of the conservative political philosophy during the campaign of 1964."[5]

No commentator was more lavish with praise than syndicated columnist Charles McDowell. He told readers Reagan had "delivered during the past campaign perhaps the greatest speech since the Gettysburg Address (Lincoln's) and who, if he had delivered it sooner and oftener, might have made the difference in what was, in retrospect, a very close election." (Whatever the correct historical comparison, there was little doubt the speech had been a major triumph—for Reagan, at least. McDowell, however, did not explain his baffling assertion that the election had been "very close.")[6]

Anyone with a passing interest in the campaign could see Reagan's communication skills far outshone Goldwater's. Political journalists and pundits who watched Reagan's speech admired his ability to articulate the conservative message. But because almost no one bothered to check his factual assertions, most viewers would never learn that much of what Reagan said was exaggerated, unsubstantiated, or false. His race for governor, two years later, would be the first time anyone subjected his rhetoric to sustained public scrutiny and criticism.

In a letter to a graduate student in 1965, Reagan came close to admitting the shaky factual ground on which he had built his nascent political career. James Todd Hayes was finishing his master's degree at Emporia State University in Kansas, researching a thesis on the factual assertions in Reagan's October 27 speech.

"To the uncritical listener," Hayes wrote in the preface to his thesis, "Ronald Reagan's 'A Time for Choosing' might seem to be the epitome of the 'logical' speech. It is a kind of rhetorical montage, bursting with 'facts and figures,' delivered . . . with earnest sincerity and conviction." What caught Hayes's eye, however, was the profusion of "unfamiliar and incongruous evidence" that Reagan presented "as if it were common knowledge, with little or no indication of source." Hayes set out to see if he could verify or locate the sources for Reagan's many assertions. His thinking was simple, but it had not occurred to most political journalists in California or elsewhere: "Whenever a man rises to prominence in politics, his public utterances are, or should be, appropriate material for rhetorical analysis. When a middle-aged screen idol and television personality suddenly becomes one of the chief hopes of a national political party, rhetorical analysis would seem to be not merely interesting but imperative."

For months, Hayes studied Reagan's speech, finally isolating sixty-three factual assertions, which he presented to the three faculty members on his thesis committee. He asked them to review the statements and tell him which they would accept as true, reject as obviously false, or would require further investigation to determine their veracity. Relying on their analyses, Hayes focused his research on the third category. Based on his study of those factual assertions, he arrived at thirty-five statements by Reagan "that seemed to require verification." Hayes then went about trying to confirm Reagan's information, even contacting individuals Reagan had mentioned in the speech, including the two U.S. senators Reagan had purported to quote. Near the end of his research, Hayes sent a questionnaire to Reagan asking him, "where possible, to indicate the sources for those statements for which [Hayes's] preliminary research had failed to disclose a source." Hayes reported that his questionnaire reached Reagan in San Diego, where the former actor, and now a presumptive candidate for governor, dutifully answered the questions. Reagan did so, as he told Hayes, without his research materials.

Asked to prove his statement, "No nation in history has ever survived a tax burden that reached a third of its national income,"

Reagan replied: "I'm sorry—this was from a summation on the history of past empires and first used by me 10 years ago—I just plain don't have the source any longer." As Hayes observed, "By implication, Reagan is now quoting himself as an authority on this point."

Discussing farm policy, Reagan had said, "In the last three years we have spent $43 in the feed grain program for every bushel of corn that we don't grow." Hayes could find no source for this statement, and Reagan, in the questionnaire, offered nothing more than "Congressional record—debate on farm legislation." Hayes could find nothing to back up Reagan's claim that the Department of Agriculture had "asked for the right to imprison farmers who wouldn't keep books as prescribed by the federal government." Reagan directed Hayes to a June 11, 1962, story in *U.S. News & World Report* that did not discuss such a request.[7]

Early in the speech, when he had attacked Lyndon Johnson's Great Society programs, Reagan quoted an unnamed "voice"— presumably a Johnson administration official who reportedly said, "The cold war will end through acceptance of a-not-undemocratic socialism." This approximated a quote by historian Arthur Schlesinger from 1947. (Reagan had repeated variations of it before.) Schlesinger, who later served as a White House aide to John F. Kennedy, had written of his doubts about the viability of capitalism in the postwar era and advocated a modified form of socialism in the United States. And he expressed concern over the United States' ability to contain Soviet aggression and avoid an all-out war with the Communist empire. "If we can avoid this war," Schlesinger wrote, "if we can contain the counter-revolution of the USSR within clearly marked limits, we have a good chance to test the possibilities of a peaceful transition into a not un-democratic socialism. But if our leadership and determination falter, neither democracy, socialism, nor anything else will have any more of a future than Hiroshima or Nagasaki." Reagan had not only implied the quote was recent—it was almost twenty years old—he also used it out of context and distorted Schlesinger's meaning.[8]

Reagan had also attacked Democratic senator J. William

Fulbright of Arkansas, who chaired the Senate Foreign Relations Committee. "Senator Fulbright has said at Stanford University that the Constitution is outmoded," he said. "He referred to the president as our moral teacher and our leader, and he said he is hobbled in his task by the restrictions in power imposed on him by this antiquated document. He must be freed so that he can do for us what he knows is best." Reagan apparently took this paraphrase of Fulbright's words from a speech the senator had delivered at Stanford University in 1961. But he misrepresented what Fulbright said and what he meant. "The President alone," the senator had told his audience, "commands the authority and the necessary forum for leading the American people to an active understanding of national objectives and to a willingness to take action necessary for their realization." When Fulbright turned to foreign policy, he advocated for the mainstream position that, in the nuclear age, the president leads and speaks for the nation in the realm of national security. "The power that is needed [to cope with worldwide revolutionary forces] is presidential power," Fulbright said. "He alone, among elected officials, can rise above parochialism and private pressures. He alone, in his role as teacher and moral leader, can hope to overcome the excesses and inadequacies of a public opinion that is all too often ignorant of the needs, the dangers, and the opportunities of our foreign relations."[9]

In the speech, Reagan also had alleged, "Senator [Hubert] Humphrey last week charged that Barry Goldwater, as president, would seek to eliminate farmers." Asked where he found such a quote, Reagan told Hayes, "Campaign speech—64 campaign—carried on all the wire services."[10] Humphrey, Johnson's running mate, did attack Goldwater's farm policies in speeches in September and October, and the Associated Press ran stories about them. Speaking in Huron, South Dakota, on September 10, Humphrey said of the nation's agricultural economy: "[Goldwater] would take away—if you let him—the limited protection your government now provides for the producers who have made this modern miracle possible."[11] In Sioux Falls, South Dakota, on October 15, Humphrey attacked Goldwater in more pointed terms, alleging the Republican nominee favored "prompt and final termination of the farm subsidy program." To that, Humphrey added, "Imagine the empty stores—the empty cash registers. Imagine the farm foreclosures—the abandoned farmhouses."[12] Contrary to what Reagan alleged, Humphrey had not said Goldwater wanted to "eliminate farmers." Instead, he commented on the imagined effects of Goldwater's farm policies. However, in his 1960 book, *The Conscience of a Conservative*, Goldwater had advocated *"prompt and final termination of the farm subsidy program* [emphasis Goldwater]."[13]

Hayes decided that, of the thirty-five disputed statements in the speech, he could not find (and Reagan could not offer) confirmation for thirteen. Hayes rejected as false or exaggerated seven more statements by Reagan; he accepted, as supported, fifteen statements—fewer than half of Reagan's thirty-five questionable assertions. In his summary, Hayes noted: "Reagan's reliance upon 'popular' sources for his information suggests to some degree a superficiality in his speech preparation. This casual attitude is certainly manifest in his handling of sources and quotations. In addition, Reagan tends to oversimplify almost every issue he chooses to discuss."[14]

DESPITE ITS QUESTIONABLE ACCURACY, Reagan's speech had been masterful. Some later viewed its main weakness—his unsubstantiated assertions—as a strength. In his 1991 rhetorical review of the speech, Harvard communications scholar Paul D. Erickson noted Reagan's speech lacked "names, dates, and other details that could be checked and then either confirmed or denied." But Erickson argued that this perceived failing was among Reagan's strongest rhetorical weapons. "Such details would be irrelevant, even counterproductive," Erickson wrote. "Reagan sought to attack not individuals but the government in general as a creature grown fat and foolish under liberal administrations." Referring to a story Reagan told in the speech about a nameless Washington bureaucrat, Erickson observed: "Reagan shows us the bureaucrat at his desk; from that image we can extrapolate to a broader vision, imagining thousands of identical scenes until the entire federal government becomes nothing but an exercise in folly and incompetence."[15]

It was not just that Reagan's rhetoric was better and more inspiring than Goldwater's. While supporting Goldwater's rigid and pure form of conservatism, Reagan was articulating something different, not just in tone but in substance. "In its tolerance of federal and state governmental power to advance the ability of the average person to live with comfort, respect, and dignity," conservative political analysist Henry Olsen wrote in 2017, "Reagan's conservatism was far more activist—and far less opposed to the principles of the New Deal—than was the Arizona senator's."[16] Historian David T. Byrne agreed: "The only New Deal programs Reagan routinely criticized were the Tennessee Valley Authority and social security. Furthermore, to be fair, the social security program that Reagan criticized in the 1960s and 1970s was far more expansive than anything FDR intended."[17] (Reagan had often criticized another New Deal initiative—FDR's farm subsidy programs.) Olson also detected another subtle difference in Reagan's rhetoric in 1964: "Reagan proclaimed that America was special because it enabled everyone to live according to his or her own choices, but Goldwater's conservatism bore the stamp of a more traditional conservative belief that America was great because it enabled the naturally great to rise." Put another way, Olsen explained, "A person following Reagan's ideas . . . could distinguish, as Reagan did, between government efforts designed to lift up and those intended to pull down."[18]

Reagan's speech had been the brightest moment for a Goldwater campaign marked by its candidate's verbal missteps and his inability to articulate, like Reagan, the rationale for his candidacy. Even had Reagan's speech been mediocre, it still might have outshone the candidate. But no matter the power of Reagan's message, it could not help Goldwater overcome the enormous odds he faced in his contest with Johnson. To no one's surprise, least of all the candidate, Johnson had swamped Goldwater on Election Day, winning 61.1 percent of the vote to Goldwater's 38.5 percent. Goldwater carried only six states. Each, except Arizona, was in the Deep South. Out of 70 million votes cast, Johnson led

Goldwater by 16 million. In California, where Reagan had worked so hard to help his friend, Johnson captured the state's forty electoral votes by winning 59 percent of the electorate, beating Goldwater by more than 1 million votes. He carried only five counties, including Orange and, narrowly, San Diego.

It was a crushing defeat for the Republican Party, especially for its conservatives. On election night, Reagan watched the returns with Goldwater's Southern California supporters at the Cocoanut Grove. "It's a shame there isn't some place in a campaign for quality to pay off," Reagan told supporters after it was clear Goldwater had lost. "Sure, we're disappointed. Sure, we didn't expect this . . . but take a look at the figure on our side and remember every one [vote] represents a conservative we didn't have when we started out." Reagan then declared, "It took thirty years to get this nation into a collective situation—and we [conservatives] are just [getting] started."[19]

In the campaign's aftermath, Goldwater and his aides took a beating in the national press for his lackluster speeches, his anemic television advertising, and his message, which was rarely optimistic, often scolding, and always moralistic. Goldwater had simply scared many voters into thinking he would start a war with the Soviet Union. The conservative cause took a beating, too, from pundits who decided the election was a referendum on conservatism. It had been, in part. But the returns were also about the stability Johnson promised as opposed to the confusion and chaos Goldwater threatened. It had been a campaign about issues, but those issues—nuclear war, the future of Social Security, and civil rights—were often proxies for the candidates' personalities and their approaches to governance.

"I've never seen a man as mad as Barry Goldwater," one California Republican advertising executive said later. "He acted like an enraged bull. I tell you he was so scary that I had second thoughts, right there, about a man with his temper sitting alone in a room next to that red button."[20] Reagan was no less a conservative than Goldwater, but his demeanor was different. "[Reagan] said a lot of the things that Barry said, but he said them differently," said Stuart Spencer, who would manage Reagan's first political campaign. "He said them in a soft way, in a more forgiving way. Style was the difference. Barry was a hard-nosed, up-front Arizonan cowboy, and that's what scared people."[21] Reagan "appeared to most of the nation as a more reasonable advocate than Goldwater," Garry Wills noted. "The actor's manner and familiar charm, the generality of his warnings, the lack of personal assault or references (even to Goldwater), made the amateur look more statesmanlike than the professional politician."[22]

But it was more than style. Goldwater's rhetoric lacked the specificity, engaging anecdotes, and telling examples that made Reagan's speeches sparkle. Stephen Shadegg observed that Goldwater's speeches "had no beginning, they did not build to a climax, they had no conclusion, and they lacked the unity necessary for victory."[23] As George Kellerman, the RNC member from Hawaii, told Dean Burch in a letter on September 15: "General statements—however sincerely or well expressed—do not impress people as much as facts that they can 'take hold of.'"[24]

Unlike Reagan, who peppered his talks with concrete language and vivid, compelling anecdotes, Goldwater's language had been ambiguous. In London, Kentucky, on October 27, the day of Reagan's first national broadcast, Goldwater had addressed a campaign rally. He struck the same themes as Reagan but with uninspiring rhetoric. "We believe in the Constitution," he told the crowd, but offered no examples of what he and Republicans thought were constitutional violations. "We believe in the individual," he said, but added nothing that might show why liberals did not. "We believe in the free enterprise system," he said, without offering an example of what conservatives believed Democrats were doing to undermine that system.[25]

An internal campaign memorandum in early October noted widespread criticism of Goldwater's campaign that the author admitted "could almost be considered constructive criticism. It is that his campaign has no central theme, and that he is not drawing a clear picture of the issues from a conservative standpoint as he has done over the years." From a source in Idaho, the Goldwater aide wrote, came this question: "What happened to the man who espoused the hard-hitting and appealing conservative philosophy in his three-times-a-week newspaper column?"[26] During the campaign Goldwater had heard this criticism and rejected it. "I refuse to go around the country discussing complicated, twisted issues," he told *Newsweek* in mid-September. "I want to talk about freedom."[27] Even before the fall campaign, Goldwater hinted he misunderstood the role of a candidate. In an interview with journalist Charles Mohr for the *Saturday Evening Post* in August, Goldwater grumbled, "It's up to the precinct workers to do the selling job and explain misunderstandings about my positions."[28]

In the December 1 issue of William F. Buckley Jr.'s *National Review*, Reagan joined other prominent conservatives—including George H. W. Bush, John Davis Lodge, and Russell Kirk—in assessing Goldwater's defeat and its meaning for the future of conservatism. "We lost a battle in the continuing war for freedom," Reagan wrote, "but our position is not untenable. First of all, there are 26 million of us and we can't be explained away as die-hard party faithfuls." Reagan argued that not every vote for Johnson was a vote against conservative philosophy. "They voted against a false image our Liberal opponents successfully mounted," Reagan asserted. "Indeed it was a double false image. Not only did they portray us as advancing a kind of radical departure from the status quo, but they took for themselves a costume of comfortable conservatism." Looking to the future, Reagan wrote: "Our job beginning now is not so much to sell conservatism as to prove that our conservatism is in truth what a lot of people thought they were voting for when they fell for the cornpone come-on. In short—time now for the soft sell to prove our radicalism was an optical illusion. We represent the forgotten American—that simple soul who goes to work, bucks for a raise, takes out insurance, pays for his kids' schooling, contributes to his church and charity, and knows there just *'ain't no such thing as a free lunch.'*"[29]

REAGAN'S FINAL FILM, *The Killers*, opened in late September 1964 to negative reviews.[30] He would remain on television screens for a little longer, after his brother, Neil, arranged for him to become the host of a long-running syndicated western anthology,

Death Valley Days. A client of Neil's advertising firm—the Pacific Coast Borax Company (producer of a laundry detergent booster, 20 Mule Team Borax)—sponsored the show. He would also film several TV commercials for Boraxo hand soap. Although he would act in twenty-one episodes of *Death Valley Days* over the next year, the fifty-three-year-old Reagan knew he was no longer an actor in great demand. As a potential politician, however, he stood on the precipice of a new career.[31]

17

The Voice of the Cubs Became the
Great Communicator

Within days of Goldwater's defeat, some California Republicans looked to Reagan as a candidate for governor in 1966 against incumbent Democrat Edmund "Pat" Brown. Toward the end of a Goldwater election-night party at the Cocoanut Grove in Los Angeles, Holmes Tuttle pulled James Kilroy, one of the California group's leaders, into an impromptu huddle of several prominent Republicans. Tuttle asked them, "Why don't we run Ron Reagan for governor? With all the political exposure and his great speeches, he'd be an excellent, well-recognized candidate and governor." Kilroy said he and the rest agreed.[1]

The first public suggestion of a Reagan candidacy came two days later. California's secretary of state—seventy-six-year-old Frank Jordan, the state's only Republican statewide elected official—told a reporter, "I'd like to see Reagan run. I don't know whether he has aspirations that way or not, but I've seen a lot of talks he made for Barry Goldwater. He makes a good appearance and talks well." To that, Jordan added this tepid endorsement of Reagan as a candidate: "Certainly don't know who else we've got. We're certainly short on talent."[2]

Asked about the race by a United Press reporter the following Sunday night, Reagan was coy. "I've never had any political aspiration as a candidate," he said. "But I'll continue to work on behalf of the philosophy of government I believe in and for those 26 million [Goldwater voters] who subscribe [to] constitutional government." When the reporter asked if he could spurn a draft by state Republican leaders, Reagan gave a careful, less-than-Shermanesque response: "I hope I could turn it down."[3]

The following Tuesday, speaking to the Los Angeles County Young Republicans, Reagan played cheerleader for the defeated conservative movement. "The conservative philosophy was not repudiated," he said, adding, "We will have no more of those candidates who are pledged to the same socialist goals of our opposition and who seek our support." Neither Reagan nor his audience were in a mood for conciliation. "The principal job now is to prove to the several million Republicans who didn't join us November 3 that our conservatism is akin to their own thinking," Reagan said to wild applause. "Turning over the party to the so-called moderates wouldn't make any sense at all."

To this audience, Reagan reflected the conservative, postelection mind-set that assigned Goldwater's loss to the betrayal of moderate Republicans more than to the failings of the candidate and his message. He claimed Goldwater was a victim of the "worst campaign of vilification and the worst betrayal of those who should have given us their trust." He added Goldwater's defeat did not mean "we would welcome as a leader those who betrayed us in the battle just fought, nor that the 27 million people who supported us should defer to the minority of Republicans who left us."[4]

Reagan may have sounded bitter to those outside the party's conservative wing, but his words were soothing to anyone who longed for an unapologetic defense of the ideology and positions most voters had rejected. Reagan no doubt sensed after this defeat there still was room in California—and national politics—for a principled, well-spoken leader who would continue promoting unabashed conservatism. Reagan later claimed he had not considered running for governor until spring 1965 when Holmes Tuttle and several friends showed up at his house to propose a campaign. "You're out of your mind," Reagan said he told him, as if the idea had never occurred to him.[5]

The problem with this version of events is the early buzz about Reagan seeking elective office. It began shortly after the November 3 presidential election, including an advertising campaign to persuade Reagan to run, launched in November by Marin County business executive Fred Ullner.[6] About the same time, Republican fans of Reagan in Michigan formed a committee to persuade him to run for president in 1968.[7] And, by month's end, Reagan admitted he entertained a race for governor. "I've never had a mail reaction like this in all my years in show business—and that goes back to 1937," he told a United Press International reporter in Los Angeles. "Honored and flattered" by the talk, Reagan insisted, "I have never aspired to public office, not looked upon a political career with any particular favor. But I have some other thoughts about where an individual's responsibility lies despite his tastes and personal desires."[8]

By the first week of December, Reagan said he leaned toward the race but hoped for a draft. Telling Hollywood columnist Sheilah Graham that "the interest for me to run is widespread," he added he wanted to assess the public's feelings about him. "I have to know if this is the best way I can serve them," he explained. "It isn't as if I wanted this kind of job, so the only way I would run would be if I were convinced that I could best be of service as the governor of California. I will give my answer a lot of soul searching." Perhaps realizing he sounded too eager to run, Reagan added, "I'm in the market for feature films."[9] As if on cue, Fred Ullner told the *Oakland Tribune* in early December that his questionnaire sent to California Republicans had already revealed substantial support for a Reagan candidacy. "It is evident that people who heard Reagan's speech in behalf of Barry Goldwater believe he could win the Republican nomination in 1966 and defeat Governor Brown," Ullner said.[10]

When Goldwater came to Los Angeles in February 1965 to speak at a dinner sponsored by the Americanism Education League, Reagan introduced him warmly. Goldwater reciprocated with an encouraging reference to Reagan's potential candidacy. "I look forward to the day when you ask me to come to California and help you campaign for your own office," he told Reagan.

Goldwater then told the audience: "I've tried to beguile him to run for office before and now the time is getting ripe. You folks keep the pressure on him."[11]

Ron Reagan believed his father was a candidate from the day someone first suggested he run. "Of course, he was already determined to run," the younger Reagan recalled. "[H]e remained uncomfortable, though, as he had always been, proclaiming grandiose ambition or seeming overeager. Even at a tender age I think I grasped that we were all indulging him in something of a charade in this regard." Reagan said it was hard to imagine what might have dissuaded his father "from any campaign he had decided, in his own mind, to mount. Yet it was equally obvious that any forthright display of naked ambition was out of the question."[12]

Not all leading California Republicans favored Reagan as their party's nominee. Two Republican legislators, hoping to lure U.S. senator Thomas Kuchel into the race, told the Associated Press in March they doubted Reagan could win.[13] And Kuchel signaled he might be open to running.[14] Former Republican governor Goodwin Knight revealed how much some in the state's party establishment feared the actor-turned-politician. At a press conference, Knight called Reagan a former "left-wing Democrat" and told reporters, "I never could understand how Reagan could be so enthusiastic in support of Helen Gahagan Douglas to defeat Richard Nixon in 1950 and then, all of a sudden, be on the other side." Having questioned Reagan's bona fides as a conservative Republican, Knight then attacked him as an extreme conservative: "I don't think some of the pronouncements of Reagan represent the broad stream of Republican thinking in California."[15]

Reagan's potency as a political figure and a legitimate contender for governor was never in doubt, but Governor Brown settled the question mid-March by attacking him: "Ronald Reagan, one of Barry Goldwater's most fervent supporters, is peddling the same old snake oil at the same old stand—'Medicare is Socialistic,' 'Washington is a hotbed of subversion,' ad nauseam."[16] Reagan's response a few days later revealed he was serious about the race. Under Brown, Reagan told 900 attendees at a Republican luncheon in Long Beach, the state had worked "more on becoming the Little Brother to the Big Brother in Washington than protecting the welfare of its own citizens."[17] The following week, in a private meeting, Brown told a group of California Democrats he would seek a third term. "The thought of Ronald Reagan sitting in that governor's chair moves me to great lengths," Brown reportedly said.[18]

If Reagan's detractors hoped their attacks would deter him, they failed. By the end of March 1965, he was all but an official candidate for the Republican nomination. At the state party convention that month, he told reporters "in a sense" he had "made my own decision" about running. He would not "be coy" about his plans, he said. Reagan's position on the race, however, was coyness squared. "The decision now is up to the people of the Republican party," he said. "They must determine who is the individual who can mobilize a unified campaign." What Reagan meant was he would stage an extensive listening tour, devoting months to speaking at events around California. "If it turns out to be me," he said, "that's not a responsibility anyone could turn down."[19] To longtime friends Lorraine and Elwood Wagner, Reagan wrote in May about his concern that Republican senator George Murphy might want to run for governor. It was not likely that Murphy, who had just won his Senate seat, would look for another office so soon. "I don't think he will," Reagan concluded in the letter, "and I'm fairly certain I will—run that is."[20]

To help him assemble the nascent campaign, Reagan hired Stuart Spencer, the Republican political consultant who had managed Nelson Rockefeller's California primary campaign the year before. "Starting roughly July 1, 1965," Reagan recalled, "I drove up and down the length and breadth of California for six months, commuting to luncheon and dinner meetings from San Diego at the southern border all the way to the coastal fishing villages near the Oregon border." Reagan spoke to Rotary clubs, chambers of commerce, and United Way organizations—the same kind of groups he had been addressing for ten years. He gave them much the same speech he had always delivered. And everywhere he went, Reagan said, people would ask him to run. Reagan later denied having any passion for the race and said he would "ask them to suggest someone who was really qualified to be governor."[21]

Reagan's recollection of his California speaking tour, however, does not match his repeated public statements—beginning in the spring of 1965 through the end of the year—about his interest in the race. As he confessed in May, several months before launching his tour, "I'm getting a little closer to the edge of the porch."[22] His listening tour was nothing but a rehearsal for the real campaign. Besides traveling the state, Reagan studied California policy and politics, topics he had ignored in his speeches over the previous decade.

AS HE PREPARED TO declare his candidacy in early January 1966—he would be the leading candidate on the day he announced—Reagan understood that his televised speech for Goldwater in October 1964 had been the most important event in his budding political career. It was more significant than the fame his movies brought him and even the notoriety of his hit television show. That one night—October 27, 1964—had changed everything.

This was something Stewart Alsop, who wrote a widely read political column for the *Saturday Evening Post*, knew as he considered Reagan's potential candidacy in late November 1965. Noting Reagan's status as "probably the hottest new product on the Republican horizon," Alsop observed Reagan "is as much in demand as a speaker as Barry Goldwater used to be, and already the conservatives are dreaming presidential dreams for him." It was "the speech" (not only Reagan's October 27 version but every other incarnation of his message) that Alsop identified as the essence of Reagan's political appeal. Alsop went to California for an interview with Reagan and listened as the former actor spoke to the Los Angeles Lions Club. Alsop told his readers:

> "The speech" is, of its kind, a masterpiece—it elicited from the Lions a long standing ovation. There is, to be sure, nothing very new or surprising in what Reagan has to say. In substance, "the speech" is simply Goldwater revisited—"The omnipotent welfare state" is threatening to rob the citizen of his freedom.

What brings audiences to their feet is not the familiar substance but the style of delivery.

Reagan's tone is infinitely sincere, his timing and modulation impeccable. . . . In a purely technical sense—in terms of delivery, timing, entertainment value—"the speech" was more effective than any political speech I have heard in years. And this, surely, is one secret of the hotness of Ronald Reagan as a political product. He not only tells his conservative audiences what they want to hear—he does so with such professional expertise that even the three-Martinis-before-lunch men stay awake.

There is another secret of the Reagan phenomenon, or so it seemed to me after the interview. The Reagan personality has a soothing effect, like a warm bath. Listening to him talk is oddly relaxing and mildly entertaining—rather like watching *Death Valley Days*, the television show in which he sometimes plays the Good Guy. . . .

There is not the faintest discernable difference between Reagan's views on all major issues and Barry Goldwater's. But there is all the difference in the world in how those views are expressed. Barry Goldwater used to say his with a harsh candor which often made him sound like God's angry man, and which certainly cost him millions of votes. Ronald Reagan is the television Good Guy come to life, and his answers to even tough questions are about as harsh as Pablum. . . .

"The speech" sounds less like a political speech than a turn, an act, a well-rehearsed performance—Ronald Reagan playing the aroused citizen saving America from the menace of creeping socialism. Yet perhaps times have changed. . . .

If Ronald Reagan wins, the effectiveness of the "Good Guy image" will be demonstrated beyond doubt. Then a nice smile and a winning manner will become more important assets to an aspiring politician than political experience or a talent for government.[23]

REAGAN DECLARED HIS CANDIDACY for governor of California in a highly produced, thirty-minute television broadcast shown around the state on the night of January 4, 1966. Relaxed and confident, he spoke to the camera from the library of his Pacific Palisades home. Reagan opened by describing his extensive travels throughout California, "answering questions and asking a few." He said the reason for his tour had been clear. "I have said I'll be a candidate for governor once I've found the answers to a few questions myself, mainly about my acceptability to you. Who'd like to be governor isn't important; who the people would like to have as governor is very important." Reagan hit some of his familiar themes from "the speech"—big government, spending, taxes—but his message this time was different. He attacked Brown indirectly about what he said was the state's high unemployment and added, "We lead the nation in bankruptcies and business failures." Reagan, however, tried to strike an optimistic tone. "A big brother or paternalistic government can solve many problems for the people," he said, "but I don't think we'll like the price it charges—ever-increasing power over us and ever-decreasing individual freedom. A great society must be a free society, and to be truly great and really free, it must be a creative society calling on the genius and power of its people."

In this speech Reagan told viewers about himself, as if most did not know him. He described his time as president of the Screen Actors Guild. At even greater length, he talked about his years as a Democrat "until I found I could no longer follow the leadership of that party as it turned from the traditional precepts of Jefferson, Jackson, and Cleveland." He was not a politician, he insisted, "in the sense of ever having held public office, but I think I can lay claim to being a 'citizen politician.' I have always had an interest in politics and been an active participant."[24] As usual, Reagan made a series of questionable assertions in the speech. Among them, he claimed the state's unemployment rate was "almost 40 percent higher than the rest of the nation," that 15 percent of Californians were on welfare, and that the state did not have residency requirements for them. All three assertions were incorrect.[25]

On the campaign trail, Reagan still fed audiences the same red meat about big government as he had done throughout his GE years. To his warnings about the federal government's threat to personal freedom, Reagan added a cautionary note about the danger to states' rights:

> The administration in Sacramento is guilty of a leadership gap. Unwilling, or unable, to solve the problems of California has reduced this state to virtually an administrative district of the Federal government. This isn't to deny the rightful place of the Federal government; but state sovereignty is an integral part of the checks and balances designed to restrain power and to restrain one group from destroying the freedom of another. We can do more by keeping California tax dollars in California than we can by running them through those puzzle palaces on the Potomac only to get them back minus a carrying charge.
>
> Federal help has neither reduced the size of the burden of our state government, nor has it solved our problems. In California, government is larger in proportion to the population than in any other state and it is increasing twice as fast as the increase in population. Our tax burden, local and state, is $100 higher per capita than it is in the rest of the nation, and the local property tax is increasing twice as fast as our increase in personal income.

Reagan called the California-focused plan that he pitched as an alternative to the Great Society programs of President Johnson "A Creative Society." To Reagan this meant "it would be the task of the entire state government to discover, enlist and mobilize the incredibly rich human resources of California, calling on the best in every field to review and revise our governmental structure and present plans for streamlining it and making it more efficient and more effective." In years past, Reagan had mentioned California only when talking about his movie days. Running for governor required plans for fighting crime in California, improving the state's economy, cutting taxes, and reforming welfare and higher education.[26]

Reagan had once closed his speeches with this declaration: "You and I have a rendezvous with destiny. We will preserve for our children this, the last best hope of man on Earth, or we will sentence them to take the last step into a thousand years of darkness." Now, on the stump across California, Reagan ended with these inspiring words: "You and I can start a prairie fire in this state that says to the people in the forty-nine other states that you don't need a big brother in Washington or the other state capitals."[27]

His usual eloquence was still there, but missing were many of the reliable, audience-pleasing antifederal government anecdotes he had used for years. While many of his well-worn lines vanished, the skills Reagan acquired and honed on the road for ten years remained. "Reagan was a competent actor with limited range," wrote Lou Cannon, who covered Reagan's governor's race for the *San Jose Mercury News*. "As a politician, however, he was so enormously gifted that he seemed a president-in-waiting almost as soon as he began campaigning."[28] Another reporter who covered Reagan's campaign, Relman Morin of the Associated Press, marveled in print about Reagan's speechmaking skill. "He makes a smooth speech, seldom using a text or pausing to reach for a word," Morin wrote in September 1966. "He says he writes all his speeches himself. They are punchy, articulate, a blend of humor, serious discussion of issues, and satirical pot shots aimed at his Democratic opponent, Gov. Edmund G. Brown."[29]

Reagan's oratory was not the only skill that impressed observers. His political instincts proved sharp, as he deftly declined Goldwater's offer of assistance to campaign on his behalf. Goldwater meant to return a favor to his old friend who had devoted months to helping his presidential campaign in California and nationally. Reagan, however, could not have missed the fact that Lyndon Johnson captured almost 60 percent of the vote in California on the same day that his former co-star, George Murphy, narrowly defeated his Democratic opponent for a U.S. Senate seat. (Reagan would later call Murphy "my John the Baptist.")[30] The message to Reagan and other Republicans was unmistakable: A Republican could win a statewide race in California, but not if he were viewed as an extreme, Barry Goldwater Republican.

Democrats were eager to remind voters of Reagan's strong ties to Goldwater. "Despite Reagan's new role of sweet reasonableness," the Los Angeles County Democratic Party chairman,

Paul Posner, said in January 1966, "he is more than ever before the leading character in the continuing assault of right-wing extremists on responsible government." Posner noted Reagan had "managed Goldwater's campaign in California and helped raise money for him in a dozen other states." Reagan, Posner said, "is a devout disciple of the Goldwater philosophy and the Goldwater views."[31] Occasionally Reagan's rhetorical subtlety reminded Republican audiences of his friendship with Goldwater. When he spoke to a religious group in Fresno late in the campaign, Reagan said, "We want a policy based on what we know in our hearts is right." To any Goldwater supporter, this was an homage to Goldwater's familiar campaign slogan from 1964: "In your heart you know he's right."[32]

California Republicans appeared not to care that Reagan distanced himself from Goldwater. The party—in state government, at least—had spent years in the wilderness. No matter how extreme his views, Reagan represented the hope of dispirited Republicans that their party could reverse its fortunes. He knew his persuasive and cheerful countenance supplanted Goldwater's growls and scowls. Many California conservatives decided their movement needed someone to deliver a hard reset—and do it with a kind face and a soothing voice. Reagan was well suited for this role. "The difference between the primaries of 1964 and your primary of 1966 is a study in contrasts," former Goldwater campaign treasurer J. William Middendorf would tell Reagan in a letter that summer. Goldwater, he observed, "permitted himself to be miscast and to let his own words be thrown back at him. He became a study in mistake-clichés that the opposition could grab hold of." Reagan, however, had "not yet made a single mistake," Middendorf said. "In a word I am absolutely amazed at the performance so far, considering the big spotlight on you."[33]

Reagan would win the Republican primary in early June, defeating his main rival, former San Francisco mayor George Christopher. His deft work on the stump helped him secure the nomination, but his celebrity and his labors for Goldwater in 1964 were also important factors in the victory. In the fall election, Reagan crushed Brown, winning a million more votes than the two-time incumbent. "I pledge a government of all the people of California," he told a cheering crowd at the Biltmore Hotel in Los Angeles. "Partisanship has ended as of today."[34]

What also began that day was speculation about Reagan's next role. The following morning, in a front-page story in the *Los Angeles Times*, the paper's Washington bureau chief, Robert J. Donovan, opined about possible "contenders or kingmakers" in the 1968 Republican presidential contest. "Among them," Donovan wrote, were Michigan governor George Romney, Illinois senator-elect Charles Percy, and former vice president Richard Nixon. Also mentioned was the man who, little more than a year before, had been hosting a syndicated western television show and pitching Borax soap powder.[35]

THE SUCCESS OF REAGAN'S speech not only transformed his life and turned him into an instant contender for California governor in 1966; it also revealed to conservative Republicans—humiliated by the voters' rejection of their message and weary of toiling in the wilderness—there might be a way out. "Reagan was now a national political voice," biographer Thomas Evans wrote. "His postgraduate education in political science had taken years and had borne fruit in a most spectacular fashion."[36] Reagan's October 1964 speech "was, to be sure, the hard-line anticommunist message," historian Jonathan Darman observed. "But it also revived the sentiment of moral clarity that [John F.] Kennedy had evoked so well—that the purpose of a meaningful life was not to avoid suffering but to find something that was worth suffering for." The message was not new, but perhaps the messenger was. With Reagan's "warm, textured voice," Darman observed, "the conservative message sounded altogether different from what had been coming from Goldwater."[37]

This is not to diminish how much Goldwater's crushing defeat depressed conservatives, who feared Johnson had destroyed their movement. Exultant liberals in both parties, meanwhile, concluded voters had delivered a decisive and deadly blow to conservatism. Reagan's stirring speech gave conservatives hope the liberals were wrong. "Although failing in its immediate goal of defeating Lyndon Johnson, [Reagan's speech] nevertheless had a profound and lasting effect on the American political scene," Paul Erickson wrote, adding, "Conservatives found a champion in this new spokesperson." Reagan would not be the only champion leading conservatives through the wilderness years of the 1960s and early 1970s. And there would be little on the national scene in the coming decade to instill in the hearts of defeated conservatives much hope their movement might triumph with the election, in 1980, of Reagan as president. No matter. Overnight Reagan was an unabashed national celebrity among those on the political Right. In the laboratory of California over the next eight years (he would serve two terms in Sacramento), Governor Reagan would prove that conservatism was plausible as a governing ideology and might one day prevail nationwide.

But it was "The Speech" that so many Republicans could not forget. "The speech came too late to rescue Goldwater, who lost in a landslide to Johnson," historian H. W. Brands noted in his biography of Reagan. "But it earned Reagan a future." Brands added, "In American political history, no speech ever did more than Reagan's to launch a national political career."[38] The only speech as important to the presidential hopes of a prospective candidate was the one Abraham Lincoln had delivered on slavery at New York's Cooper Union on February 27, 1860. As Goldwater aide Stephen Shadegg wrote in his memoir of Goldwater's campaign, Reagan had given "by far the most effective exposition of conservative concern for the future of the nation offered by anyone in the 1964 campaign."[39]

Reagan's message in the 1960s was a forerunner of his effective appeals to working-class Democrats in the 1980 presidential campaign. "The entire speech had been directed at one audience," Henry Olsen wrote in his 2017 book on Reagan, *The Working-Class Republican*, "the men and women who, like Reagan, had once believed the Democratic Party was their vehicle but now had to face the truth that it had become wedded to another cause."[40] Writing in his history of the conservative movement, Jonathan M. Schoenwald observed: "As much as Goldwater and his campaign had come to be recognized as a defining moment among conservatives, Reagan too became an object of reverence. If Goldwater had articulated the need for a broad-based conservative coalition, Reagan succeeded in demonstrating that it was possible to assemble one that would not only refrain from offending liberal Republicans and conservative Democrats but would actually attract them too."[41]

Conservatives had long "hungered for a national spokesman with political sex appeal," journalist Joseph Lewis wrote several years after the 1964 election. "Goldwater was too blunt and abrasive for all but a committed few. But when thousands of people watched Reagan saying essentially the same things, the message was much more palatable. His manner was friendly and engaging, devoid of the bitterness that often crept into conservative speeches."[42] To Shadegg, Reagan's speech had been simply "the most effective exposition of conservative concern for the future of the nation offered by anyone in the 1964 campaign."[43]

"Few may have recognized it at the time," historian Gary Donaldson wrote, "but it was the passing of the baton from one leader in the conservative movement to another."[44] As Lou Cannon put it succinctly: "'The Speech' was such a beacon for conservatives that Reagan was soon being touted as a probable candidate for governor with the clear intimation that he might someday become president."[45]

For Reagan, it had been the defining event of his early political life—the moment that time, chance, and preparation transformed him in the minds of many conservatives from fading actor into rising political star. Ten years after the 1964 election—in the last of his eight years as governor—Reagan traveled the country campaigning for Republican candidates for Congress and governor. Along the way, one of his speechwriters recalled, voters and campaign workers would mention to Reagan his 1964 speech. "In state after state," Peter Hannaford recalled, "we would run into volunteer drivers and event coordinators who said that it was Reagan's 1964 speech that first caused them to get actively involved in politics."[46]

But it was more than a speech. It was the spark and later the ballast of Reagan's early political career. In another sense, however, the speech was the culmination of a decade of training and experimentation on the minor-league "fields" of General Electric plants, small-town chambers of commerce, and Rotary clubs. When many viewers first heard him speak in 1964, Reagan had polished his message to near perfection. Going back further, Reagan's training for his October 1964 triumph began in the radio studios of Davenport and Des Moines, Iowa. There he practiced communicating not to vast crowds but to isolated baseball fans. In these early years, Reagan perfected the art of speaking to the individual, not the crowd. Over time, Paul Erickson concluded, "The Voice of the Cubs became the Great Communicator and approached his own rendezvous with destiny."[47] Reagan may have put it best in his postpresidential memoir: "Of course, I didn't know it then, but that speech was one of the most important milestones in my life—another one of those unexpected turns in the road that led me onto a path I never expected to take."[48]

Epilogue

Ron, Would You Come Down?

Reagan surveyed the sea of delegates on the floor of Kansas City's Kemper Arena on the night of Thursday, August 19, 1976—the final day of the Republican National Convention. From their VIP box, he and Nancy had watched President Gerald Ford accept the party's presidential nomination. The day before, Reagan had been Ford's rival for that nomination. Tonight he was destined to leave the arena a bit player in the evening's drama, a sixty-five-year-old former California governor whose political career had sputtered to a disappointing, dispiriting end. To those in the hall and in the nationwide television audience, the convention appeared to be over.

And then Reagan's fortunes changed. As the band played, Ford stepped to the podium, leaned into the microphone, and invited his conquered opponent to the dais. "Ron," he bellowed, "would you come down and bring Nancy?" The president wanted Reagan to deliver the convention's final words.[1]

It would be an unusual end to a long and bitter campaign. Ford and his advisers had feared the struggle over the Republican nomination might cost the incumbent the election, and Reagan had ignored his critics who urged him to concede. He fought on, even after a string of early primary defeats suggested he had little chance to win. By the time he rolled into Kansas City, however, Reagan had won ten of the twenty-two contested primaries—a remarkable feat for a challenger. After a contentious convention, Ford had prevailed with 1,187 delegates to Reagan's 1,070. In voting on Wednesday, Reagan fell 117 delegates short.

Ford had the nomination, but now he needed Reagan's endorsement. More than that, he needed Reagan to bless him as the legitimate leader of a conservative movement that sometimes doubted the accidental president's bona fides. For Reagan, this last-minute speech to delegates would likely be his political swan song. The next day's *New York Times* would declare him "defeated and apparently at the end of his political career." Reagan knew that whatever he told the convention must be strong and memorable. "Mike, I have no idea what I'm going to say," he told his longtime, trusted aide Michael Deaver as they left the box.[2]

As he hustled to the dais to unify the party that his insurgent candidacy had helped divide, Reagan knew the press would listen for any hint of lingering discord between him and Ford. If Ford lost to former Georgia governor Jimmy Carter—the Democratic Party's nominee—Reagan knew he could share the blame. He knew tens of millions would watch on television as he spoke. He knew the drama in the convention hall would be palpable. And despite the anxiety he expressed to Deaver, Reagan knew exactly what he wanted to say.

And Ford's aides knew exactly what role they wanted Reagan to play: reproduce the magic of Carter's convention, at which the Reverend Martin Luther King Sr. closed the festivities with an electrifying benediction. The scene was riveting television and sent delegates home unified around their nominee.[3] Now Ford's staff hoped Reagan would help them create a similar emotional ending.

Ford's thirty-six-minute acceptance speech had been a departure from his usual plodding style. "Ford had come alive," commentator William F. Buckley Jr. wrote in a column after the convention. "It was in itself an electrifying performance. And it was in the circumstances something very nearly miraculous, as if Joe Palooka had appeared in the Roman Senate and outshone Cicero. There was determination, fluency, and a sense of spirit in the message."[4] *Time* called the speech "one of the president's finest hours."[5] For what Ford lacked in easy command of the podium he compensated with commanding presentation. "You at home listening tonight," Ford said, "you are the people who pay the taxes and obey the laws. You are the people who make our system work. You are the people who make America what it is. It is from your ranks that I come and on your side that I stand." Delegates loved it, and for many, it stood briefly as the week's rhetorical highlight and a harmonious conclusion to a fractious convention. What came next, however, would make Ford's oration seem pedestrian by comparison.

Once delegates saw Reagan at the dais, Nancy recalled, he got "the largest, loudest ovation I had ever heard."[6] Journalist Elizabeth Drew, who watched from the press gallery, believed the applause was louder than what delegates gave Ford.[7] As Reagan "took the microphone at Ford's bidding," *Time* wrote, "the eyes of many delegates shimmered with tears."[8] A United Press International reporter noted, "Some openly wept."[9]

After Ford's brief introduction, Reagan strode to the microphone "with the sureness of a salmon returning to home waters," his biographer Edmund Morris wrote.[10] He would give an abbreviated version of an acceptance speech he had already composed. "There are cynics who say that a party platform is something that no one bothers to read and it doesn't very often amount to much," Reagan said in an unmistakable reference to that week's struggle over a foreign policy plank, included at Reagan's urging, that tacitly rebuked Ford for negotiating with the Soviet Union. Rather than fight and lose, Ford agreed to the plank's language.[11] Reagan continued: "Whether it is different this time than it has ever been before, I believe the Republican Party has a platform that is a banner of bold, unmistakable colors, with no pastel shades." Delegates roared with approval. "We have just heard a call to arms based on that platform, and a call to us to really be successful in communicating and reveal to the American people the difference between this platform and the platform of the opposing party, which is nothing but a revamp and a reissue and a running of a late, late show of the thing that we have been hearing from them for the last forty years."

That last line, from an actor whose black-and-white movies many Americans had watched on late-night television, spurred raucous applause. The audience that rose to applaud Reagan's arrival at the podium would not sit.[12] Then Reagan arrived at the heart of his short speech and its most riveting and emotional moments. To a near-silent convention hall he told a story:

> I had an assignment the other day. Someone asked me to write a letter for a time capsule that is going to be opened in Los Angeles a hundred years from now, on our Tricentennial.
>
> It sounded like an easy assignment. They suggested I write something about the problems and the issues today. I set out to do so, riding down the coast in an automobile, looking at the blue Pacific out on one side and the Santa Ynez Mountains on the other, and I couldn't help but wonder if it was going to be that beautiful a hundred years from now as it was on that summer day.
>
> Then as I tried to write—let your own minds turn to that task. You are going to write for people a hundred years from now, who know all about us. We know nothing about them. We don't know what kind of a world they will be living in.
>
> And suddenly I thought to myself if I write of the problems, they will be the domestic problems the president spoke of here tonight; the challenges confronting us, the erosion of freedom that has taken place under Democratic rule in this country, the invasion of private rights, the controls and restrictions on the vitality of the great free economy that we enjoy. These are our challenges that we must meet.
>
> And then again, there is that challenge of which he spoke that we live in a world in which the great powers have poised and aimed at each other horrible missiles of destruction, nuclear weapons that can in a matter of minutes arrive at each other's country and destroy, virtually, the civilized world we live in.
>
> And suddenly it dawned on me, those who would read this letter a hundred years from now will know whether those missiles were fired. They will know whether we met our challenge.

Whether they have the freedoms that we have known up until now will depend on what we do here.

Will they look back with appreciation and say, "Thank God for those people in 1976 who headed off that loss of freedom, who kept us—now one hundred years later—free, who kept our world from nuclear destruction"?

And if we failed, they probably won't get to read the letter at all because it spoke of individual freedom, and they won't be allowed to talk of that or read of it.

This is our challenge, and this is why, here in this hall tonight—better than we have ever done before—we have got to quit talking to each other and about each other and go out and communicate to the world that we may be fewer in numbers than we have ever been, but we carry the message they are waiting for.

Reagan spoke every word from memory. Unlike Ford, he required no teleprompter. He never broke eye contact with delegates. The passion and emotion of his earnest words, his perfect timing, and his supreme self-assurance before one of the largest crowds of his career had not intimidated him. Reagan drew strength from the crowd's silent adulation. After the applause died, he closed his oration with a familiar line from the late Gen. Douglas MacArthur: "We must go forth from here united, determined that what a great general said a few years ago is true: There is no substitute for victory, Mr. President." As Reagan backed away from the lectern, the convention hall went wild. The band again struck up "California Here We Come." Vice President Nelson Rockefeller grasped Reagan's hand and told him, "That was beautiful."[13]

Praise for Reagan's speech was immediate and lavish. Writing in the *Nashville Tennessean*, publisher John Seigenthaler noted, "It was the final oration by Ronald Reagan that stole the show."[14] In the *Washington Evening Star* the next day, columnist Mark Shields wrote that "many Americans were finally introduced to Ronald Reagan and found him to be somebody you would not mind having season tickets next to."[15] Columnist Robert Donovan observed, "The sight, sound, and spirit" of the convention "made the Republicans look more like the party of Reagan" than of Ford. "If Reagan had wanted the vice presidential nomination for himself, which he did not," Donovan added, "the convention might well have forced him on Ford, no matter what the President wished."[16] Wrote the *Chicago Tribune*'s Washington bureau chief: "On almost every day and in every way, the Republican National Convention demonstrated that the symbol of the Grand Old Party is Ronald Reagan."[17]

Reagan's remarkable speech was significant in at least one other way: It would be the second time in twelve years he had delivered the best speech of a presidential campaign—for the losing candidate. Now, as in October 1964, Reagan's rare ability to deliver the conservative message captured the imagination of Republican voters. Reporter Bob Schmidt reflected in the *Independent Press-Telegram* of Long Beach a few days after the Kansas City convention: "Reagan's 1964 speech for [Goldwater] was a skilled exhortation for the free enterprise system, and was written and delivered with such mastery that it was easily the most upbeat, memorable moment in the otherwise downbeat, disastrous campaign." That 1964 speech, Schmidt added, had propelled Reagan into "a meteoric ascendancy" that resulted in his election as governor in 1966, "and to another speech [the coda of the 1976 convention], perhaps the briefest, most impressive speech of all."[18]

In 1964 some Republicans had watched Reagan's powerful speech on television and wondered if they had chosen the wrong candidate. The same fleeting remorse reappeared as Reagan ceded the spotlight to Ford at the end of the 1976 convention. As Reagan's Texas co-chair Ernie Angelo later said, "I personally heard a number of people say, 'We've nominated the wrong man.' And I'd look around and I'd see somebody wearing a Ford button saying that. It wasn't just one or two."[19] Reagan knew that although Ford would leave town with the nomination, he would depart Kansas City with delegates' hearts.

The morning after the speech, some supporters unfurled a

large banner from Reagan's hotel. "Goodbye GOP. You Blew It," it said.[20] As she and her husband headed for the airport to return to California, Nancy Reagan looked out the window of their car. On the roadside stood a lonely supporter waving a simple, hand-painted sign that echoed the banner hanging from their hotel: "GOODBYE REPUBLICANS. YOU PICKED THE WRONG MAN."[21]

Notes

Abbreviations

DBP   Dean Burch Papers
GHDP Government History Documentation Project
LCRRP Lou Cannon–Ronald Reagan Papers
LRBP Lemuel R. Boulware Papers
RRPL Ronald Reagan Presidential Library
SGC   Shadegg/Goldwater Collection
VTV   Vanderbilt TV News Archive

1. My Heart Is a Ham Loaf

1. "Ronald for Real," *Time*, October 6, 1966.

2. Ronald Reagan, "Remarks during a Homecoming and Birthday Celebration in Dixon, Illinois," February 6, 1984, in Gerhard Peters and John T. Woolley, *The American Presidency Project*, http://www.presidency.ucsb.edu.

3. Reagan, *Reagan: A Life in Letters*, 35.

4. Ron Reagan, *My Father at 100*, 61.

5. Ronald Reagan, *An American Life*, 25.

6. Reagan, *Where's the Rest of Me?* 7.

7. Reagan, *Where's the Rest of Me?* 7.

8. Reagan, *An American Life*, 21.

9. A. Edwards, *The Reagans*, 28.

10. Reagan, *An American Life*, 22.

11. Reagan, *An American Life*, 21–23, 27–28.

12. Reagan, *An American Life*, 35.

13. Morgan, *Reagan*, 7; Morrell, *Reagan's Journey*, 19–20.

14. Reagan, *An American Life*, 35.

15. Reagan, *An American Life*, 41.

16. Morgan, *Reagan*, 11–12; Hannaford, *Reagan's Roots*, 62–64.

17. "'Dutch' Reagan Had Made Fine Mark as Guard," *Dixon Evening Telegraph*, July 23, 1932.

18. Morris, *Dutch*, 11.

19. Ron Reagan, *My Father at 100*, 8.

20. Reagan, *An American Life*, 31.

21. Reagan, *An American Life*, 47; A. Edwards, *Early Reagan*, 88–89.

22. A. Edwards, *Early Reagan*, 90.

23. Reagan, *An American Life*, 47–48.

24. Wills, *Reagan's America*, 58.

25. Reagan, *An American Life*, 47–48; L. Cannon, *Governor Reagan*, 25–27.

26. Morgan, *Reagan*, 14.

27. Reagan, *Where's the Rest of Me?* 28–29.

28. Ron Reagan, *My Father at 100*, 173.

29. Reagan, *Where's the Rest of Me?* 29.

30. Hannaford, *Reagan's Roots*, 77–78; Reagan, *Where's the Rest of Me?* 38.

31. Reagan, *An American Life*, 42.

32. Reagan, *Reagan: A Life in Letters*, 19.

33. Reagan, *An American Life*, 9, 27.

34. Reagan, *An American Life*, 22.

35. Reagan, *Where's the Rest of Me?* 7.

36. Reagan, *Reagan: A Life in Letters*, 33–34.

37. Reagan, *Where's the Rest of Me?* 7, 41.

38. Reagan, *Where's the Rest of Me?* 42, 52.

39. Reagan, *Where's the Rest of Me?* 54.

40. Wills, *Reagan's America*, 83.

41. Reagan, *An American Life*, 66–67.

42. Reagan, *Reagan: A Life in Letters*, 36.

43. Reagan, *An American Life*, 66–67.

44. Ron Reagan, *My Father at 100*, 165; Reagan, *Reagan: A Life in Letters*, 27.

45. Reagan, *Where's the Rest of Me?* 7, 46.

46. "Hired for Season," *Dixon Evening Telegraph*, October 26, 1932; A. Edwards, *Early Reagan*, 123, 125; Reagan, *Reagan: A Life in Letters*, 29–31.

47. Reagan, *Where's the Rest of Me?* 59; "May Get Radio Job," *Dixon Evening Telegraph*, January 28, 1933.

48. "'Dutch' Reagan Winning Place in Radio World," *Dixon Evening Telegraph*, August 11, 1934.

49. Reagan, *Where's the Rest of Me?* 59.

50. Reagan, *Where's the Rest of Me?* 70; Spitz, *Reagan*, 138.

51. A. Edwards, *Early Reagan*, 149

52. "Ronald Reagan's Fine Work Rewarded with Top Film Roles," *Dixon Evening Telegraph*, September 12, 1941.

53. Reagan, *Where's the Rest of Me?* 74; "Dutch Reagan Gets Contract in Hollywood," *Des Moines Register*, April 3, 1937; "Ronald Reagan Reveals His Reaction over Success," *Dixon Evening Telegraph*, April 16, 1937.

2. Mr. Norm Is My Alias

1. Reagan, *An American Life*, 89; Reagan, *Where's the Rest of Me?* 83; "Dutch Does First Scene Over Again," *Des Moines Register*, July 4, 1937.

2. "Dutch Is Hit in First Film," *Des Moines Register*, August 22, 1937.

3. "'Dutch' Makes His First Scene," *Des Moines Register*, June 27, 1937.

4. Smith, *Who Is Ronald Reagan?* 55; Reagan, *An American Life*, 85–89.

5. Reagan, *An American Life*, 92–93; "Ronald Reagan's Fine Work Rewarded with Top Film Roles," *Dixon* (IL) *Evening Telegraph*, September 12, 1941.

6. Reagan, *An American Life*, 89.

7. A. Edwards, *Early Reagan*, 185.

8. Vaughn, *Ronald Reagan in Hollywood*, 37.

9. Smith, *Who Is Ronald Reagan?* 55.

10. Vaughn, *Ronald Reagan in Hollywood*, 231.

11. Ron Reagan, *My Father at 100*, 9.

12. Wills, *Reagan's America*, 205–6, 211; Quirk, *Jane Wyman*, 63.

13. A. Edwards, *Early Reagan*, 16.

14. Williams, "The Disordered Memories of a Movie Actor," *Westport* (CT) *News*, October 31, 1980.

15. Reagan, *An American Life*, 25.

16. Williams, "The Disordered Memories of a Movie Actor."

17. Earl Dunckel oral history, 1982, GHDP.

18. Jessica Mitford, "The Rest of Ronald Reagan," *Ramparts*, November 1965, 36

19. McClelland, *Hollywood on Ronald Reagan*, 228.

20. A. Edwards, *Early Reagan*, 228, 230.

21. L. Cannon, *President Reagan*, 128.

22. Williams, "The Disordered Memories of a Movie Actor."

23. McClelland, *Hollywood on Ronald Reagan*, 225.

24. A. Edwards, *Early Reagan*, 246.

25. Allyson, *June Allyson*, 96; A. Edwards, *Early Reagan*, 229.

26. Colacello, *Ronnie and Nancy*, 288.

27. Yager, *Ronald Reagan's Journey*, 62.

28. Reagan, *Where's the Rest of Me?* 139.

29. L. Cannon, *Governor Reagan*, 93–94.

30. Lewis, *What Makes Reagan Run?* 43–44.

31. Reagan, *An American Life*, 96; Peretti, *The Leading Man*, 188; Rose, *The Agency*, 81.

32. "Ronald Reagan's Fine Work."

33. Stephen Vaughn, "Spies, National Security, and the 'Inertia Projector': The Secret Service Films of Ronald Reagan," *American Quarterly* 39, no. 3 (Autumn 1987): 366.

34. "RAF's Yanks Shown in Film at the Strand," *New York Daily News*, November 14, 1941.

35. Thomas, *The Films of Ronald Reagan*, 124–27, 137–40; Klein and Villines, *Ronald Reagan's Road to the White House*, 87–91.

36. Vaughn, "Spies, National Security, and the 'Inertia Projector,'" 366.

37. Vaughn, *Ronald Reagan in Hollywood*, 35.

38. Vaughn, *Ronald Reagan in Hollywood*, 103.

39. "Reagan Departs to Report for Army Service," *Los Angeles Times*, April 20, 1942; "Ronald Reagan Gets Transfer to Burbank," *San Bernardino County Sun*, June 11, 1942; "Many Previously Rejected Now Acceptable, Army Says," *Pittsburgh Press*, November 4, 1942; "Defends AFMP Unit No. 1," *El Paso Times*, December 18, 1942; Doherty, *Show Trial*, 166; "World War II: The Movie," *Air & Space Magazine*, March 2012, https://www.airspacemag.com/history-of-flight/world-war-ii-the -movie-21103597/?c=y&page=2; Spitz, *Reagan*, 196; Friedrich, *City of Nets*, 155–56; "History of the 11th Armored Cavalry Regiment," http://www.irwin.army.mil/ Pages/Units/11thACR/History14.html; "Military Service of Ronald Reagan," RRPL, https://www.reaganlibrary.gov/sreference/military-service-of-ronald-reagan.

40. Klein and Villines, *Ronald Reagan's Road to the White House*, 98.

41. Vaughn, *Ronald Reagan in Hollywood*, 112–18.

42. Vaughn, *Ronald Reagan in Hollywood*, 118; Spitz, *Reagan*, 201.

43. Morris, *Dutch*, 210.

44. Reagan, *An American Life*, 102.

45. Spitz, *Reagan*, 206.

46. Reagan, *Where's the Rest of Me?* 139–40.

47. Reagan, *Where's the Rest of Me?* 139.

48. Reagan, *An American Life*, 105, 161.

49. Van Ells, *To Hear Only Thunder Again*, 31, 135, 176, 188.

50. Morris, *Dutch*, 228.

51. Reagan, *An American Life*, 106.

52. Reagan, *Where's the Rest of Me?* 165; "American Veterans Committee," *Van Nuys News*, May 9, 1946.

53. Morris, *Dutch*, 221.

54. "Links Republicans to Reds, Fascists," *New York Times*, December 15, 1946.

55. Morris, *Dutch*, 229.

56. Smith, *Who Is Ronald Reagan?* 63; Eliot, *Reagan*, 174.

57. Reagan, *Where's the Rest of Me?* 142; Reagan, *An American Life*, 105–7.

58. "Film Chiefs Organize to Battle Communism," *San Francisco Examiner*, February 4, 1944.

59. Eliot, *Reagan*, 153, 172–75.

60. Reagan, *Where's the Rest of Me?* 167; Spitz, *Reagan*, 215; Morris, *Dutch*, 233.

61. Reagan, *Where's the Rest of Me?* 166–67.

62. Reagan, *An American Life*, 111–13

63. Reagan, *An American Life*, 113; Eliot, *Reagan*, 177; Morris, *Dutch*, 233–34; Spitz, *Reagan*, 215.

64. Wills, *Reagan's America*, 292–93.

65. Neil Reagan oral history, GHDP.

66. Bunch, *Tear Down This Myth*, 33.

67. Vaughn, *Ronald Reagan in Hollywood*, 35.

68. Reagan, *An American Life*, 110.

3. Have You Ever Heard Him Talk?

1. Holden, *The Making of the Great Communicator*, 104.

2. McClelland, *Hollywood on Ronald Reagan*, 158.

3. Day, *Doris Day*, 121.

4. A. Edwards, *Early Reagan*, 229.

5. Arthur Bell, "Bell Tells," *Village Voice*, November 12–18, 1980.

6. Eliot, *Reagan*, 176.

7. Reagan, *An American Life*, 105.

8. Brands, *Reagan*, 61–62; McDougal, *The Last Mogul*, 138–39; Kleinknecht, *The Man Who Sold the World*, 40; Sperber and Lax, *Bogart*, 330.

9. Holden, *The Making of the Great Communicator*, 104.

10. Reagan, *An American Life*, 89.

11. Jack Dales oral history, GHDP; A. Edwards, *Early Reagan*, 231; "Ronald Reagan," SAG website: https://www.sagaftra.org/ronald-reagan.

12. "Ronald Reagan," SAG website; SAG-AFTRA records.

13. Doherty, *Show Trial*, 46.

14. Thomas, *The Films of Ronald Reagan*, 159.

15. Brands, *Reagan*, 68.

16. Hedda Hopper, "Don't Give Him the Ronnie-round," *Honolulu News*, June 22, 1947; Prindle, *The Politics of Glamour*, 48.

17. Prindle, *The Politics of Glamour*, 48; Reagan, *An American Life*, 108; Reagan, *Where's the Rest of Me?* 174–75.

18. Reagan, *An American Life*, 109.

19. Ceplair and Englund, *The Inquisition in Hollywood*, 215–25; Moldea, *Dark Victory*, 66–67.

20. Horne, *Class Struggle in Hollywood*, 15–17.

21. Morris, *Dutch*, 157–58.

22. Reagan, *An American Life*, 111; L. Cannon, *Governor Reagan*, 90; A. Edwards, *Early Reagan*, 306.

23. Reagan, *An American Life*, 110.

24. L. Cannon, *Governor Reagan*, 94–95; Wills, *Reagan's America*, 291.

25. "Men of the Year: Ronald Reagan & Yuri Andropov," *Time*, January 2, 1984.

26. Wills, *Reagan's America*, 293, 297.

27. Betty Glad, "Reagan's Midlife Crisis and the Turn to the Right," *Political Psychology* 10, no. 4 (December 1989): 620.

28. McClelland, *Hollywood on Ronald Reagan*, 170.

29. Morella and Epstein, *Jane Wyman*, 104–5.

30. Farrell, *Nixon*, 98.

31. "Reagan, Ronald," box 6, Exhibits, Evidence, Etc. Re: Committee Investigations: Hollywood Blacklist, Records of the Investigative Section, National Archives.

32. Transcript of Reagan House committee testimony, October 23, 1947, Ronald Reagan Presidential Foundation, https://www.reaganfoundation.org/media/51313 /red-scare.pdf; A. Edwards, *Early Reagan*, 338–49; Doherty, *Show Trial*, 167.

33. Doherty, *Show Trial*, 168; Vaughn, *Ronald Reagan in Hollywood*, 148.

34. "Mr. Reagan Airs His Views," *Chicago Tribune*, May 18, 1947.

35. Jack Dales interview, August 18, 2002, box 2, LCRRP.

36. Reagan, *An American Life*, 119–20.

37. McClelland, *Hollywood on Ronald Reagan*, 152.

38. Reagan, *An American Life*, 119–20.

4. An Ambassador of Goodwill

1. Erskine Johnson, "Ronald Reagan Rebels at 'Boy Scout' Roles," *Gastonia* (NC) *Gazette*, February 7, 1950.

2. Bob Thomas, "Ronald Reagan Has New Plans for His Film Career," *Mt. Vernon* (IL) *Register-News*, January 6, 1950.

3. A. Edwards, *Early Reagan*, 361.

4. Neal, *As I Am*, 113.

5. Reagan, *Where's the Rest of Me?* 232.

6. Morella and Epstein, *Jane Wyman*, 92.

7. McClelland, *Hollywood on Ronald Reagan*, 166.

8. Eliot, *Reagan*, 153.

9. Richard Schickel, "No Method to His Madness," *Film Comment*, May/ June 1987, https://www.filmcomment.com/article/ronald-reagan-film-career -actor-president/.

10. M. Reagan, *First Father, First Daughter*, 44.

11. M. Reagan, *First Father, First Daughter*, 44–45.

12. Jerry Asher quoted in Quirk, *Jane Wyman*, 42.

13. "Jane Wyman Is Granted Divorce; Blames 'Politics,'" *Cumberland* (MD) *News*, June 29, 1948; "Jane Wyman Divorces Ronald Reagan," *Freeport* (IL) *Journal-Standard*, June 30, 1948.

14. Schweizer, *Reagan's War*, 15.

15. Vaughn, *Ronald Reagan in Hollywood*, 227.

16. Eliot, *Reagan*, 211–12.

17. "Searchlight Spectacle Lights Gilmore Stadium," *Los Angeles Times*, September 24, 1948.

18. Reagan, *Reagan: A Life in Letters*, 36; "Truman Tells Crowd Sole Hope for U.S. Lies in His Re-election," *Los Angeles Times*, September 24, 1948; Jessel, *The World I Lived In*, 161–64.

19. "Reagan Heads Union Drive to Aid Truman," *Los Angeles Times*, October 5, 1948.

20. L. Edwards, *The Essential Ronald Reagan*, 40; audio of Reagan radio speech, https://www.youtube.com/watch?v=uJDhS4oUm0M.

21. L. Cannon, *Governor Reagan*, 101.

22. McClelland, *Hollywood on Ronald Reagan*, 229.

23. Douglas, *A Full Life*, 323.

24. Leuchtenburg, *In the Shadow of FDR*, 217.

25. Reagan, *An American Life*, 132.

26. A. Edwards, *Early Reagan*, 418.

27. L. Cannon, *Governor Reagan*, 101–2.

28. Ronald Reagan, "Inside on Labor," *Evening Review* (East Liverpool OH), July 27, 1951.

29. "Russ Imperialism Seen by Veteran," *Los Angeles Times*, July 17, 1951.

30. "Ronald Reagan Fighting Hollywood Communists," *Shreveport Times*, July 20, 1951.

31. "Film Freedom Held Cut by Political Censorship," *Los Angeles Times*, February 19, 1952.

32. Vaughn, *Ronald Reagan in Hollywood*, 234.

33. L. Cannon, *Governor Reagan*, 102.

34. "Ronald Reagan Top Labor Leader of Hollywood Actors," *Courier* (Waterloo IA), May 12, 1952.

35. Reagan, *An American Life*, 133.

36. To Sam Harwood Jr., December 1952, quoted in Morris, *Dutch*, 292.

37. Morris, *Dutch*, 292.

38. Evans, *The Education of Ronald Reagan*, 16.

39. Speech text, "America the Beautiful," 1980 Campaign Papers, 1965–80, series XXII: Tony Dolan Files: RR Speeches (Reference File), box 873, RRPL.

40. Speech text, "America the Beautiful."

41. Maier, *American Scripture*, 150–57; McCullough, *John Adams*, 136–37.

42. Lippard, *Legends of the American Revolution*, 395–97.

43. Ronald Reagan, "Your America to Be Free," commencement address at Eureka College, June 9, 1957, transcript online: https://patriotpost.us/pages/425-ronald-reagan-your-america-to-be-free.

44. Reagan, *The Greatest Speeches of Ronald Reagan*, 19–22.

45. David Broder, "The Great Persuader," *Washington Post*, June 7, 2004; "Reagan Praises Role Played by Small Liberal Arts Schools," *Pantagraph* (Bloomington IL), June 10, 1957.

46. "'Wing, Prayer' Air Thriller," *Star Tribune* (Minneapolis), August 13, 1944; Fitzgerald, *Way Out There in the Blue*, 22; Suid, *Guts and Glory*, 89–90.

47. Michael Deaver oral history interview, Miller Center, University of Virginia, September 12, 2002, https://millercenter.org/the-presidency/presidential-oral-histories/michael-deaver-oral-history-deputy-chief-staff.

48. "The Telling Tale," *Washington Post*, April 21, 1991; McClelland, *Hollywood on Ronald Reagan*, 38.

49. Evans, *The Education of Ronald Reagan*, 18.

50. McClure, *Ronald Reagan*, 157–74.

51. "The American Film Industry in the Early 1950s," *History of the American Cinema*, Thomson Gale: 1990, https://www.encyclopedia.com/arts/culture -magazines/american-film-industry-early-1950s.

52. Becker, *It's the Pictures That Got Small*, 48.

53. Prindle, *The Politics of Glamour*, 78.

54. Bruck, *When Hollywood Had a King*, 119.

55. Prindle, *The Politics of Glamour*, 78–79; Moldea, *Dark Victory*, 98–99.

56. McDougal, *The Last Mogul*, 184.

57. McDougal, *The Last Mogul*, 186.

58. Transcript of Chester B. "Chet" Migden, June 3, 1998, for SAG Documentary Project, courtesy Screen Actors Guild–American Federation of Television and Radio Artists.

59. SAG biography of Walter Pidgeon, https://www.sagaftra.org/walter -pidgeon.

60. McDougal, *The Last Mogul*, 186.

61. Moldea, *Dark Victory*, 5.

62. "The Monopolist," *New Yorker*, April 21, 2003; Bruck, *When Hollywood Had a King*, 123.

63. Prindle, *The Politics of Glamour*, 81.

64. Migden transcript.

65. McDougal, *The Last Mogul*, 187.

66. A. Edwards, *Early Reagan*, 436; McDougal, *The Last Mogul*, 184–88.

67. Colacello, *Ronnie and Nancy*, 252.

68. Reagan, *Where's the Rest of Me?* 234.

69. Colacello, *Ronnie and Nancy*, 252.

70. A. Edwards, *The Reagans*, 57.

71. N. Reagan, *My Turn*, 100.

72. Colacello, *Ronnie and Nancy*, 278–79.

73. Eliot, *Reagan*, 288.

5. That's the Way, Ron

1. History of Malibu Lake Mountain Club, http://www.maliboulake.com/ History.html.

2. "Bowron Interview on Radio Tonight," *Van Nuys News*, May 10, 1953; Sitton, *Los Angeles Transformed*, 184.

3. Buntin, *L.A. Noir*, 198–99.

4. "Fiery Ronald Reagan's Political Mixing Clipped His Movie Career," *Star Press* (Muncie IN), June 19, 1953.

5. Reagan interview by GHDP, January 19, 1979, copy in box 51, LCRRP.

6. N. Reagan, *My Turn*, 124–25.

7. "The Week the Gipper Played Vegas," *Tampa Bay Times*, April 25, 1984; Spitz, *Reagan*, 3.

8. N. Reagan, *My Turn*, 124–25.

9. Holden, *The Making of the Great Communicator*, 98.

10. Erskine Johnson, "Cornell Ready to Listen," *Elmire* (NY) *Advertiser*, March 10, 1953.

11. Erskine Johnson, "In Hollywood," *Independent Record* (Helena MT), October 1, 1954.

12. Brooks and Marsh, *The Complete Directory to Prime Time Network and Cable TV Shows, 1946–Present*, 1031; Hyatt, *Short-Lived Television Series*, 46–47; Timberg and Erler, *Television Talk*, 274–75; "Day and Night with Radio and Television," *San Francisco Examiner*, May 30, 1953.

13. Reagan, *Reagan: A Life in Letters*, 137, 142.

14. Colacello, *Ronnie and Nancy*, 270; "Reagan Happy over Night Club Success," *Los Angeles Times*, February 26, 1954; "Ronald Reagan Charges Studios Driving Stars into Other Mediums," *Newport* (RI) *Daily News*, February 15, 1954; "The Week the Gipper Played Vegas," *Tampa Bay Times*, April 25, 1984.

15. Reagan, *An American Life*, 125.

16. "Ronald Reagan Charges Studios Driving Stars into Other Mediums."

17. Reagan, *An American Life*, 125.

18. Eliot, *Reagan*, 268; "Tonight's TV," *Akron Beacon Journal*, July 18, 1953.

19. McDougal, *The Last Mogul*, 189; Newcomb, *Encyclopedia of Television*, 676.

20. Kelly, *Nancy Reagan*, 103.

21. Eliot, *Reagan*, 276.

22. Colacello, *Ronnie and Nancy*, 288.

23. Earl Dunckel interview, April 27, 1982 (from Bancroft Library, University of California, Berkeley), found in Gubernatorial Papers, 1966 Campaign, box 029, RRPL.

24. Hedda Hopper, "Reagan to Introduce Notable Stars on TV," *Los Angeles Times*, April 27, 1954.

25. Raphael, *The President Electric*, 162.

26. McDougal, *The Last Mogul*, 190–91; A. Edwards, *The Reagans*, 51.

27. Dunckel interview.

28. "Ronald Reagan Favors Filmed Drama for TV," *Cleveland Plain Dealer*, September 25, 1954; "Ronald Reagan's Duties More than Host for GE," *Boston American*, September 23, 1954; Morris, *Dutch*, 304–5; McDougal, *The Last Mogul*, 191; Eliot, *Reagan*, 276–77; A. Edwards, *Early Reagan*, 453; Phillips-Fein, *Invisible Hands*, 87.

29. Reagan, *An American Life*, 126–27.

30. Raphael, *The President Electric*, 179.

31. Reagan, *An American Life*, 126–27.

32. Dunckel interview.

33. Evans, *The Education of Ronald Reagan*, 58.

34. Dunckel interview.

35. "Ronald Reagan Charms All Comers during Bridgeport Visit," *Bridgeport* (CN) *Telegram*, October 3, 1955.

6. Progress Is Our Product

1. "Ronald Reagan Favors Filmed Drama for TV," *Cleveland Plain Dealer*, September 25, 1954; "Reagan Gets New Fall Show," *Bluefield* (WV) *Daily Telegraph*, April 25, 1954.

2. "TV Topics," *Asbury Park* (NJ) *Press*, October 3, 1954.

3. Newspaper ad, *Troy* (NY) *Record*, October 9, 1954.

4. "Lookin' and Listenin'," *Daily Reporter* (Dover OH), October 30, 1954.

5. Eliot, *Reagan*, 277; ad for GE *Theater* in *Troy* (NY) *Record*, September 25, 1954.

6. The show would not fall from the top thirty until the 1961–62 season. It would rank seventh for 1957–58 (31.5 share), twenty-sixth for 1958–59 (26.7 share), twenty-third for 1959–60 (24.4 share), and twentieth for 1960–61 (23.4 share). Nielsen Media Research ratings in Brooks and Marsh, *The Complete Directory to Prime Time Network and Cable TV Shows, 1946–Present*, 1680–83.

7. Earl Dunckel oral history, GHDP.

8. "Film Star Traffic to TV on Increase," *New York Times*, December 25, 1954.

9. "Ronald Reagan Tells Secret of Lining Up the Top Stars," *Los Angeles Times*, October 27, 1957.

10. "General Electric Theatre: It's Trying a Fresh Approach as a Film-and-Live Series," *Broadcasting*, January 10, 1955.

11. Clotworthy, *Saturday Night Live*, 6.

12. Becker, *It's the Pictures That Got Small*, 108.

13. Morris, *Dutch*, 305.

14. Newcomb, *Encyclopedia of Television*, 678; "TV Highlights," *Arizona Republic*, February 17, 1957.

15. A. Edwards, *Early Reagan*, 459.

16. Newcomb, *Encyclopedia of Television*, 677; "A Super-Satisfied Customer," *Broadcasting*, July 28, 1958.

17. "A Super-Satisfied Customer."

18. Reagan, *Where's the Rest of Me?* 257.

19. Reagan, *Where's the Rest of Me?* 257, 261.

20. Dunckel interview.

21. Reagan, *An American Life*, 128.

22. Wills, *Reagan's America*, 336–37.

23. L. Cannon, *Governor Reagan*, 123.

24. "Regimented Schools," *Miami News*, October 21, 1954.

25. Milton R. Bass, "The Lively Arts," *Berkshire Evening Eagle* (Pittsfield MA), April 5, 1955.

26. "The President from GE," *Nation*, January 31, 1981.

27. Joyce Thompson, "Reagan—Busy, Pleasant," *Decatur Daily Review*, October 12, 1955.

28. "A Recommended Audience Promotion Plan for THE GENERAL ELECTRIC THEATER," Batten, Barton, Durstine & Osborn, May 17, 1955, box 1, Jim Brown Papers.

29. "General Electric Theatre: It's Trying a Fresh Approach as a Film-and-Live Series."

30. Dunckel interview.

31. "The President from GE."

32. Reagan, *An American Life*, 128.

33. Deaver, *A Different Drummer*, 53.

7. He Had That Little Computer

1. Ronald Reagan interview by GHDP, January 19, 1979, found in box 51, LCRRP.

2. Reagan, *Where's the Rest of Me?* 263.

3. "3,000 Pickets Crash Police Lines in Phila. General Electric Strike," *Mauch Chunk* (PA) *Times-News*, February 28, 1946; "Back-to-Work Trend Spreads across the Country," *Tampa Times*, March 14, 1946; "Union Withdraws Injunction Petition as General Electric Strike Is Ended," *Mercury* (Pottstown PA), March 15, 1946.

4. Hoopes, *Corporate Dreams*, 76–77; Schatz, *Electrical Workers*, 169.

5. Phillips-Fein, *Invisible Hands*, 89.

6. Hoopes, *Corporate Dreams*, 76–77.

7. Boulware, *Truth about Boulwarism*, 168, 3.

8. Northup, *Boulwarism*, 26–27, 57.

9. Carbone and Lubar, *Brown and Sharpe and the Measure of American Industry*, 234.

10. Edward Langley, "How Reagan Hit Road for GE and Met His Destiny," *Chicago Tribune*, July 13, 1980.

11. Patrick Owens, "The President from GE," *Nation*, January 31, 1981; Reagan-Boulware correspondence, box 48, folder 1435, LRBP.

12. Dunckel interview.

13. A. Edwards, *The Reagans*, 53.

14. Langley, "How Reagan Hit Road for GE."

15. Boulware speech, January 10, 1952, box 13, folder 293, LRBP.

16. Boulware, *The Truth about Boulwarism*, 31–39; Nye, *Image Worlds*, 60; Langley, "How Reagan Hit Road for GE."

17. Hoopes, *Corporate Dreams*, 78–79; Patrick Owens, "The President from GE," *Nation*, January 31, 1981; Evans, *Education of Ronald Reagan*, 50.

18. Newspaper ad, "What Is a Speed-up?" *Decatur* (IL) *Daily Review*, May 31, 1949.

19. Newspaper ad, "21 GE Job Dividends," *Elmira* (NY) *Advertiser*, August 15, 1952.

20. Brands, *Reagan*, 126; General Electric, *Supervisor's Guide*, 31; Boulware speech, January 10, 1952, box 13, folder 293, LRBP; Boulware, *The Truth about Boulwarism*, 30–39; Byron, *Testosterone, Inc.*, 101; Hoopes, *Corporate Dreams*, 80; Kim Phillips-Fein, "'If Business and the Country Will Be Run Right': The Business Challenge to the Liberal Consensus, 1945–1964," *International Labor and Working-Class History*, no. 72 (Fall 2007): 203; Schatz, *The Electrical Workers*, 172.

21. Hazlitt, *Economics in One Lesson*, 26, 133

22. Address by President Ronald Reagan to the Conservative Political Action Conference, March 20, 1981, https://www.reaganlibrary.gov/research/speeches /32081b.

23. Haney, *How You Really Earn Your Living*, 168, 197, 230, 239–40.

24. Flynn, *The Road Ahead*, 7, 93.

25. Phillips-Fein, *Invisible Hands*, 101.

26. Byrne, *Ronald Reagan*, 25–26.

27. Remarks at Eureka College, February 6, 1984, RRPL, https://www .reaganlibrary.gov/research/speeches/20684b.

28. Perlstein, *Before the Storm*, 122.

29. Reagan, *Reagan: A Life in Letters*, 281.

30. Dunckel interview.

31. "A Constitutional President: Ronald Reagan and the Founding," January 26, 2012, Heritage Foundation forum: www.heritage.org/political-process/ report/constitutional-president-ronald-reagan-and-the-founding.

32. Deroy Murdock, "Reagan Was Avid Reader, Intellectual," *Town Talk* (Alexandria LA), June 13, 2004.

33. "The President from GE," *Nation*, January 31, 1981.

34. Hedda Hopper, "In Hollywood," *Valley Morning Star* (Harlingen TX), February 15, 1956.

35. Hoopes, *Corporate Dreams*, 80.

36. Reagan, *An American Life*, 129.

37. Langley, "How Reagan Hit Road for GE."

38. "Film Industry to Fight Crime," *San Francisco Examiner*, October 15, 1949; "Actors May Aid Film Council," *Los Angeles Times*, February 23, 1949; "Film Council Gets Art Directors' Aid," *Los Angeles Times*, March 4, 1949.

39. "Reagan Ends Tour Here," *Decatur* (IL) *Daily Review*, October 13, 1955.

40. "Ronald Reagan Wows Burlington Groups," *Burlington Free Press*, March 9, 1956.

41. "Clerics Castigate Stars' Divorce Rate," *Courier-Journal* (Louisville KY), February 18, 1947.

42. Hedda Hopper, "In Hollywood," *Newark* (OH) *Advocate*, December 18, 1947; Erskine Johnson, "The Question: How Immoral Is Hollywood," *Tallahassee Democrat*, December 5, 1951.

43. Hedda Hopper, "In Hollywood," *Hartford Courant*, August 23, 1947.

44. Reagan, *Speaking My Mind*, 17–21; "Film Freedom Held Cut by Political Censorship," *Los Angeles Times*, February 19, 1952; "Film Star Reagan Tells Pittsfield Clubs of Hollywood," *North Adams* (MA) *Transcript*, April 7, 1955; "Reagan to Rotary: How Film Stars Fought," *Pantagraph* (Bloomington IL), October 21, 1955; "M'Innes Asks End to State Site Row," *Tampa Tribune*, March 22, 1957; "E. H. Jackson Named New C of C head," *Shreveport Times*, December 3, 1958; "Filmland Wrong—Reagan," *Star-Gazette* (Elmira NY), October 2, 1958.

45. U.S. Department of Health, Education and Welfare, *Vital Statistics of the United States, 1951*, xxix; National Center for Health Statistics, *100 Years of Marriage*, 22.

46. U.S. Department of Health, Education and Welfare, *Vital Statistics of the United States, 1950*, 71.

47. National Center for Health Statistics, *100 Years of Marriage*, 22.

48. "Marriage, Divorce Rate Slump through Nation," *Los Angeles Times*, April 19, 1950.

49. "Divorce Rate Down 40 Pct. from Record Set in 1946," *Corpus Christi Caller-Times*, December 29, 1954.

50. "Rise in Marriages Disclosed by U.S.," *New York Times*, October 31, 1955.

51. Reagan, *Where's the Rest of Me?* 266.

52. Reagan, *An American Life*, 129.

8. Ronald Reagan, Businessman

1. "Actor Ronald Reagan Urges Unity against Censorship," *Providence Journal*, March 17, 1956.

2. Hal Humphrey, "Host Ronald Reagan Checks TV's Pulse," *Dallas Morning News*, November 23, 1956.

3. Reagan, *Speaking My Mind*, 17–21.

4. "U.S. Reaction Rules Films, Russian Says," *New York Times*, May 13, 1947.

5. "Chamber Told of Reds' Attempts to Infiltrate," *Times Record* (Troy NY), April 12, 1955.

6. "Tough U.S. Policy toward Russia Advocated by Actor," *Coshocton* (OII) *Democrat*, October 13, 1956.

7. "A Case of Liking People," *Trenton Evening Times*, March 1, 1957.

8. Hedda Hopper, "In Hollywood," *Valley Morning Star* (Harlingen TX), February 15, 1956.

9. "Actor Lashed Stiff U.S. Tax," *Asheville* (NC) *Citizen-Times*, March 20, 1957.

10. "Federal Individual Income Tax Rates History," Tax Foundation, online: https://files.taxfoundation.org/legacy/docs/fed_individual_rate_history_nominal&adjusted-20110909.pdf; Bureau of the Census, "Consumer Income."

11. "Reagan: Regulations Hurting Hollywood," *Asbury Park* (NJ) *Press*, June 10, 1957.

12. Eliot, *Reagan*, 258; Reagan, *Where's the Rest of Me?* 247.

13. "Reagan: Regulations Hurting Hollywood."

14. "Liberties Group Scores Film Code," *New York Times*, April 24, 1957; "ACLU Director Raps Self-Styled Censors," *Quad-City* (Davenport IA) *Times*, April 24, 1957.

15. "Movies' Self-Censorship Code Blasted, Defended at Hearing," *Baltimore Sun*, June 17, 1955; "Catholic Critic Calls Movie Censors Lax," *New York Daily News*, June 17, 1955.

16. "High Taxes Kill Dreams, Film Star Tells House Unit," *Morning News* (Wilmington DE), January 28, 1958; Reagan testimony in Houck and Kiewe, *Actor, Ideologue, Politician*, 10–18.

17. Houck and Kiewe, *Actor, Ideologue, Politician*, 10–18.

18. "Big Government No. 1 Opponent of Freedom, Reagan Reports," *Jefferson City* (MO) *Post-Tribune*, May 8, 1958.

19. Bureau of the Census, *Statistical Abstract of the United States*, 1957, 10; Bureau of the Census, *1957 Census of Governments*, 1.

20. "600 Volunteers Hear TV, Film Star at Kickoff," *Press and Sun-Bulletin* (Binghamton NY), October 2, 1958.

21. "Red Fight Cited," *Elmira* (NY) *Advertiser*, October 3, 1958.

22. "Actor's Fame Outshines His Businessman's Role," *Shreveport Times*, December 3, 1958.

23. "Ronald Reagan's Speech," *Shreveport Times*, December 7, 1958.

24. "Reagan Articulate and Well-Informed," *Abilene* (TX) *Reporter-News*, April 12, 1959.

25. Reagan, *Reagan: A Life in Letters*, 702.

26. "Ron Reagan Spews Facts Like IBM Machine," *Honolulu Star-Bulletin*, July 21, 1960.

27. "Ronald Reagan Wants No Part of Nikita's Party," *El Paso Herald-Post*, September 18, 1959; Carson, *K Blows Top*, 150.

28. "Gossip in Gotham," *Pittsburgh Post-Gazette*, September 25, 1959.

29. Reagan, *Reagan: A Life in Letters*, 146.

30. Dunckel interview.

31. "TVA, General Electric in Row over Speech by Ronald Reagan," *St. Louis Post-Dispatch*, June 12, 1960.

32. Reagan, *Where's the Rest of Me?* 269–70.

9. He Used to Be a Liberal

1. Wills, *Reagan's America*, 336–37.

2. Edward Langley, "How Reagan Hit Road for GE"; Langley, "How the Star Changed His Stripes," *Politics Today*, January/February 1980.

3. Reagan, *An American Life*, 133–34.

4. Eliot, *Reagan*, 304.

5. Reagan, *Reagan: A Life in Letters*, 702, 705.

6. Donaldson, *Liberalism's Last Hurrah*, 29.

7. Kelley, *Nancy Reagan*, 126.

8. Reagan, *An American Life*, 133–34.

9. "No Longer Jefferson Party, Says Reagan," *Press and Sun-Bulletin* (Binghamton NY), October 15, 1960.

10. Kelley, *Nancy Reagan*, 126.

11. Ronald Reagan filmography, online: IMDb.

12. "'Socialistic' Trends Blasted by Reagan," *Clarion-Ledger* (Jackson MS), October 15, 1960.

13. Text of Reagan speech, "Your America to Be Free," at Eureka College, June 9, 1957, online: https://patriotpost.us/reagan.

14. Text of Reagan speech in Houck and Kiewe, *Actor, Ideologue, Politician*, 18–27, online at the Reagan Speech Preservation Society: www.poorrichardsprintshop.com/wiki/(X(1)S(u4lz0j2cqj1l4e55qi1wyh55))/Business,%20Ballots%20and%20Bureaus.ashx?Code=1

15. Radio listings, *Arizona Republic*, April 3, 1961; "Anti-Red Meeting to Tear Reagan Tape," *Arizona Republic*, April 21, 1961.

16. "Khrushchev Could Have Said It," *New Republic*, May 7, 1962.

17. Text of Reagan speech, "Encroaching Control," to Phoenix Chamber of Commerce, March 30, 1961, 1980 Campaign Papers, Series XXII: Tony Dolan Files: RR Speeches, box 871, RRPL, online: https://archive.org/details/RonaldReagan-EncroachingControl.

18. Congressional Research Service, "Individual Tax Rates and Tax Burdens: Changes since 1960," February 29, 2008, https://www.everycrsreport.com/files/20080229_RL33786_edeaad27254d7b597345675ed45d11542b1e2e1b.pdf; John Karl Scholz, "Taxation and Poverty: 1960–2006," *Focus* 25, no. 1 (Spring–Summer 2007): 53, online at https://www.irp.wisc.edu/publications/focus/pdfs/foc251h.pdf.

19. Goldwater, *The Conscience of a Conservative*, 55.

20. Reagan speech, "Encroaching Control."

21. Reagan speech texts, 1980 Campaign Papers, Series XXII: Tony Dolan Files: RR Speeches, box 873, RRPL.

22. N. Reagan, *My Turn*, 118.

23. Sasala, "A Case Study of Ronald Reagan's October 27, 1964, Address," 48.

24. Reagan, *American Life*, 130.

25. Schweizer, *Reagan's War*, 33.

26. Reagan and Brinkley, *The Notes*, xiv.

27. Speeches-Handwritten drafts (no date), Series I: Hannaford/California Headquarters, Ronald Reagan Files, box 20, RRPL.

28. Neil Reagan interview, box 2, LCRRP.

29. Bruck, *When Hollywood Had a King*, 107–8.

30. Deaver, *A Different Drummer*, 53–54.

31. Roger Rosenblatt, "Out of the Past, Fresh Voices for the Future," *Time*, January 5, 1981.

32. Darman, *Landslide*, 134.

10. Operation Coffeecup

1. "Ronald Reagan Gets California GOP Bid," *Wisconsin State Journal* (Madison), February 2, 1961.

2. "How Medicare Was Made," *New Yorker*, February 15, 2015; "Medical Insurance for the Aged," *CQ Almanac 1961*, 262–65.

3. Skidmore, "Ronald Reagan and 'Operation Coffeecup,'" 89–96.

4. "Reagan Lashes State Medicine," *Arizona Republic*, March 31, 1961.

5. "Sittin' In with the Athletes," *Des Moines Register*, April 9, 1957.

6. See Snopes.com: https://www.snopes.com/politics/quotes/socialism.asp.

7. St. Onge, "Operation Coffeecup," 236.

8. Skidmore, "Ronald Reagan and 'Operation Coffeecup,'" 89–96.

9. Drew Pearson, "Ronald Reagan Stirs Opposition to Medical Aid Bill for AMA," *Quad-City Times* (Davenport IA), June 17, 1961.

10. McClelland, *Hollywood on Reagan*, 152.

11. "Senate Kills Social Security Health Care Plan," *CQ Almanac 1962*, 189–96.

12. Skidmore, "Ronald Reagan and 'Operation Coffeecup,'" 89–96.

13. "Americans Are Slowly Losing Their Freedom through Federal Controls," *Daily Nonpareil* (Council Bluffs IA), November 17, 1961.

14. "Chamber Speaker Says Americans in Danger of Losing Their Freedom," *Oregonian*, September 26, 1961.

15. "Star's Talk Called JFK Attacks," *Oregonian*, October 16, 1961.

16. Patrick Owens, "The President from GE," *Nation*, January 31, 1981.

11. Bobby Kennedy Is Behind It

1. "Reagan Sees New Communist Threat in Hollywood," *Herald* (Jasper IN), July 8, 1961.

2. Reagan speech, "Encroaching Control." Also see "Complete Text of Speech by Ronald Reagan," *Ames* (IA) *Daily Tribune*, November 22, 1961; "Louisiana Freedom by Installment," *Daily World* (Opelousas LA), November 28, 1961; "Round Town and the Clock," *Tipton* (IN) *Daily Tribune*, May 29, 1963.

3. Welch, *The Blue Book of the John Birch Society*, 1959, online: https://archive.org/details/TheBlueBook; "The Elusive Lenin," *New York Times*, October 8, 1985.

4. Reagan to Hefner, in Reagan, *Reagan: A Life in Letters*, 146–49.

5. "School to Give Facts on Reds," *Philadelphia Daily News*, November 14, 1960.

6. "One-Day Course Tickets Available for Local Anti-Communism School," *Valley News* (Van Nuys CA), August 22, 1961; "Anti-Communist School Opens Sessions in L.A.," *Los Angeles Times*, November 8, 1960.

7. "Probe into 'Muzzling' of Military Asked" and "Anti-Red Talks to Be Telecast," *Los Angeles Times*, August 31, 1961; "Anti-Red Youth Night Draws Overflow Crowd at Arena," *Independent* (Long Beach CA), August 31, 1961; newspaper ad, *Los Angeles Times*, August 28, 1961.

8. Villeneuve, "Teaching Anticommunism," 11.

9. "Probe into 'Muzzling' of Military Asked," *Los Angeles Times*, August 31, 1961.

10. "Anti-Communism School Packs 16,000 in Arena," *Desert Sun* (Palm Springs CA), August 31, 1961.

11. Villeneuve, "Teaching Anticommunism," 9, 11.

12. "Anti-Red Rally Told to Seek 'Total Victory,'" *Los Angeles Times*, October 17, 1961; "Anti-Red Schools Will Be Started throughout Nation," *San Bernardino County Sun*, October 18, 1961; newspaper ads on November 2, 1961, in *New York Daily News* and *Journal News* (White Plains NY).

13. "Dr. Fred C. Schwarz's Anti-Communist Crusade Fails to Stir Up Much Enthusiasm in New York," *St. Louis Post-Dispatch*, July 1, 1962.

14. "Ministers Charge Anti-Red School Is Freedom Threat," *News-Review* (Roseburg OR), February 12, 1962.

15. George Sokolsky, "Have We Ganged Up?" *Traverse City* (MI) *Record-Eagle*, February 21, 1962; George Sokolsky, "Loud Shouting Not Answer to Communism," *Standard-Speaker* (Hazelton PA), February 24, 1962.

16. "Dr. Fred C. Schwarz's Anti-Communist Crusade."

17. "Schwarz' Anti-Red 'School' Draws 50," *Akron Beacon Journal*, October 2, 1962.

18. "Actor Reagan Attacks Coexistence Theories," *Arizona Daily Star*, February 20, 1962.

19. "Embarrassed Underdogs," *Courier-Journal* (Louisville KY), October 19, 1962; "Rousselot Criticizes Kennedy's Cuba Policy," *Los Angeles Times*, August 31, 1962.

20. Reagan, *Where's the Rest of Me?* 297

21. "Reagan Fights Communists in TV Drama," *Detroit Free Press*, March 16, 1962.

22. Bruck, *When Hollywood Had a King*, 179–91.

23. L. Cannon, *Governor Reagan*, 112–13.

24. L. Cannon, *Governor Reagan*, 113; "It Was a Hard Fight, but 'Bonanza' Won," *Mason City* (IA) *Globe-Gazette*, January 1, 1962; "GE Theater Grist in the Rumor Mill," *Los Angeles Times*, January 5, 1961; "GE Theater Starts Final Re-run Series," *Daily Reporter* (Dover OH), June 9, 1962; "Jack Webb Supplies Crop of New Faces," *Daily Capital News* (Jefferson City MO), November 24, 1962.

25. Davis, *The Way I See It*, 67.

26. Reagan, *An American Life*, 137.

27. "GE Ends Host Spot for Reagan," *Omaha World-Herald*, May 24, 1963.

28. Bill Clotworthy oral history, August 24, 2004, RRPL.

29. L. Edwards, *Reagan: A Political Biography*, 73.

30. Davis, *The Way I See It*, 68.

31. "Jane Wyman Will Sue Ronald Reagan for Divorce Soon," *San Bernardino County Sun*, February 9, 1948; "Reagan Heads Cal. Campaign," *Press and Sun-Bulletin* (Binghamton NY), February 26, 1962.

32. "Wright Assails Jarvis for Attacking Chairman," *Los Angeles Times*, March 3, 1962.

33. "Medical Wives Carry on 'Operation Coffee Pot,'" *Daily Herald* (Chicago), April 5, 1962.

34. Reagan, *Reagan: A Life in Letters*, 281.

35. Eliot, *Reagan*, 326.

36. Wills, *Reagan's America*, 339.

12. Have You Reregistered Yet?

1. Ad in *Tucson Daily Citizen*, February 21, 1962.

2. Ad in *La Grande* (OR) *Observer*, February 23, 1962.

3. Ad in *Shreveport* (LA) *Times*, March 22, 1962.

4. "Public Invited to Hear Talk by Ronald Reagan," *Amarillo Globe-Times*, March 2, 1962.

5. "Reagan's Speech to Be Rebroadcast," *Longview News-Journal*, April 22, 1962; Lone Star Steel Company ads: "The Way I See It," *Gilmer* (TX) *Mirror*, March 29, 1962, and *Longview News-Journal*, April 12, 1962.

6. Louella Parsons, "Edie Adams Conquering Sorrow, Has Role in New Caesar Comedy," *Albuquerque Journal*, March 6, 1962.

7. "Rotarians Hear Actor's Speech," *Port Angeles* (WA) *Evening News*, January 11, 1962.

8. "Kiwanians Hear Speech Attacking Federal Medicine," *Tribune* (Seymour IN), January 19, 1962; "Chapter to Hear Recorded Talk by Ronald Reagan," *Star Tribune* (Minneapolis), March 18, 1962.

9. "Ronald Reagan at Benefit for GOP Candidate Thomas," *San Bernardino County Sun*, March 17, 1962; "A Question of Political Interest," *Signal* (Santa Clarita CA), September 20, 1962; "Reagan to Campaign Here for Controller" and "Major Figures in Both Parties Due This Week," *San Diego Union*, October 6 and 7, 1962; "GOP Report Urges Brown to Talk Issues," *Los Angeles Times*, October 8, 1962; "Reagan Stresses Loyalty," *Petaluma Argus-Courier*, October 10, 1962; "Actor Reagan Stirs the Emotions of GOP Crowd at Gold Clubhouse," *Daily Independent Journal* (San Rafael CA), October 10, 1962; "Actor Ronald Reagan Takes Dim View of Democrats," *Press Democrat* (Santa Rosa CA), October 10, 1962; "Actor Reagan Will Speak on Freedom," *Los Angeles Times*, October 28, 1962.

10. Reagan, *An American Life*, 135–36.

11. "Brown Says State to Become Richest," *Oakland Tribune*, October 9, 1962.

12. Ads by Judge Tom Coakley in *San Francisco Examiner*, November 3 and 4, 1962; *Los Angeles Times*, November 4, 1962; and *The Californian* (Salinas CA), November 5, 1962.

13. Reagan television address, November 4, 1962, in Houck and Kiewe, *Actor, Ideologue, Politician*, 27–35.

14. Homer Bigart, "Embarrassed Underdogs," *Courier-Journal* (Louisville KY), October 10, 1962.

15. "Ronald–Bess Again to Host 'Rose Parade,'" *Sandusky* (OH) *Register*, December 7, 1962.

16. "Reagan, Astaire to Quit Television for Movies," *Omaha World-Herald*, February 17, 1963.

17. "Ronald Reagan Back in Cavalry Garments," *Lima* (OH) *News*, June 3, 1963; McClure, *Ronald Reagan*, 181, 194.

18. "Red Treachery on 'Peace' Front Documented in TV Film," *Daily Capital News* (Jefferson City MO), October 11, 1963.

19. "Panning and Scanning," *Springfield* (MO) *Leader and Press*, October 13, 1963.

20. "Film on Communism," *Los Angeles Times*, January 15, 1963; "Actor to Narrate Film Smuggled out of Russia," *Los Angeles Times*, January 24, 1963; "Group to Show Smuggled Film," *Los Angeles Times*, January 27, 1963.

21. Misc. newspaper advertisements via Newspapers.com; "A Revealing Reagan Film," *San Francisco Examiner*, November 7, 1983.

22. "Film Clips," *Film News*, January/February 1962, 30.

23. Video, "The Ultimate Weapon: The Minds of Free Men," 1963 documentary, online: https://www.youtube.com/watch?v=_yVzQB9y3GE.

24. TV listings, *Chicago Tribune*, December 28, 1963; "BPW Club Honors 1963 'Girl of Year,'" *Evening Standard* (Uniontown PA), March 29, 1963; "Lioness Club Meets Tonight," *Press Democrat* (Santa Rosa CA), March 28, 1963; "Mormons Slate Benefit Films Friday Evening," *Pensacola News*, May 29, 1963.

25. "Young Republicans to Meet Tonight," *Arlington Heights* (IL) *Herald*, July 11, 1963; "Town Goldwater Boosters to Show Movie at Rally," *Hartford Courant*, November 20, 1963; "Maj. Edgar Bundy to Begin Crusade," *Independent* (Long Beach CA), July 13, 1963; *Valley Morning Star* (Harlingen TX), December 11, 1963; "Pro America Sees Welfare State Film," *Oshkosh* (WI) *Northwestern*, January 11, 1964; "Tampa Electric Withdraws Film Attacked by Democrats," *Tampa Tribune*, October 23, 1964.

26. Video, *Heritage of Splendor*, 1963 documentary, accessed online: https://archive.org/details/youtube-2AShgCQ4wgw; "Color Movie Shows Scenery," *Pittsburgh Post*, December 22, 1963.

27. "Reagan Speech Available Here," *Mt. Pleasant* (IA) *News*, March 7, 1963.

28. Harry T. Everingham, "Everyman's Problem," *San Marino* (CA) *Tribune*, April 25, 1963.

29. "Ronald Reagan Hits at 'Big Government' in Dixon Address," *Daily Gazette* (Sterling–Rock Falls IL), April 30, 1963.

30. "Ronald Reagan Sets Mt. Morris Bells Ringing," *Morning Star* (Rockford IL), May 1, 1963.

31. "'Government Is Watchdog, Not Cow to Be Milked,' Ronald Reagan Tells Audience," *Arkansas City* (KS) *Daily Traveler*, May 6, 1963.

32. Rusher, *The Rise of the Right*, 61.

33. Kim Eisler, "Eisenhower's Mistakes," *New York Times*, July 28, 1997.

34. Donaldson, *Liberalism's Last Hurrah*, 9.

35. L. Edwards, *Goldwater*, 132; Goldberg, *Barry Goldwater*, 119–20.

36. Rusher, *The Rise of the Right*, 88.

37. Colacello, *Ronnie and Nancy*, 262, 318.

38. Goldberg, *Barry Goldwater*, 252.

39. Reagan, *An American Life*, 138.

40. "Reagan: I Am a Liberal Supporting Goldwater; Semantics, He Explains," *Omaha World-Herald*, April 26, 1963.

41. Reagan to Linda West, October 1, 1963, in Reagan, *Reagan: A Life in Letters*, 149–50.

42. Thomas, *The Films of Ronald Reagan*, 222–24.

43. "Sunday Afternoon with the Ronald Reagans," *Saturday Evening Post*, April 1974.

44. Colacello, *Ronnie and Nancy*, 322

45. Goldwater, *Goldwater*, 198.

46. Goldberg, *Barry Goldwater*, 176–80.

47. "Toward the Day of Reckoning," *Time*, January 10, 1964.

48. Barry M. Goldwater presidential announcement, January 3, 1964, online: http://www.4president.org/speeches/1964/barrygoldwater1964announcement.htm.

49. Kopelson, *Reagan's 1968 Dress Rehearsal*, 59.

50. "Who Are the Goldwaterites?" *Time*, July 24, 1964.

51. "The Non-Candidates," *Time*, January 24, 1964.

52. "Senator Goldwater's Bid," *New York Times*, January 4, 1964.

53. "Goldwater Wins Wide Lead in Poll," *New York Times*, November 3, 1963.

54. Faber, *The Road to the White House*, 12–13.

55. Donaldson, *Liberalism's Last Hurrah*, 78.

56. Goldwater, *Goldwater*, 202

57. "Welfare Programs Get Top Billing in Politics," *Portsmouth* (NH) *Herald*, January 10, 1964.

58. "Goldwater Favors Sharing Atom Arms with NATO Allies," *New York Times*, January 14, 1964.

59. Stuart K. Spencer interview, 1979, GHDP.

60. Schuparra, *Triumph of the Right*, 96.

61. McGirr, *Suburban Warriors*, 134–35; Schuparra, *Triumph of the Right*, 95.

62. Darman, *Landslide*, 154.

63. "Extremists Took Over, Rockefeller Charges," *Redlands* (CA) *Daily Facts*, March 16, 1964; "Use A-arm in Viet War—Goldwater," *Cincinnati Inquirer*, May 25, 1964.

64. "Oregon Victory Gives Moral Boost to Rockefeller Camp," *Oshkosh* (WI) *Northwestern*, May 27, 1964.

65. Goldberg, *Barry Goldwater*, 189.

13. Which One Was the Candidate?

1. "Rockefeller Rushes Home for Birth of Nelson Jr.," *Battle Creek Enquirer*, May 31, 1964; "Happy Told to Give Up Her Youngest," *Times* (San Mateo CA), October 17, 1964.

2. "Rockefeller's Remarriage Hit," *Los Angeles Times*, May 29, 1964.

3. Shadegg, *What Happened to Goldwater?* 122–23.

4. Novak, *The Agony of the GOP 1964*, 391.

5. Buckley, *Flying High*, 114.

6. Novak, *The Agony of the GOP 1964*, 391–93; Goldwater, *Goldwater*, 202.

7. Schuparra, *Triumph of the Right*, 94.

8. Ad for "Goldwater Kickoff Dinner," *Los Angeles Times*, March 10, 1964; "Goldwater Backers Start Drives Here," *Pasadena Independent*, March 11, 1964; "A Tradition Spoiler," *Long Beach Press Telegram*, March 25, 1964.

9. "Goldwater Cancels Visit to Monterey," *Oakland Tribune*, March 28, 1964; "Leading Republicans," *San Mateo Times*, April 1, 1964; "Goldwater Due Back

for California Tour," *Los Angeles Times*, April 24, 1964; "Reagan to Speak for Goldwater," *San Diego Union*, May 1, 1964; "Reagan Talk Slated Tonight," *San Diego Union*, May 6, 1964; "Goldwater Berry Farm Rally Set," *Long Beach Independent*, May 28, 1964; "Goldwater Breakfast Due in Westchester," *Los Angeles Times*, May 24, 1964.

10. "Reagan Warns of Federal Inroads," *San Diego Union*, May 7, 1964.

11. "Attacks Provoke Goldwater Camp," *New York Times*, May 30, 1964.

12. Lewis, *What Makes Reagan Run*, 8–9.

13. Perlstein, *Before the Storm*, 340, 350.

14. Schuparra, *Triumph of the Right*, 95; "How Counties Voted," *Redlands Daily Facts*, June 3, 1964.

15. "Goldwater: Party Victory," *Los Angeles Times*, June 3, 1964.

16. Reagan interview, 1979, GHDP.

17. Middendorf, *A Glorious Disaster*, 101.

18. "Rocky Says Ike, Nixon Should Support Scranton," *Redlands* (CA) *Daily Facts*, June 17, 1964.

19. "The Disenchanted," *Time*, July 24, 1964.

20. "Gov. Romney Threatens Bid to Stop Goldwater," *Los Angeles Times*, June 8, 1964.

21. "Text of Senator's Acceptance Speech," *Los Angeles Times*, July 17, 1964.

22. "Goldwater Does Little to Placate GOP Liberals," *Fresno Bee*, July 17, 1964.

23. Kabaservice, *Rule and Ruin*, 114.

24. "Goldwater Forces Score Win in Crucial Platform Battle," *Portland Oregonian*, July 15, 1964.

25. White and Gill, *Why Reagan Won*, 14; Totton J. Anderson and Eugene C. Lee, "The 1964 Election in California," *Western Political Quarterly* 18 (June 1965): 451–74.

26. Reagan, *An American Life*, 139.

27. Jamieson, *Packaging the President*, 173; Nofziger, *Nofziger*, 29–31.

28. Reagan interview, 1979, GHDP.

29. Reagan questionnaire quoted in Baird, "A Time for Choosing by Ronald Reagan," 69.

30. "Capacity Crowd Expected at Goldwater Rally Tonight," *Valley News* (Van Nuys CA), September 8, 1964.

31. "Cheering Throng Hails Candidate at Stadium," *Los Angeles Times*, September 9, 1954; "Goldwater Blasts Democrats' Fiscal Policy," *Valley News* (Van Nuys CA), September 10, 1964.

32. "Ronald Reagan Assails the Johnson Administration for Waste and Woes," *Santa Cruz Sentinel*, September 24, 1964.

33. "Ronald Reagan Assails"; "Better than 400 Humboldt County Republicans Gathered," *Eureka Humboldt Standard* (Eureka CA), October 6, 1964; "Actor Reagan Stumps Marin for Goldwater," *Daily Independent Journal* (San Rafael), October 23, 1964.

34. "College, Graduate Schools Will Raise Tuition in 1964," *Harvard Crimson*, May 21, 1963.

35. April 23, 1985, Reagan speech in *Public Papers of the Presidents of the United States: Ronald Reagan, 1985*.

36. "Here Is Text of Address by Ronald Reagan," *Shreveport Times*, March 1, 1964.

37. "Actor Reagan Stumps Marin for Goldwater."

38. "Reagan Talks against Elite Group, for Barry," *Daily Independent Journal* (San Rafael CA), October 24, 1964.

39. Bill Strobel, "Actor Star Spokesman for Barry," *Oakland Tribune*, October 30, 1964.

40. Dallek, *The Right Moment*, 64.

41. White and Gill, *Why Reagan Won*, 15.

42. Middendorf, *A Glorious Disaster*, 178

43. "Russia, N-arms Top Presidential Issues," *Honolulu Star-Bulletin*, October 12, 1964; "Study Backs Goldwater's Arms Policy," *Baltimore Sun*, October 6, 1964.

44. "Military Leaders Back Goldwater on Nuclear Issue," *Burlington* (VT) *Free Press*, October 7, 1964.

45. "Demos Pick Up Tab for President's Trip," *Pocono Record* (Stroudsburg PA), September 8, 1964.

46. "Reagan Claims Administration Weapons 'Lies,'" *San Diego Union*, October 14, 1964.

47. "Reagan Talks against Elite Group, for Barry."

48. "Better than 400 Humboldt County Republicans Gathered."

49. "So They Tell Me with Bill Soberanes," *Petaluma* (CA) *Argus Courier*, October 10, 1964.

50. "Actor Ronald Reagan Backs Goldwater Drive," *Auburn* (CA) *Journal*, October 15, 1964.

51. "GOP Planning $1,000-a-Plate Dinner Series," *Los Angeles Times*, September 2, 1964; Colacello, *Ronnie and Nancy*, 326–27; Holmes Tuttle interview by Lou Cannon, LCRRP; "A Time for Credit: The Men Who Put Reagan on the Air in '64," CONELRAD ADJACENT, October 27, 2014, http://conelrad.blogspot .com/2014/10/a-time-for-credit-men-who-put-reagan-on.html.

52. Reagan, *An American Life*, 139.

53. Leamer, *Make Believe*, 193.

54. Holmes Tuttle interview by Lou Cannon, LCRRP.

55. Reagan, *An American Life*, 140.

56. Kilroy, *Kialoa-US1*, 78; "Jim Kilroy, Real Estate Developer Renowned as a Yachtsman, Dies at 94," *New York Times*, October 7, 2016.

57. "TV Gets Workout for Political Perpetuity," *Broadcasting*, October 12, 1964.

58. "Saltonstall to Present Goldwater," *Boston Globe*, September 24, 1964; "Author of 'Treason' Will Address Rally for Captive Nations," *Valley News* (Van Nuys CA), September 27, 1964; "TV Gets Workout for Political Perpetuity," *Broadcasting*, October 12, 1964.

59. "A Time for Credit: The Men Who Put Reagan on the Air in '64"; Gardiner Johnson Oral history, 1983, GHDP, https://archives.cdn.sos.ca.gov/oral-history/pdf/johnson.pdf.

60. "1964 Campaign Receipts and Spending Reported by 164 Groups," CQ *Almanac 1965*, 1564–70.

61. Report #13, Erwin Wasey, Ruthrauff & Ryan memo, September 14, 1964, box 3H514, SGC.

62. "Goldwater Films Find No Sponsor," *Tennessean*, July 4, 1965; Roland Evans and Robert Novak, "President Runs with GOP's Suggestion for Confidence," *Daily Plainsman* (Huron SD), May 10, 1965; Schuparra, *Triumph of the Right*, 184fn; "A Time for Credit: The Men Who Put Reagan on the Air in '64."

63. Report #46, EWR&R memo, October 23, 1964, box 3H514, SGC.

64. Baird, "A Time for Choosing by Ronald Reagan," 70.

65. Sasala, "A Case Study of Ronald Reagan's October 27, 1964, Address," 112.

14. A Rendezvous with Destiny

1. Bunch, *Tear Down That Myth*, 38.

2. As secretary of the U.S. Senate from 1953 to 1963, Baker had been a close associate of Lyndon Johnson. In 1963 Baker became embroiled in scandal after allegations emerged he had bribed members of Congress and arranged sexual favors in return for government contracts for his private business. In 1967 a federal jury convicted Baker on charges of tax evasion, theft, and fraud. He served eighteen months in prison.

3. "The Rise and Reign of the Welfare Queen," *New America*, September 22, 2016, https://www.newamerica.org/weekly/edition-135/rise-and-reign-welfare-queen/; "The Welfare Queen," *Slate*, December 19, 2013, http://www.slate.com/articles/news_and_politics/history/2013/12/linda_taylor_welfare_queen_ronald_reagan_made_her_a_notorious_american_villain.html.

4. "French Deny Charge Made by Goldwater," *New York Times*, October 3, 1964.

5. Vestal, *The Lion of Judah in the New World*, 120–21.

6. Raisbeck cut whatever Reagan said next because the completed speech was too long. This is the only place he edited out any of Reagan's words.

7. Franklin D. Roosevelt, "Acceptance Speech for the Renomination for the Presidency, Philadelphia," June 27, 1936, online by Gerhard Peters and John T. Woolley, *The American Presidency Project*: http://occonline.occ.cccd.edu/online/vmarcina/Franklin%20Delano%20Roosevelt%20Speech.pdf.

8. Evans, *The Education of Ronald Reagan*, 60.

9. Text of Reagan speech, https://www.americanrhetoric.com/speeches/ronaldreaganatimeforchoosing.htm; video of Reagan speech, RRPL, https://www.youtube.com/watch?v=qXBswFfh6AY; Abraham Lincoln, "Second Annual Message," December 1, 1862, online by Miller Center, University of Virginia, https://millercenter.org/the-presidency/presidential-speeches/december-1-1862-second-annual-message.

10. Video of Reagan speech, RRPL, https://www.youtube.com/watch?v=qXBswFfh6AY.

15. Why Didn't Goldwater Talk Like That?

1. *A Time for Credit*, CONELRAD Adjacent, http://conelrad.blogspot.com /2014/10/a-time-for-credit-men-who-put-reagan-on.html; Shadegg, *What Happened to Goldwater?* 248.

2. Radio programming schedule, *Sacramento Bee*, October 20, 1964; "TV's Reagan Speaks Up Tonight for Barry," *Chicago Tribune*, October 27, 1964; newspapers advertisements for Reagan speech in *Independent* (Long Beach CA), October 23, 1964; *Los Angeles Times*, October 23, 1964; *Sacramento Bee*, October 23, 1964; *Eureka Humboldt Standard*, October 24, 1964; *Independent Press-Telegram* (Long Beach CA), October 25, 1964; "Tonight's TV Political Schedule," *Oakland Tribune*, October 24, 1964.

3. Telegram, George F. Wilson to Dean Burch, October 27, 1964, box 12, DBP.

4. Pawluk telegram to Burch, October 25, 1964, and Randles to Burch, October 26, 1964, box 12, DBP.

5. Barstow telegram, October 23, 1964, Gubernatorial Papers, 1966 Campaign, box C35, RRPL.

6. Telegrams to Reagan and Goldwater campaign, Gubernatorial Papers, 1966 Campaign, box C35, RRPL.

7. Report #42 and Report #45, Erwin Wasey, Ruthrauff & Ryan, box 3H510, SGC.

8. Report #46, Erwin Wasey, Ruthrauff & Ryan, box 3H510, SGC.

9. Reagan TV spot for Goldwater, accessed on YouTube: https://www.youtube .com/watch?v=FzAJZjxxauU.

10. Perlstein, *Before the Storm*, 500; Shadegg, *What Happened to Goldwater?* 252; Reagan, *An American Life*, 140.

11. Middendorf, *A Glorious Disaster*, 207.

12. Perlstein, *Before the Storm*, 500.

13. Reagan, *An American Life*, 140–41.

14. Shadegg, *What Happened to Goldwater?* 253.

15. Evans and Novak, "Anderson's Worlds," *Greensboro Daily News*, November 17, 1964.

16. Cushon to Burch, October 27, 1964, box 12, DBP.

17. Telegrams to Burch, box 13, DBP.

18. Middendorf, *A Glorious Disaster*, 175.

19. Report #29, October 2, 1964, and Report #30, October 3, 1964, Erwin Wasey, Ruthrauff & Ryan, box 3H510, SGC.

20. Middendorf, *A Glorious Disaster*, 175.

21. Morreale, *The Presidential Campaign Film*, 70.

22. Jamieson, *Packaging of the Presidency*, 173; "UN Delegate Charles Lichenstein, 75, Dies," *New York Times*, August 31, 2002.

23. Bruce Reagan to Kitchel, September 30, 1964, box 12, DBP.

24. "Ronald Reagan on TV for Goldwater," *Oakland Tribune*, October 25, 1964.

25. "TV's Reagan Speaks Up Tonight for Barry," *Chicago Tribune*, October 27, 1964.

26. Reagan, *An American Life*, 142–43.

27. Baird, "A Time for Choosing by Ronald Reagan," 74; A Time for Credit, CONELRAD, http://conelrad.blogspot.com/2014/10/a-time-for-credit-men-who-put-reagan-on.html.

28. Baird, "A Time for Choosing by Ronald Reagan," 118.

29. Telegrams to Reagan and Goldwater campaign, Gubernatorial Papers, 1966 Campaign, box C35, RRPL.

30. Kopelson, Reagan's 1968 Dress Rehearsal, 67

31. Telegrams to Reagan and Goldwater campaign, Gubernatorial Papers, 1964 Campaign, box C35, RRPL.

32. Reagan, An American Life, 143; Hess and Broder, The Republican Establishment, 253; "$12 Million Left in GOP Treasury after Campaign," New York Times, November 10, 1964; "1964 Campaign Receipts and Spending Reported by 164 Groups," CQ Almanac 1965, 1564–70; Alexander, Financing the 1964 Election, 108–9.

33. "Record $47.8 Million Reported Spent in 1964 Elections," CQ Almanac 1965, 1549–58.

34. "Ronald Reagan Backs Barry on TV," Rockford Register Republic, October 27, 1964.

35. Advertisement in Quad-City Times (Davenport IA), October 30, 1964.

36. "Goldwater Campaign Bulletin," Journal and Courier (Lafayette IN), October 30, 1964; "The Last Stand," Sheboygan (WI) Press, November 2, 1964; "Did You See Ronald Reagan's TV Speech?" Ames Daily Tribune, November 2, 1964.

37. Telegrams about Reagan speech, box 12, DBP.

38. "Time for Choosing," Sandusky Register, October 30, 1964.

39. Larry Wolters, "NBC-TV to Air Barry Talk by Actor Reagan," Chicago Tribune, October 31, 1964.

40. Post-campaign letters to Shadegg, box 3H510, SGC.

16. The Brightest Spot of the Campaign

1. "Goldwater Saved GOP Money as Defeat Became Apparent," Evansville Courier and Press, November 12, 1964.

2. "Decision of the Majority," Garden City (KS) Telegram, November 4, 1964.

3. Fulton Lewis Jr., "Ronald Reagan Gave Best Campaign Speech," Lebanon (PA) Daily News, November 12, 1964.

4. Evans and Novak, "Bob Anderson . . . for LBJ . . . Softly," Boston Globe, November 15, 1964.

5. Arthur Krock, "Farley's View of the Constitutional Function," Boston Herald, November 19, 1964.

6. McDowell, "Wheels Turning for Republicans," Newark Star-Ledger, December 16, 1964.

7. Hayes, "Ronald Reagan as a 'Thoughtful' Speaker."

8. Schlesinger quoted in Partisan Review 14 (May/June 1947): 242; Silver, Coolidge and the Historians, 98; "How Far Can We Go," Herald (Bessemer MI), September 20, 1962.

9. Hayes, "Ronald Reagan as a 'Thoughtful" Speaker,' 44.

10. Hayes, "Ronald Reagan as a 'Thoughtful" Speaker,' 45.

11. "Humphrey Raps Barry's Farm Stand," *Daily Plainsman* (Huron SD), September 11, 1964.

12. "Hubert Lauds Achievements of REA in SD," *Argus-Leader* (Sioux Falls SD), October 16, 1964.

13. Goldwater, *The Conscience of a Conservative*, 37.

14. Hayes, "Ronald Reagan as a 'Thoughtful' Speaker," 18–23, 43–66.

15. Erickson, *Reagan Speaks*, 26–27.

16. Olsen, *The Working-Class Republican*, 54–55

17. Byrne, *Ronald Reagan*, 56.

18. Olsen, *The Working-Class Republican*, 54–55.

19. "GOP Assesses Self in Lieu of Victory Party," *Los Angeles Times*, November 4, 1964.

20. Lewis, *What Makes Reagan Run?* 71.

21. Knott and Chidester, *At Reagan's Side*, 19.

22. Wills, *Reagan's America*, 346.

23. Shadegg, *What Happened to Goldwater?* 219.

24. Kellerman to Burch, September 15, 1964, box 3H510, SGC.

25. Transcript of Goldwater speech, London, Kentucky, October 27, 1964, Series 11, 1964 Presidential Campaign, box 120, Arizona Historical Foundation.

26. Memo, Jody Baldwin to Pam Rymer, box 3H510, SGC.

27. "Goldwater in the Old Confederacy," *Newsweek*, September 29, 1964.

28. Charles Mohr, "Goldwater: A Close Look at a 'Damned Cowboy,'" *Saturday Evening Post*, August 8, 1964.

29. "Ronald Reagan," *National Review*, December 1, 1964, 1055.

30. "Sick Film Not Worthwhile," *Fort Lauderdale News*, September 25, 1964; "Angie Dickinson Enriches 'Killers,'" *Indianapolis Star*, September 17, 1964.

31. Neil Reagan interview, GHDP; "Commercial Production Includes Reagan, Borax," *Sponsor*, September 1, 1964.

17. The Great Communicator

1. Kilroy, *Kialoa-US1*, 80.

2. "'Reagan for Governor,' Jordan Says," *Eureka Humboldt Standard*, November 5, 1964.

3. "Ronald Reagan 'Nixes' Politics," *Lead* (SD) *Daily Call*, November 9, 1964.

4. "Young GOP Reaffirms Support of Goldwater," *Los Angeles Times*, November 11, 1964; "Reagan Promises to Keep Up Fight," *Dallas Morning News*, November 11, 1964.

5. Reagan, *An American Life*, 144.

6. "Accent on Youth from Marin Courthouse to State Capitol," *Daily Independent Journal* (San Rafael CA), November 20, 1964.

7. "Ronald Reagan for President, Group's Goal," *Ironwood* (MI) *Daily Globe*, November 23, 1964.

8. "Ronald Reagan May Try Politics," *Odessa* (TX) *American*, November 25, 1964; "Ronald Reagan Urged to Seek Public Office," *Pasadena Independent*, November 26, 1964.

9. Sheilah Graham, "Hollywood," *Washington Evening Star*, December 2, 1964.

10. "Reagan Gaining in Governor Candidacy Draft, Aide Says," *Oakland Tribune*, December 3, 1964.

11. "Barry Boosts Ronald Reagan in LA Speech," *Fresno Bee*, February 23, 1965.

12. Ron Reagan, *My Father at 100*, 134.

13. "GOP Legislators Indicate Kuchel in Governor's Race," *Pasadena Independent*, March 5, 1965.

14. "Kuchel Wants 'Door Open' to Governor Race," *Independent* (Long Beach CA), March 5, 1965.

15. "Reagan Once Left-Wing Democrat, Knight Says," *Independent* (Long Beach CA), March 6, 1965.

16. "Pat Brown, under Fire, Steps Up Third Term Plans," *Fresno Bee*, March 14, 1965.

17. "Reagan Fire Shifted to Gov. Brown," *Independent* (Long Beach CA), March 17, 1965.

18. "Brown to Run Again to Keep Reagan Out," *Press Democrat* (Santa Rosa CA), March 23, 1965; "Brown Remains an Undeclared Candidate," *Press Democrat* (Santa Rosa CA), March 24, 1965.

19. "Reagan Says He's Ready to Enter Governor Race," *San Bernardino County Sun*, March 28, 1965.

20. Reagan, *Reagan: A Life in Letters*, 170.

21. Reagan, *An American Life*, 146–47.

22. "Reagan Gets Star Role in 'Will He Run?' Saga," *Los Angeles Times*, May 10, 1965.

23. Stewart Alsop, "The Good Guy," *Saturday Evening Post*, November 20, 1965.

24. Reagan, "A Plan for Action," January 4, 1966, 1966 Campaign, Speeches, and Statements, box C30, RRPL; L. Cannon, *Governor Reagan*, 141.

25. "Demos Blast Reagan 'Distortion, Falsities,'" *Fresno Bee*, January 5, 1966; "State Officials Correct Reagan's Jobless Figures," *Fresno Bee*, January 5, 1966; "Welfare Group Leader Slams Reagan 'Errors,'" *Fresno Bee*, January 13, 1966; "Statewide Reaction to Reagan," *Ukiah Daily Journal*, January 5, 1966; "Brown Accuses Reagan of False Statements," *San Mateo Times*, January 6, 1966; "Brown, Reagan Trade Challenges on Facts," *Fresno Bee*, January 7, 1966.

26. Reagan speech, "The Creative Society," April 19, 1966, 1980 Campaign Papers, Series XXII: Tony Dolan Files: Ronald Reagan Speeches, box 873, RRPL.

27. "And Now, the 'Prairie Fire' of Reagan's Creative Society," *Santa Cruz Sentinel*, November 13, 1966.

28. L. Cannon, *Governor Reagan*, 140.

29. "Ronald Reagan Demonstrates He's Political Box Office," (San Mateo) *Times*, September 29, 1966.

30. Peretti, *The Leading Man*, 188.

31. "Will the Real Ronnie Reagan Please Stand Up?" *Fresno Bee*, January 9, 1966.

32. "Ronald Reagan Demonstrates He's Political Box Office."

33. Dallek, *The Right Moment*, 214.

34. "Government of All the People Pledged by Gov.-Elect Reagan," *Los Angeles Times*, November 9, 1966.

35. "GOP's Gains Spark Interest in 1968 Presidential Campaign," *Los Angeles Times*, November 9, 1966.

36. Evans, *The Education of Ronald Reagan*, 169.

37. Darman, *Landslide*, 218–19.

38. Brands, *Reagan: The Life*, 5–6.

39. Shadegg, *What Happened to Goldwater?* 253.

40. Olsen, *The Working-Class Republican*, 61.

41. Schoenwald, *A Time for Choosing*, 216.

42. Lewis, *What Makes Reagan Run?* 7.

43. Shadegg, *What Happened to Goldwater?* 253.

44. Donaldson, *Liberalism's Last Hurrah*, 288.

45. L. Cannon, *Governor Reagan*, 125.

46. Hannaford, *The Reagans*, 10–11.

47. Erickson, *Reagan Speaks*, 30.

48. Reagan, *An American Life*, 143.

Epilogue

1. CBS News broadcast, August 19, 1976, CBS-2259, VTV.

2. Deaver, *A Different Drummer*, 46; "Reagan, on Dais, Spurs Party On," *New York Times*, August 20, 1976.

3. Trent, Friedenberg, and Denton, *Political Campaign Communication*, 59–60.

4. William F. Buckley Jr., "Closing Night," *Shreveport Times*, August 25, 1976.

5. John Margolis, "Instant Replay: How Ford Won It," *Time*, August 30, 1976, 20.

6. N. Reagan, *My Turn*, 197.

7. Elizabeth Drew, *American Journey*, 410; CBS News broadcast, August 19, 1976, CBS-2259, VTV.

8. Margolis, "Instant Replay."

9. "Vanquished Challenger Touches Republicans' Hearts," *Lebanon* (PA) *Daily News*, August 20, 1976.

10. Morris, *Dutch*, 403.

11. J. Cannon, *Gerald Ford*, 419.

12. "'It Was Riotous,'" *Politico*, April 5, 2016.

13. CBS broadcast, August 19, 1976, CBS-2259, VTV.

14. John Seigenthaler, "Ford to Run Like Truman," *Nashville Tennessean*, August 22, 1976.

15. Mark Shields, "How Television Put on the Republican Airs," *Washington Evening Star*, August 22, 1976.

16. Robert J. Donovan, "Did Reagan Pull GOP Too Far Right?" *Sunday Advocate* (Baton Rouge LA), August 22, 1976.

17. "Not Everyone Went Home Happy," *Chicago Tribune*, August 22, 1976.

18. "Reagan, a Touch of Class," *Independent Press-Telegram* (Long Beach CA), August 22, 1976.

19. "'It Was Riotous,'" *Politico*, April 5, 2016.

20. "Aftermath of a Convention," *Corpus Christi Caller-Times*, August 22, 1976.

21. N. Reagan, *My Turn*, 201.

Bibliography

Archives and Manuscript Materials

Boulware, Lemuel R. Papers. Kislak Center for Special Collections, Rare Books and Manuscripts, University of Pennsylvania.

Brown, Jim. Papers. John W. Hartman Center for Sales, Advertising, and Marketing History, David M. Rubenstein Rare Book and Manuscript Library, Duke University.

Burch, Dean. Papers. FM MSS 142, Arizona Collection, Arizona State University Library.

Cannon, Lou, and Ronald Reagan. Papers. Department of Special Collections, University of California Santa Barbara.

Goldwater, Barry M. Personal and Political Papers. Series 11, 1964 Presidential Campaign, Arizona Historical Foundation.

Government History Documentation Project, Ronald Reagan Gubernatorial Era, California State Government Oral Histories, California State Archives.

House Un-American Activities Committee, 1945–1975. Records. RG 233, National Archives.

Ronald Reagan Presidential Library, Simi Valley CA.

Shadegg/Goldwater Collection. Briscoe Center for American History, University of Texas at Austin.

Vanderbilt TV News Archive. Vanderbilt University.

Published Works

Alexander, Herbert E. *Financing the 1964 Election*. Princeton NJ: Citizens' Research Foundation, 1966.

Allyson, June. *June Allyson*. New York: G. P. Putnam's Sons, 1982.

Baird, John William. "A Time for Choosing by Ronald Reagan: A Rhetorical Analysis." Master's thesis, Miami University, Oxford, Ohio, 1967.

Becker, Christine. *It's the Pictures That Got Small: Hollywood Film Stars on 1950s Television*. Middletown CT: Wesleyan University Press, 2008.

Boulware, Lemuel. *The Truth about Boulwarism: Trying to Do Right Voluntarily*. Washington: Bureau of National Affairs, 1969.

Brands, H. W. *Reagan: The Life.* New York: Anchor Books, 2015.

Brooks, Tim, and Earle Marsh. *The Complete Directory to Prime Time Network and Cable TV Shows, 1946–Present.* New York: Ballantine, 2007.

Bruck, Connie. *When Hollywood Had a King: The Reign of Lew Wasserman, Who Leveraged Talent into Power and Influence.* New York: Random House, 2003.

Buckley, William F. *Flying High: Remembering Barry Goldwater.* New York: Basic Books, 2008.

Bunch, William. *Tear Down This Myth: The Right-Wing Distorting of the Reagan Legacy.* New York: Free Press, 2009.

Buntin, John. *L.A. Noir: The Struggle for the Soul of America's Most Seductive City.* London: Orion, 2014.

Bureau of the Census, *1957 Census of Governments: Summary of Public Employment.* Vol. 2, no. 1. Washington: U.S. Department of Commerce, 1958.

———. *Current Population Reports: Consumer Income.* Series P-60, no. 3. Washington: U.S. Department of Commerce, December 1958.

———. *Statistical Abstract of the United States: 1957.* Washington: U.S. Department of Commerce, 1957.

Byrne, David T. *Ronald Reagan: An Intellectual Biography.* Lincoln: Potomac Books, 2018.

Byron, Christopher. *Testosterone, Inc.: Tales of CEOs Gone Wild.* New York: Wiley, 2004.

Cannon, James M. *Gerald Ford: An Honorable Life.* Ann Arbor: University of Michigan Press, 2013.

Cannon, Lou. *Governor Reagan: His Rise to Power.* New York: Public Affairs, 2005.

———. *President Reagan.* New York: Public Affairs, 2000.

Carbone, Gerald M., and Steven Lubar. *Brown and Sharpe and the Measure of American Industry: Making the Precision Machine Tools That Enabled Manufacturing.* Jefferson NC: McFarland, 2017.

Carlson, Peter. *K Blows Top: A Cold War Comic Interlude Starring Nikita Khrushchev, America's Most Unlikely Tourist.* New York: Public Affairs, 2009.

Ceplair, Larry, and Steven Englund. *The Inquisition in Hollywood: Politics in the Film Community, 1930–60.* Urbana: University of Illinois Press, 2003.

Clotworthy, William G. *Saturday Night Live: Equal Opportunity Offender.* N.p.: AuthorHouse, 2001.

Colacello, Bob. *Ronnie and Nancy: Their Path to the White House.* New York: Grand Central, 2014.

CQ Almanac 1961. 17th ed. Washington DC: Congressional Quarterly, 1961.

CQ Almanac 1962. 18th ed. Washington DC: Congressional Quarterly, 1962.

CQ Almanac 1965. 21st ed. Washington DC: Congressional Quarterly, 1966.

Dallek, Matthew. *The Right Moment: Ronald Reagan's First Victory and the Decisive Turning Point in American Politics.* New York: Free Press, 2000.

Darman, Jonathan. *Landslide: LBJ and Ronald Reagan at the Dawn of a New America.* New York: Random House, 2014.

Davis, Patti. *The Way I See It: An Autobiography.* New York: Putnam, 1992.

Day, Doris. *Doris Day: Her Own Story*. London: Star Books, 1977.

Deaver, Michael. *A Different Drummer: My Thirty Years with Ronald Reagan*. New York: William Morrow, 1999.

Doherty, Thomas. *Show Trial: Hollywood, HUAC, and the Birth of the Blacklist*. New York: Columbia University Press, 2018.

Donaldson, Gary A. *Liberalism's Last Hurrah: The Presidential Campaign of 1964*. New York: Skyhorse, 2016.

Douglas, Helen Gahagan. *A Full Life*. Garden City NY: Doubleday, 1982.

Drew, Elizabeth. *American Journey: The Events of 1973–1974*. New York: Macmillan, 1984.

Edwards, Anne. *Early Reagan*. Lanham MD: Taylor Made, 2012.

——— . *The Reagans: Portrait of a Marriage*. New York: St. Martin's Press, 2003.

Edwards, Lee. *The Essential Ronald Reagan: A Profile in Courage, Justice, and Wisdom*. Lanham MD: Rowan and Littlefield, 2007.

——— . *Goldwater: The Man Who Made a Revolution*. Washington: Regnery, 1995.

——— . *Reagan: A Political Biography*. San Diego: Viewpoint Books, 1967.

Eliot, Marc. *Reagan: The Hollywood Years*. Waterville ME: Thorndike Press, 2009.

Erickson, Paul D. *Reagan Speaks: The Making of an American Myth*. New York: New York University Press, 1991.

Evans, Thomas W. *The Education of Ronald Reagan: The General Electric Years and the Untold Story of His Conversion to Conservatism*. New York: Columbia University Press, 2006.

Faber, Harold. *The Road to the White House: The Story of the 1964 Election by the Staff of the New York Times*. New York: Berkley, 1966.

Farrell, John. *Nixon: The Life*. New York: Vintage, 2017.

Fitzgerald, Frances. *Way Out There in the Blue: Reagan, Star Wars, and the End of the Cold War*. New York: Touchstone, 2000.

Friedrich, Otto. *City of Nets: A Portrait of Hollywood in the 1940s*. New York: Harper and Row, 1986.

General Electric. *Supervisor's Guide to General Electric Job Information*. General Electric, 1947.

Gold, Vic. *PR as in President*. Garden City NY: Doubleday, 1977.

Goldberg, Robert Alan. *Barry Goldwater*. New Haven: Yale University Press, 1995.

Goldwater, Barry. *The Conscience of a Conservative*. Princeton: Princeton University Press, 2007.

——— . *Goldwater*. New York: Doubleday, 1988.

Hannaford, Peter. *Reagan's Roots: The People and Places That Shaped His Character*. Bennington VT: Images from the Past, 2012.

Hayes, James Todd. "Ronald Reagan as a "Thoughtful" Speaker: The Sources of Evidence for Selected Assertions from His Campaign Speech of October 27, 1964. Master's thesis, Department of Speech, Kansas State Teachers College, August 1965.

Hazlitt, Henry. *Economics in One Lesson*. New York: Pocket Books, 1948.

Hess, Stephen, and David S. Broder. *The Republican Establishment: The Present and Future of the* GOP. New York: Harper and Row, 1967.

Holden, Kenneth. *The Making of the Great Communicator: Ronald Reagan's Transformation from Actor to Governor.* Guilford CT: Lyons Press, 2013.

Hoopes, James. *Corporate Dreams: Big Business in American Democracy from the Great Depression to the Great Recession.* New Brunswick NJ: Rutgers University Press, 2011.

Horne, Gerald. *Class Struggle in Hollywood, 1930–1950: Moguls, Mobsters, Stars, Reds and Trade Unionists.* Austin: University of Texas Press, 2001.

Houck, Davis W., and Amos Kiewe. *Actor, Ideologue, Politician: The Public Speeches of Ronald Reagan.* Westport CT: Greenwood Press, 1993.

Hyatt, Wesley. *Short-Lived Television Series, 1948–1978: Thirty Years of More than 1,000 Flops.* Jefferson NC: McFarland, 2003.

Jamieson, Kathleen Hall. *Packaging the President: A History and Criticism of Presidential Campaign Advertising.* New York: Oxford University Press, 1996.

Jessel, George. *The World I Lived In.* Chicago: Henry Regnery, 1975.

Kabaservice, Geoffrey M. *Rule and Ruin: The Downfall of Moderation and the Destruction of the Republican Party, from Eisenhower to the Tea Party.* New York: Oxford University Press, 2013.

Kelley, Kitty. *Nancy Reagan: The Unauthorized Biography.* New York: Simon and Schuster, 1991.

Kilroy, James. *Kialoa-US1: Dare to Win: In Business, in Sailing, in Life.* Brooklin ME: Smith Kerr, 2012.

Klein, J. Herbert, and Melanie Villines. *Ronald Reagan's Road to the White House: How Hollywood Prepared America's 40th President for the World Stage.* Los Angeles: International FA, 2011.

Kleinknecht, William. *The Man Who Sold the World: Ronald Reagan and the Betrayal of Main Street America.* New York: Basic Books, 2009.

Knott, Stephen F., and Jeffrey L. Chidester. *At Reagan's Side: Insiders' Recollections from Sacramento to the White House.* Lanham MD: Rowman and Littlefield, 2009.

Kopelson, Gene. *Reagan's 1968 Dress Rehearsal: Ike, RFK, and Reagan's Emergence as a World Statesman.* Los Angeles: Figueroa Press, 2016.

Leamer, Laurence. *Make Believe: The Story of Nancy and Ronald Reagan.* New York: Dell, 1983.

Leuchtenburg, William E. *In the Shadow of FDR: From Harry Truman to Ronald Reagan.* Ithaca NY: Cornell University Press, 1992.

Lewis, Joseph. *What Makes Reagan Run? A Political Profile.* New York: McGraw-Hill, 1968.

Lippard, George. *Legends of the American Revolution; or, Washington and His Generals.* Philadelphia: T. B. Peterson, 1847.

Maier, Pauline. *American Scripture: Making the Declaration of Independence.* New York: Knopf, 1997.

McClelland, Doug. *Hollywood on Ronald Reagan: Friends and Enemies Discuss Our President, the Actor.* Winchester MA: Faber and Faber, 1983.

McClure, Arthur F., et al. *Ronald Reagan: His First Career.* Lewiston NY: Edwin Mellen Press, 1988.

McCullough, David. *John Adams.* New York: Simon and Schuster, 2001.

McDougal, Dennis. *The Last Mogul: Lew Wasserman and the Hidden History of Hollywood.* New York: Crown, 1998.

McGirr, Lisa. *Suburban Warriors: The Origins of the New American Right.* Princeton: Princeton University Press, 1998.

Middendorf, John William. *A Glorious Disaster: Barry Goldwater's Presidential Campaign and the Origins of the Conservative Movement.* New York: Basic Books, 2006.

Moldea, Dan E. *Dark Victory: Ronald Reagan, MCA, and the Mob.* New York: Viking, 1986.

Morella, Joe, and Edward Z. Epstein. *Jane Wyman: A Biography.* New York: Delacorte, 1985.

Morgan, Iwan. *Reagan: An American Icon.* London: I. B. Tauris, 2016.

Morreale, Joanne. *The Presidential Campaign Film: A Critical History.* Westport CT: Praeger, 1993.

Morrell, Margot. *Reagan's Journey: Lessons from a Remarkable Career.* New York: Threshold, 2011.

Morris, Edmund. *Dutch: A Memoir of Ronald Reagan.* New York: Random House, 1998.

National Center for Health Statistics. *100 Years of Marriage and Divorce Statistics, United States, 1867–1967,* series 21, no. 24. Rockville MD: DHEW, 1973.

Neal, Patricia. *As I Am: An Autobiography.* New York: Simon and Schuster, 1988.

Newcomb, Horace, ed. *Encyclopedia of Television.* New York: Routledge, 1977.

Nofziger, Lyn. *Nofziger.* Washington: Regnery Gateway, 1992.

Northrup, Herbert R. *Boulwarism: The Labor Relations Policy of the General Electric Company.* Ann Arbor: Bureau of Industrial Relations, 1965.

Novak, Robert M. *The Agony of the GOP 1964.* New York: Macmillan, 1965.

Nye, David E. *Image Worlds: Corporate Identities at General Electric, 1890–1930.* Cambridge: MIT Press, 1985.

Olsen, Henry. *The Working-Class Republican: Ronald Reagan and the Return of Blue-Collar Conservatism.* New York: Broadside Books, 2017.

Peretti, Burton W. *The Leading Man: Hollywood and the Presidential Image.* New Brunswick NJ: Rutgers University Press, 2012.

Perlstein, Rick. *Before the Storm: Barry Goldwater and the Unmaking of the American Consensus.* New York: Hill and Wang, 2001.

———. *The Invisible Bridge: The Fall of Nixon and the Rise of Reagan.* New York: Simon and Schuster, 2015.

Phillips-Fein, Kim. *Invisible Hands: The Businessmen's Crusade against the New Deal.* New York: W. W. Norton, 2009.

Prindle, David F. *The Politics of Glamour: Ideology and Democracy in the Screen Actors Guild.* Madison: University of Wisconsin Press, 1988.

Public Papers of the Presidents of the United States: Ronald Reagan, 1985. Washington: Government Printing Office, 1988.

Quirk, Lawrence J. *Jane Wyman: The Actress and the Woman.* New York: Dembner Books, 1986.

Raphael, Timothy. *The President Electric: Ronald Reagan and the Politics of Performance.* Ann Arbor: University of Michigan Press, 2009.

Reagan, Maureen. *First Father, First Daughter: A Memoir.* Boston: Little, Brown, 1989.

Reagan, Nancy. *My Turn: The Memoirs of Nancy Reagan.* New York: Random House, 1989.

Reagan, Ron. *My Father at 100.* New York: Viking, 2011.

Reagan, Ronald. *An American Life.* New York: Simon and Schuster, 1990.

———. *The Greatest Speeches of Ronald Reagan.* Boca Raton FL: Humanix Books, 2003.

———. *Reagan: A Life in Letters.* Edited by Kiron K. Skinner, Annelise Graebner Anderson, and Martin Anderson. London: Simon and Schuster, 2005.

———. *Speaking My Mind: Selected Speeches.* New York: Simon and Schuster, 1989.

———. *Where's the Rest of Me? The Autobiography of Ronald Reagan.* New York: Karz-Seigel, 1981.

Reagan, Ronald, and Douglas Brinkley. *The Notes: Ronald Reagan's Private Collection of Stories and Wisdom.* New York: Harper, 2011.

Roberts, Randy, and James S. Olson. *John Wayne: American.* New York: Free Press, 1995.

Rose, Frank. *The Agency: William Morris and the Hidden History of Show Business.* New York: HarperBusiness, 1995.

Rusher, William. *The Rise of the Right.* New York: National Review, 1993.

Sasala, Steven Richard. "A Case Study of Ronald Reagan's October 27, 1964, Address: 'A Time for Choosing.'" Master's thesis, Bowling Green State University, August 1967.

Schatz, Ronald W. *The Electrical Workers: A History of Labor at General Electric and Westinghouse, 1923–60.* Urbana: University of Illinois Press, 1983.

Schuparra, Kurt. *Triumph of the Right: The Rise of the California Conservative Movement.* Armonk NY: Sharpe, 1998.

Schweizer, Peter. *Reagan's War: The Epic Story of His Forty-Year Struggle and Final Triumph over Communism.* New York: Anchor Books, 2003.

Shadegg, Stephen C. *What Happened to Goldwater? The Inside Story of the 1964 Republican Campaign.* New York: Holt, Rinehart and Winston, 1965.

Shearer, Stephen Michael. *Patricia Neal: An Unquiet Life.* Lexington: University Press of Kentucky, 2006.

Shirley, Craig. *Reagan's Revolution: The Untold Story of the Campaign That Started It All.* Nashville: Nelson, 2010.

Sitton, Tom. *Los Angeles Transformed: Fletcher Bowron's Urban Reform Revival, 1938–1953.* Albuquerque: University of New Mexico Press, 2005.

Skidmore, Max J. "Ronald Reagan and 'Operation Coffeecup': A Hidden Episode in American Political History." *Journal of American Culture* 12, no. 3 (Fall 1989).

Smith, George H. *Who Is Ronald Reagan?* New York: Pyramid, 1968.

Sperber, A. M., and Eric Lax. *Bogart.* New York: William Morrow, 1997.

Spitz, Bob. *Reagan: An American Journey.* New York: Penguin Press, 2018.

St. Onge, Jeffrey. "Operation Coffeecup: Ronald Reagan, Rugged Individualism, and the Debate over Socialized Medicine." *Rhetoric and Public Affairs,* July 2017.

Suid, Lawrence H. *Guts and Glory: The Making of the American Military Image in Film.* Lexington: University Press of Kentucky, 2015.

Thomas, Tony. *The Films of Ronald Reagan.* Secaucus NJ: Citadel Press, 1980.

Timberg, Bernard M., and Bob Erler. *Television Talk: A History of the TV Talk Show.* Austin: University of Texas Press, 2002.

Trent, Judith S., Robert V. Friedenberg, and Robert E. Denton, *Political Campaign Communication: Principles and Practice.* Lanham MD: Rowman and Littlefield.

U.S. Department of Health, Education, and Welfare. *Vital Statistics of the United States, 1950.* Vol. 1. Washington: U.S. Department of Commerce, 1954.

———. *Vital Statistics of the United States, 1951.* Vol. 1. Washington: U.S. Department of Commerce, 1954.

Van Ells, Mark D. *To Hear Only Thunder Again: America's World War II Veterans Come Home.* Lanham MD: Lexington Books, 2001.

Vaughn, Stephen. *Ronald Reagan in Hollywood: Movies and Politics.* Cambridge: Cambridge University Press, 1994.

Vestal, Theodore M. *The Lion of Judah in the New World: Emperor Haile Selassie of Ethiopia and the Shaping of Americans' Attitudes toward Africa.* Westport CT: Praeger, 2001.

Villeneuve, Hubert. "Teaching Anticommunism: Fred C. Schwarz, the Christian Anti-Communism Crusade, and American Postwar Conservatism." Master's thesis, McGill University, Department of History, August 2011.

Welch, Robert. *The Blue Book of the John Birch Society, 1959.* Appleton WI: Western Islands, 1961.

White, F. Clifton, and William J. Gill, *Why Reagan Won.* Chicago: Regnery, 1981.

Wills, Garry. *Reagan's America: Innocents at Home.* New York: Penguin, 2000.

Yager, Edward M. *Ronald Reagan's Journey: Democrat to Republican.* Lanham MD: Rowan and Littlefield, 2006.

Index